ASSISTIVE TECHNOLOGY FOR PEOPLE WITH DISABILITIES

DIANE PEDROTTY BRYANT

The University of Texas at Austin

BRIAN R. BRYANT

Psycho-Educational Services

Boston • New York • San Francisco • Mexico City • Montreal •
Toronto • London • Madrid • Munich • Paris • Hong Kong •
Singapore • Tokyo • Cape Town • Sydney

Executive Editor: *Virginia Lanigan*
Editorial Assistant: *Robert Champagne*
Executive Marketing Manager: *Amy Cronin*
Editorial-Production Administrator: *Beth Houston*
Editorial-Production Service: *Walsh & Associates, Inc.*
Composition Buyer: *Linda Cox*
Manufacturing buyer: *JoAnne Sweeney*
Cover Administrator: *Kristina Mose-Libon*

Between the time Website information is gathered and then published, it is not unusual for some sites to have closed. Also, the transcription of URLs can result in typographical errors. The publisher would appreciate notification where these occur so that they may be corrected in subsequent editions.

Library of Congress Cataloging-in-Publication Data

Bryant, Diane Pedrotty.
   Assistive technology for people with disabilities / Diane Pedrotty Bryant,
Brian R. Bryant.
     p. cm.
   Includes bibliographical references and index.
   ISBN 0-205-32715-X
   1. Self-help devices for people with disabilities.   2. Rehabilitation technology.
I. Bryant, Brian R. II. Title.

RM950.B79   2003
617'.03—dc21

                           2002018547

Printed in the United States of America

10 9 8 7 6 5   06

Within a 12-month period, we lost two friends and colleagues in the College of Education at The University of Texas at Austin. Whenever we ran into Tom Tyree and Candy Bos in the hallways of the Sanchez Building, it was as if the hallway lights shone a bit brighter. We learned much from them. Tom was an advocate for people with disabilities and an AT user. Candy dedicated her life to helping people with learning disabilities and to helping students become excellent teachers. They left us all too soon. This book is dedicated to their memories and their work.

CONTENTS

CHAPTER 6

Assistive Technology Devices to Enhance Access to Information   111

CHAPTER 7

Integrating Assistive Technology Adaptations into Academic Instruction   134

CHAPTER 8

Anchoring Instruction for Students with Disabilities   174

CHAPTER 9

Assistive Technology Devices to Enhance Independent Living   194

PREFACE

This textbook is intended to provide readers with a wide range of information about assistive technology adaptations with an emphasis on devices and services. Assistive technology (AT) is an area that is characterized by rapid development and innovation as a result of work done by researchers, engineers, educators, users and families, therapists, and rehabilitation specialists to inform and provide better and more promising devices to meet the needs of technology users. We know more than ever about the benefits of assistive technology to enhance the lives of individuals with disabilities to promote independence, access, and equity.

PURPOSE AND AUDIENCE

This textbook presents information about assistive technology adaptations to educators, therapists, users and families, and rehabilitation specialists. By providing information that is grounded in research and supported by individuals who use technology, decision makers, users, and their families will obtain information to better inform choices made about technology and individual needs. This book is intended for undergraduate and graduate students who are taking an assistive technology course and for individuals who are working in the rehabilitation and therapy fields. The focus of the book is on the lifespan, various disabilities, and the environments in which all individuals function as a part of life. Assistive technology makes activities possible for many people and, as our colleague Dr. Peg Nosek noted, it is liberating! It is this message of possibility, liberation, access, and independence that we hope serves as an underpinning theme throughout the chapters.

FEATURES

There are several noteworthy features that are intended to enrich the content and assist readers in learning about assistive technology adaptations. First, we have included instructional features such as Objectives, Making Connections, and Discussion Questions to help readers think about the content before and after reading each chapter. Second, we have included the feature Focus on . . . that provides application activities for many sections of each chapter. This feature is intended to help readers use the information in a practical way as they engage in activities requiring application of the content. Third, the Personal Perspective feature highlights the viewpoints of individuals who either use technology, have children who use technology, provide professional development, and/or serve as advocates for assistive technology. We think this feature helps to personalize the information presented in the chapters and illustrate the impact of assistive technology on the lives of individuals who benefit most.

CONTENT AND ORGANIZATION

The nine chapters in the book address a variety of topics related to assistive technology devices and services. Topics include an introduction to assistive technology, the Adaptations Framework, assessment, mobility, communication, access to information, academic instruction, anchoring instruction, and independent living. Each topic was chosen because of its contribution to assistive technology and the effects of AT on the lives of individuals with disabilities across the lifespan.

The first three chapters of the book provide introductory material and assessment information about assistive technology. The Adaptations Framework is introduced and is applied throughout the book as a means of considering assistive technology and matching adaptations, such as AT devices, with individuals' needs in various settings. Next, we provide chapters on mobility, communication, and access to the information pervasive in our society—these are basic life requirements. We provide two chapters that focus on assistive technology during the school years because of the importance of ensuring that all students have access to the curriculum and that teachers examine ways to make instruction more meaningful for learning. Finally, we conclude the book with a chapter on independent living. We think this represents a good culminating chapter that focuses on how assistive technology is applicable across all environments. We hope you enjoy the book!

ACKNOWLEDGMENTS

When we first talked about writing a book on assistive technology, we were the first to admit that we didn't know everything there was to know about AT devices and services and that considerable research would have to be conducted if we were going to do the topic justice. One of the biggest challenges was to identify content that would not be outdated immediately. We hope that we have captured the "big ideas" in assistive technology and that the examples we provided will illustrate the ideas successfully. Throughout this book, you see Personal Perspectives and references to a number of colleagues whom we have met and worked with over the years. We would like to acknowledge and thank them at this time: Diana Carl, Anne Corn, Bess Althaus Graham, Mike Haynes, Pat MacGregor, Tony McGregor, Peg Nosek, Sean Slattery, Jamie Judd-Wall, and Joy Zabala. We believe that the reflections offered in the Personal Perspectives will help readers understand the application of assistive technology from different viewpoints.

In addition, we would like to recognize Tricia Legler and Marshall Raskind, two friends, who have taught us much about assistive technology from their professional and personal experiences working with AT users and their families. Much of what we know has come from working closely with these two professionals. We would also like to express our appreciation to our editor, Virginia Lanigan, and Erin Kathleen Liedel, editorial assistant, for their assistance, support, and patience. We would like to acknowledge and thank our reviewers whose insight and helpful feedback strengthened the content of this book. Thank you to Beatrice Babbitt—University of Nevada, Las Vegas; Jami M. Goetz—University of Colorado at Denver; Michael Hudson—Michigan State University; Marshall H. Raskind—Frostig Center; and Loraine J. Spenciner—University of Maine, Farmington. Hopefully, the combined efforts of all we have mentioned have made this book an informative and pleasant reading experience for you.

Finally, we would like to acknowledge the students and parents with whom we have worked over the years. They are the people who are most affected by AT's promise. They have taught us much over the years, and we hope that, for them, AT eventually fulfills its potential as a tool for accessibility and full participation in all of life's activities.

CHAPTER ONE

INTRODUCTION TO ASSISTIVE TECHNOLOGY DEVICES AND SERVICES

CHAPTER AT A GLANCE

ASSISTIVE TECHNOLOGY DEFINED
- Focus on 1.1

HISTORICAL OVERVIEW OF ASSISTIVE TECHNOLOGY

- Personal Perspective 1.1
- Focus on 1.2

MULTIDISCIPLINARY NATURE OF AT SERVICE PROVISION

OBJECTIVES

1. Examine definitions of key assistive technology terms.
2. Demonstrate knowledge concerning the history of assistive technology.
3. Identify key professionals involved in assistive technology service delivery.

MAKING CONNECTIONS

Think about how inventions have changed people's lives over the past 100 years. Some inventions, such as computers and airplanes, have dramatically altered our way of life. Others, such as remote control units and electric can openers, have certainly made our lives easier on a daily basis. Think about inventions that make things possible for people with disabilities. What are they and how are they used? What capabilities are they designed to enhance?

Now think about legislation that has been passed to help secure people's civil rights. How might these laws apply to people with disabilities? What laws are specifically designed for people with disabilities?

Some time ago, International Business Machines (IBM, 1991) provided a training package for assistive technology (AT), in which they noted, "For people without disabilities, technology makes things easier; for people with disabilities, technology makes things possible" (p. 2). Of all we have read concerning AT and its application, this statement seems to be the most succinct. There is no doubt that technological advances have made most people's lives considerably easier in the past 40 years or so. Many of us can recall the first pocket calculators in the 1970s and how they sold for several hundred dollars. Seemingly overnight these minicomputers were being offered free of charge to car owners who purchased at least eight gallons of gasoline. Presto—balancing a checkbook, or at least attempting to do so, became that much easier. For people with math disabilities, balancing a checkbook became possible, because their computational weaknesses make such a task nearly impossible to perform independently. This is but one example of the "easier . . . possible" comparison. We might also recall how speaking into a computer's microphone and having the words magically appear on paper was once a pipedream to those of us who labored at typing a term paper. Thanks to voice-to-text technology, such a task is accomplished simply using a computer and specialized software. For most of us, writing was made easier; for a person with a severe motor or vision difficulty who would otherwise struggle inputting text into a computer, writing not only became possible but somewhat simple to perform (if writing is ever simple). Advances in technology have benefited most of society, but it could be argued that for people with disabilities, technology has provided a means to an end, which is independence. That is, AT devices serve as a vehicle to help individuals with disabilities do what they want to do when they want to do it, thereby reducing the need to depend on others to do things for them. This chapter provides background information that sets the stage for the central themes (i.e., access and independence) that run throughout this text: From where has AT use evolved, where is AT used currently, and where will AT use take us? In this chapter, we provide opening cues to these questions by (a) defining assistive technology (more specifically, AT device, AT service, and instructional technology); (b) providing a historical overview of AT development; and (c) discussing the multidisciplinary nature of AT service delivery.

ASSISTIVE TECHNOLOGY DEFINED

Interestingly, the term *assistive technology* is not defined in any dictionary we could find. But the term *assist* is defined in *Webster's Universal College Dictionary* (1997) as "to give support or aid to; help" (p. 48); and *technology* is defined by the same source as "1. the branch of knowledge that deals with applied science, engineering, the industrial arts, etc. 2. the application of knowledge for practical ends. 3. a technological process, invention, or method" (p. 808). Thus, we could be relatively safe in stating that AT is "the applications of science, engineering, and other disciplines that result in processes, methods, or inventions that support people with disabilities." We have added "people with disabilities" to tie AT specifically to disabilities and to differentiate helpful technology from assistive technology, in keeping with the IBM reference earlier. We realize that some may disagree somewhat with this definition, but the key point is that AT is really a concept, a perspective as it were, that leads one down the road to making practical decisions about specific devices, services, and adaptations that can be used by people with disabilities, their advocates, and their family members to make independence possible. With this in mind, it would be helpful to examine the definitions of assistive technology device, assistive technology service, instructional technology, and adaptations, because they are the primary focus of this text.

Assistive Technology Device

"Assistive technology device" was defined first in the Technology-Related Assistance for Individuals with Disabilities Act of 1988 (P.L. 100-407), better known as the "Tech Act," and the definition was included later in the 1990 reauthorization of the Individuals with Disabilities Education Act. According to the sources, an assistive technology device refers to "any item, piece of equipment, or product system, whether acquired commercially off-the-shelf, modified, or customized, that is used to increase, maintain or improve the functional capabilities of individuals with disabilities" (U.S. Congress, 1988). This definition is sufficiently broad to include just about any item or system, from electronic wheelchairs for people with mobility impairments to remedial reading software programs for children with dyslexia. As can be seen, there are three components of the definition of an AT device: *What* it is, *how* it's made, and its *use*.

The *what* obviously refers to the unit itself, which can either be an item (e.g., a Hoover cane to help a person who is blind move about), a piece of equipment (e.g., a corner chair that supports a child's torso in extension, which helps the shoulders and arms to move freely), or a product system (e.g., a computer with speech recognition software and a microphone attachment that allows a person to speak into the computer and have the spoken words translated to text in a word processing program).

The *how* refers to whether the device is purchased as an "as-is" item in a store (e.g., a motorized wheelchair from a mobility vendor), modified (e.g., the same chair, but with "special features," such as balloon tires for beach access), or customized (e.g., the same type of chair but one that is created specially for a person with very specific needs). The key ingredient to this section of the definition is that the device can be bought from an available vendor, adapted from another device to tailor it to specific customer features, or made from scratch.

Finally, the *use* deals with the purpose of the device as it pertains to the user. The device has to be able to be used either to enhance a person's functioning or to maintain the functional level at its current level, that is, to prevent a condition from worsening. This means that the device allows a person with a disability either to do something that he or she couldn't do without the device or to keep doing what is currently being done. A practical interpretation of the federal definition could be as follows: An AT device is anything that is bought or made that helps a person with a disability accomplish tasks that would be otherwise difficult or impossible to perform. We hope that this simpler description captures the essence of the term "assistive technology device."

Just what types of devices are used? Some might argue this point, but for our purposes, we group AT devices into seven categories: positioning, mobility, augmentative and alternative communication, computer access, adaptive toys and games, adaptive environments, and instructional aids. Considerable space is devoted throughout this text for each AT category; here, we introduce the concepts inherent in each category.

Positioning refers to finding the best posture for a person to be in for a particular function. This function might entail moving about from one place to another, sitting during conversation, eating, sleeping, and so on. Because some people with disabilities have idiosyncratic physical conditions, their specific body features must be adapted to allow for maximum efficiency and comfort during typical functioning. Physical and occupational therapists are key professional contacts who deal with positioning issues.

Mobility refers literally to the act of movement. Humans are active creatures and mobility allows us to do everything from flip the pages of a book to boarding an airplane. Thus, AT devices that facilitate mobility help people move about in various environments. When most people think of mobility AT devices, they think of wheelchairs, but mobility devices also include children's scooter boards, vehicular modifications, white canes, electronic direction-finding/mobility aids, and other adaptations and devices. Rehabilitation engineers, physical therapists, orientation and mobility specialists, and engineers are vital team members when mobility issues are discussed.

Augmentative and alternative communication ("aug com") devices help people to communicate with each other, even if they have speech difficulties. Professionals once used the term "nonverbal" to describe individuals who could not speak. Thanks to "aug com" devices, use of the term "nonverbal" is antiquated and largely inappropriate today. Stories of people's use of aug com devices to communicate with one another are sometimes profound and inspiring. We have heard several accounts of a child and a parent communicating verbally their love for each other for the first time; it is not difficult to see the power of augmentative and alternative communication when used for this and many other purposes.

Computer access devices are those that allow people to use the computer, even if their disability inhibits typical access. For example, instead of using a conventional keyboard to input information into a computer, people with physical impairments can use beams of light to activate or simulate a terminal. Or they can speak into a microphone and tell the computer what functions to employ. Or a stick can be held in one's mouth and a key depressed on the keyboard by applying pressure. People who are blind require alternative output methodologies for computer use, and text to speech offers a critical access feature. Access to computers allows for all sorts of uses, from general word processing to data analysis to communication with people in other countries. Educators and rehabilitation specialists typically are called upon to assist in this area.

It is usually agreed upon that early cognitive development occurs as children play. *Adaptive toys and games* is an area of assistive technology that provides children with disabilities the opportunity to play with toys, games, and one another, thus allowing children to develop cognitive skills associated with these activities. Anyone who has seen groups of children playing while a child with a disability sits or stands excluded from the activities is well aware of the social and cognitive repercussions of such exclusion. Conversely, children playing together, despite physical or sensory differences, is a joyous sight to behold. (Note: We recognize that some readers may find our use of the term "joyous sight to behold" a bit of an overstatement; we would challenge those readers to watch children at play, especially those children who have been typically excluded from such an activity, and arrive at another conclusion.)

Adaptive environments refer to the use of devices and approaches that allow a person to manipulate the environment to allow for daily living, working, schooling, playing, and so forth. For instance, most people use remote control units to change channels on their television sets without having to get up from the couch. People with disabilities can do the same thing and also can use the same units to turn lights on and off, respond to a ring of the doorbell, adjust their beds, and carry on a number of other activities in the home, school, or workplace. We typically consider "gadgets" as helpful toys; in reality, these "toys" become AT devices when they help a person with a disability "increase, maintain, or improve" capabilities in various environments.

Instructional aids help educate a person in school or during employment training. Instructional aids also can be used during functional living skills training in an adult's new home. Whatever the application, this broad category involves devices and adaptations that help facilitate learning in one way or another. Instructional aids include technology that is used to compensate for a person's functional limitations (e.g., screen reader programs that allow for information access) or technology that is used for remediation purposes (e.g., math or reading instructional programs).

It is important to note that the types of AT devices often overlap. For example, positioning and mobility are closely intertwined, as are adaptive toys and games and instructional aids. We categorized the devices to aid in discussion, but one must always maintain a broad perspective when considering AT devices, whether discussing categories or seeking alternative adaptations.

Assistive Technology Service

Assistive technology service is a term that has been defined in federal legislation. According to federal guidelines (U.S. Congress, 1988),

> the term "assistive technology service" refers to any service that directly assists an individual with a disability in the selection, acquisition, or use of an assistive technology device:
>
>> a functional evaluation of the person in the individual's customary environment;

purchasing and/or leasing;
selecting, designing, fitting;
coordinating and using other therapies or interventions;
training or technical assistance for an individual with disabilities or the
family;
training or technical assistance for a professional.

When considering AT services, it is best to think in terms of devices existing outside of a vacuum. That is, devices are simply "things" that are available for use. Without AT services, these devices would exist on catalog pages only, with no apparent use or even the ability to acquire the devices, in many instances. The phrase "refers to any service that directly assists an individual with a disability in the selection, acquisition, or use of an assistive technology device" provides the essence of the definition. The services are provided to decide what device to select, how to get the device, and how to use it; or how a person can use the device so that his or her goals can be met though the device's use. We discuss briefly the elements included in the definition. Many of the definition's elements are discussed in detail elsewhere in the text, so this section is intended as an overview of each definitional element.

The phrase "a functional evaluation of the person in the individual's customary environment" refers to what is commonly considered the "person-technology match." Assistive technology devices are not "one size fits all"; that is, one specific device is not appropriate for everyone, and each must be matched with a person for correct application. You do not enter a shoe shop and immediately buy a pair of shoes because you like how they look on another person. You try on the shoes. Do the shoes fit? Are they comfortable? Do they give you freedom of movement so that you can do what you want while the shoes are on your feet? Do they look good on you? Analogously, AT evaluations are conducted so that people can be reasonably sure that the devices match the user's needs, attributes, and the tasks to be done. The phrase "individual's customary environment" merits particular attention. Back to the shoe analogy, if you live on a ranch with rocky terrain and you are looking for a good work boot, the store's cushiony carpet will tell little about how the shoe will feel in your normal workplace. So it would be best to try the shoe in your customary environment. Although the shoe store is unlikely to give you that luxury, AT evaluators should consider such a factor; in fact, this element of the definition mandates such a consideration. It should be added that a plural form "environment" may be more appropriate for this element of the definition, given that people function in multiple environments, and AT devices are usually used across these multiple environments.

The "purchasing and/or leasing" phrase of the definition is critical. There is an old saying that goes something like "Given unlimited resources, we can do anything." Well, "unlimited resources" are unrealistic when it comes to purchasing AT devices, so people allocate the resources that are available. This is of particular relevance when purchasing or leasing AT devices. Usually, there are several devices that can be useful to an individual. Identifying ways to secure funding for the devices is critical if these device are to be acquired (i.e., bought or leased). Personal health insurance benefits, special education funds, and Medicaid are but three of a variety of options that can be used, but knowing about and accessing these options requires expertise. Social workers are particularly adept in this area, as are rehabilitation counselors and special education personnel; thus, decisions about purchasing and/or leasing should be made after close consultation with these or other knowledgeable professionals.

Once the need for AT devices has been determined, the "selecting, designing, fitting" element of the definition comes into play. Clearly, this element coincides with the AT evaluation because each word describes a portion of the evaluation process. A device might have to be designed from scratch or a design modification might have to be identified for an intact unit. In a broad sense, the "person-technology match" is an effort to identify the perfect "fitting" of a device to an individual; but in a more restrictive sense positioning also would fall into this category.

We mentioned earlier that AT devices do not exist in a vacuum. This is the predominant issue when considering the "coordinating and using other therapies or interventions" element of the definition. When a child is matched with an aug com device, for example, the device becomes a tool to be used by the child and his or her speech-language pathologist as part of a speech-language therapy program. As another example, using voice-to-text as a means to access a computer is but one part of what might be an effort to enhance a student's writing skills. Instructional intervention on idea generation, syntax, vocabulary selection, and editing must incorporate the device—the device itself cannot be expected to "teach" these writing skills. Voice-to-text technology allows for access to writing instruction, but it does not replace writing instruction.

Some AT devices are simple to use and some are complicated, but *all* devices require training of the user in order to maximize use. This is the basic notion behind the "training or technical assistance for an individual with disabilities or the family" element. Anyone who has bought a VCR and has tried to program the device, or worse yet, an automatic lawn sprinkler system, knows that some devices are complicated and are difficult to learn to use without special training. Most AT practitioners can recount stories of AT users being inept with the device, and therefore the device does not get used or is used inefficiently or ineffectively. To prevent or reduce such an occurrence, it is necessary for training to be done on the device. Preferably this training occurs during the AT evaluation and is supplemented once the device is selected.

In addition to training the AT user, training also must be conducted for family members, who generally serve as the primary support system for the user. When the user has difficulties with the device, family members step in to assist, but they can do so only if they know how the device operates. Also, because the device is a tool for independence and the family is critical to fostering independence, it is vital that members know how the device is used to facilitate integration into family and community activities. Without such training, the chance for full implementation of the device is unlikely.

The final element of the definition, "training or technical assistance for a professional," is one that is particularly challenging. As educators, we have walked into many classrooms where a device is left sitting on a counter because the teacher has not received training on how the device can be used in the classroom. Contrast this scenario with one in which the teacher is knowledgeable about the AT device and integrates the device, and hence the student, into the curricular activities. But education is only one setting where training is needed. Employers and fellow employees require device training for maximum workplace efficiency. Further, speech-language pathologists require training on the latest aug com devices, and social workers, rehabilitation counselors, and other professionals who work in disability-related fields must receive ongoing training on devices. Training on the benefits of AT should be offered, and when a person with an AT device participates in a program or activity, significant participants in that program/activity should have specialized training in the use and integration of the devices being utilized.

If all AT services are implemented, there is greater likelihood for success, no matter what the context of the device's use. In particular, it should be noted that AT services are ongoing, with periodic training updates, evaluations, and monitorings to ensure that the device is being used appropriately. Although AT service implementation cannot guarantee success, such implementation makes success possible.

Instructional Technology

Instructional technology refers to any technology that is used in the education of an individual. The term includes presentation hardware and software used by teachers and students, including overhead transparencies and projectors, multimedia software and tools, and Internet technology for watching real-time activities, and the like. The term also includes instructional software that is used to *remediate* academic weaknesses. Although we stated earlier that, in its broadest sense, the term "AT device" could include instructional software, generally instructional software is classified with instructional technology. Our point that instructional technology can be considered AT is illustrated by the case of two students, Maria and Phil, who use a reading instructional software program. Phil has no reading difficulties and uses the instructional software to improve his skills. Maria, on the other hand, has dyslexia, and uses the instructional software and hardware (a computer) to "increase her functional (reading) capabilities." For Phil, the technology is helpful; for Maria the software is assistive, that is, an AT device.

Instructional technology also can include such techniques as anchoring instruction, when the technique involves the use of CD-ROMs, video, or some other technological feature. This and other instructional approaches and devices provide the educator with innovative ways to instruct, whether that instruction occurs in a classroom, a workplace, at home, or elsewhere.

Adaptations

In the next chapter, we argue that AT is but one of many adaptations that are available to help a person with a disability accomplish a task. For our purposes, adaptations are *alterations that are made so that a task can be accomplished by a person who does not possess the requisite abilities needed for task completion.* In this way, adaptations are access vehicles that facilitate participation and inclusion in everyday activities. As described in the next chapter, not every adaptation need requires AT devices. Yet a mind-set for making adaptations is necessary for anyone who interacts with people who have disabilities. Otherwise, people with disabilities are destined to be excluded from activities in which they could otherwise participate.

It is also important to understand that adaptations can be either remedial or compensatory in nature. Our earlier example of the instructional program being used by Maria and Phil to improve their reading skills would be an example of remedial adaptations. But if Maria uses a screen reader program to access her e-mail by bypassing her area of weakness (i.e., reading), then the adaptation would be compensatory in nature. Many of the devices and approaches discussed in these chapters are compensatory in scope, but it should not be assumed that remediation and compensation are mutually exclusive concepts. For instance, one never gives up trying to teach a nonreader how to read, so AT devices can be used for remediation purposes throughout the lifespan. But it is also important that a person have access to print, so the use of a compensatory strategy concurrently with remedial efforts is reasonable.

FOCUS ON 1.1

Visit a school or interview a teacher to identify AT devices that are used at the school. What categories (e.g., augmentative and alternative communication, computer access) of AT are represented? Are some categories more represented than others? Is there a relationship between the disabilities (e.g., visual impairments, learning disabilities) students have and the categories of AT that are used?

HISTORICAL OVERVIEW OF ASSISTIVE TECHNOLOGY

Like all fields of study, AT has a history from which it has evolved and that changes dramatically, seemingly on a daily basis. For sake of chronological convenience, we look at the history of AT in three periods: (a) that which occurred prior to 1900, which we call the Foundation Period; (b) that which occurred from 1900 through 1972, which we term the Establishment Period; and (c) the years from 1973 to the present, which we call the Empowerment Period. Some of the information, such as the invention of a particular AT device, has a direct connection for AT use. Other significant events, such as the opening of special schools or the beginning of a periodical, have an indirect connection to AT, either as a venue or an opportunity for AT service delivery or as a means to disseminate information pertaining to AT use.

Foundation Period: Pre-1900s

In their excellent text, titled *Assistive Technologies: Principles and Practices,* Cook and Hussey (1995) recounted the fictional case of Borg, a Stone Age resident who broke his leg on a hunting trip. The authors make the point that, for all intents and purposes, AT began with man's attempt to "make do" after a debilitating injury, whether temporary or permanent. In Borg's case, his leg healed improperly, leaving him with a noticeable limp. Reaching down, he found a stick, which he cut to proper length and used to help him walk more easily. Certainly the stick fits the definition of an AT device in that it is an *item* that was *customized* and that helped him *maintain* one of his functional capabilities. One can easily agree with Cook and Hussey's assertion that AT devices existed as soon as human beings began making "things" to help them adapt to the functional limitations imposed by disabilities, whether those disabilities were acquired or congenital.

If one assumes that AT development paralleled the disability field, then one can look to history to see indications that adaptations of some kind were needed as far back as 1000 B.C., when speech and language difficulties were first recorded. One of the earliest incidences of acquired learning disabilities can be traced to A.D. 33, when Mecurial reported the case of a man losing his memory for letters after being hit on the head with an ax during a skirmish (Wiederholt and Bryant, 1987). We also know that the first recorded spinal surgery occurred around A.D. 600, providing evidence that individuals existed with acquired physical conditions that undoubtedly required postsurgical adaptations for remaining functional limitations. Those may have been as simple as special feeding utensils and techniques or as complex as specially designed wheeled mobility mechanisms. Further examination of historical accounts show autopsies being performed on deceased veterans in the 1600s and 1700s to examine causal factors for physical and mental conditions (Cook & Hussey, 1995). And, of course, there are literary accounts of seafarers with wooden legs and hooks continuing to go to sea long after injuries caused the loss of extremities. There is little doubt that human ingenuity helped such people perform their tasks in a way that would keep them of value to their crewmates. At the end of the 18th century, special education began with Dr. Jean-Marc-Gaspard Itard's efforts to teach Victor, nicknamed "The Wild Boy of Aveyron" because of his early years spent in seclusion in the woods of France.

The 1800s began a period of service for individuals with disabilities that has continued to this day and laid the foundation for disability services as we know it. During this century, in 1817, Thomas Hopkins Gallaudet opened his school for students who were deaf. The name of the school, the American Asylum for Education of the Deaf and Dumb (later, the American School for the Deaf), provides an indication of how terminology has changed over the last 200 years. Twelve years later, a Frenchman by the familiar name of Louis Braille introduced an adaptation of Barbier's "Ecriture Nocturne" (night writing, originally developed for the French military) embossed code so that people who were blind could decode the printed word. In 1834, he perfected the literary code that bears his name.

At about the same time, Dr. J. G. Blomer established an institute for people with physical disabilities where he maintained a workroom for devising apparatus, bandages, and artificial limbs, early AT devices (McNurtrie, 1980). Samuel Gridley Howe started the New England Asylum for the Blind (later the Perkins School for the Blind) in 1832, providing educational services that utilized a variety of techniques specially tailored to the students' visual needs. In 1836, Taylor devised what was thought to be the first tangible math apparatus that could be used by individuals who were blind. The *American Annals of the Deaf* was first published in 1847, followed a year later by the opening of the first residential institution for people with mental retardation (the Perkins Institution in Boston).

The latter half of the 19th century found several significant events that indirectly affected AT by benefiting individuals with disabilities. The first occurred in 1855, when Kentucky set up a printing house for people who were blind, which several years later was incorporated as the American Printing House for the Blind. In 1860, the *Gallaudet Guide and Deaf Mute's Companion* became the first publication written especially for people with disabilities. Four years later, in 1864, Gallaudet University was founded as the National Deaf Mute College (Smith, 1998).

In 1869, a patent was filed for the basic design for the manual wheelchair in use to this day (Pelka, 1997). The wheelchair had been introduced in the United States during the Civil War, when wooden chairs and wooden wheels provided mobility for soldiers who had legs amputated. In 1877, Thomas Edison invented the phonograph, a significant event for those who would later benefit from learning through listening to material on recordings. A short two years later, Public Law 45-186 provided a subsidy to provide books in Braille; the same law also funded the American Printing House for the Blind. Then, in 1884, the Home of the Merciful Savior opened its doors in Philadelphia to children with physical disabilities. Finally, in 1892, Frank Hall invented the Braille typewriter.

To summarize the Foundation Period from the perspective of the 21st century, one sees seemingly small steps occurring in the disabilities field that led the way for major breakthroughs in the 20th century. But the steps taken up to 1900 were anything but minor. Rather, the dedicated leaders of their time (a) worked to ensure that people with sustained injuries survived those injuries; (b) studied the relationships or resulting limitations to neurological damage; and (c) developed programs to teach academics and life skills to people with cognitive, sensory, and motor limitations. No doubt some of the programs involved what could be now termed AT devices.

Establishment Period: 1900–1972

We label the seventy-two-year period from 1900 through 1972 the Establishment Period because these years established the disability disciplines as specific entities, and the policies, laws, and litigation that were established ushered in an era of unprecedented gains for people with disabilities, their families, and their advocates. Throughout this period, educational, scientific, and psychological advances were made concerning the causes, preventions, and ramifications of disabilities. In addition, people's viewpoints concerning disabilities and the capabilities of people with disabilities changed dramatically. Devices and techniques were devised to help people with disabilities utilize their strengths to compensate for their limitations. In addition, legal and procedural barriers that discriminated against people seen as "different" were addressed. Finally, organizations such as the currently named Council for Exceptional Children, American Speech-Language-Hearing Association, American Association on Mental Retardation, Easter Seals, United Cerebral Palsy, the ARC, and Learning Disability Association of America to name but a few, were formed to advocate for people with disabilities and the professionals and families associated with the disability movement. Our discussion here is intended to introduce readers to events that led to a rapid development of AT devices and services, years before those terms officially existed.

We mentioned in the Foundation Period the impact of war on disabilities, that is, battles led to injuries that led to physical, language, sensory, and cognitive conditions. Shortly after World War I, the United States Congress recognized the results of battle-caused disabilities when it passed the Soldier Rehabilitation Act (also known as the Smith-Sears Veterans Rehabilitation Act) in 1918. This significant legislation was intended to assist veterans with disabilities resume life, postdisability, and included the first vocational rehabilitation provision. The work of people like Kurt Goldstein and other injured veterans stimulated service delivery and enhancement and brought a focus on people who had served their country and who now needed their countrymen's assistance to reenter American life. Two years later, the Smith-Fess Citizens Vocational Rehabilitation Act was passed, extending vocational rehabilitation services to nonveterans whose challenges were similar to their military counterparts. Funds were provided for vocational guidance, training, job adjustment, prostheses, and placement services (Bryant, 1996). Clearly, recognition of functional capabilities and people's assets became the rule rather than the exception; rehabilitation professionals focused on using techniques and devices to help people compensate for their functional limitations. Not surprisingly, this new focus brought about a new emphasis on compensatory strategies and equipment that would change the face of disabilities forever.

In 1920 Barr, Stroud, and Fournier d'Albe patented the first reading machine, the Optophone, for use by people who were blind. Three years later, Barr and colleagues expanded their apparatus facilities to deal with the increased demands for their services.

By the end of the decade, guide dogs had been introduced to America, providing mobility independence potential to people who were blind. Breakthroughs in blindness continued, including the National Institute for the Blind's introduction of a high-speed rotary press for embossed type and the Library of Congress' 1931 decision to distribute Braille reading materials under its auspices. The next year, long-standing debate as to the "preferred" Braille style partially was settled when Standard English Braille was adopted by British and American committees as uniform type. In 1933, the American Printing House for the Blind adopted Standard English Braille Grade 2 for junior and senior high school textbooks. A few years later, the first talking books on long-playing records were produced and disseminated. By 1936, the American Printing House for the Blind had produced and disseminated its first recorded materials.

The passage of the Social Security Act in 1935 provided, among other things, grants to states for assisting (a) individuals who were blind and (b) children with disabilities. The decade of the 1930s also produced the Coyne Voice Pitch Indicator, which allowed people's speech patterns to appear as visual images. The year 1937 brought a patent for the X-frame folding wheelchair by Herbert A. Everest and Harry C. Jennings. In 1939, Lowenfeld began his six-year exploration of the educational role of talking books, which resulted in the demonstrated value of these tools in the teaching-learning process.

The 1940s continued to see service delivery breakthroughs, as the United States military began providing its members with speech and hearing services. The Bardon-LaFollette Act, also known as the Rehabilitation Act of 1943, introduced training funds for physicians, nurses, rehabilitation counselors, physical therapists, occupational therapists, social workers, psychologists, and other rehabilitation specialists. World War II provided the impetus for the foundation of Recording for the Blind (later called Recording for the Blind and Dyslexic) in 1918. Annie T. McDonald established the organization to help veterans who had lost their sight during the war obtain an education under the GI Bill of Rights. The year 1947 brought about the introduction of the Hoover cane, which was developed as part of a comprehensive approach to orientation and mobility training that was known as the "touch cane technique" and was designed in part to assist veterans who became blind during World War II (Sauberger, 1996). World War II also saw the development of battery-operated hearing aids, but their bulk presented great difficulty in their use.

Several events of the 1950s assisted communication and educational skills for people who were blind. The initial contribution occurred in 1951 with the availability of the Perkins Brailler, a device still in use today. The year 1952 saw the introduction of the Tellatouch communication device for people who were both deaf and blind. The following year the Megascope was invented and the Nemeth Braille Mathematics Code was introduced.

Computerized Braille was first demonstrated in 1955, and the following year the American Printing House for the Blind first made materials available for day school students. By 1957, the Visotonor and Visotactor were available; the first device transformed musical sounds to letters and the second was a reading machine that produced vibrations that could be felt by the fingers in order to facilitate decoding.

The end of the 1950s introduced PL 85-905, which allowed funding for captioned films, and 1958 saw its first application on a motion picture film (Hardman, Drew, & Egan, 1996). The 1960s saw legislation intended for students who were bilingual (the Bilingual Education Act of 1968) and who had learning disabilities (the Specific Learning Disabilities Act of 1969). South Carolina passed the nation's first statewide architectural access code in 1963. The year 1965 saw the establishment of the National Commission on Architectural Barriers, which led to the passage of the Architectural Barriers Act of 1986. The lasercane, which emitted beams of light to detect objects deterring unobstructed movement, was invented in 1966 and helped people receive advanced notice of obstacles and detect items that were not detected by a traditional white cane (e.g., things that would hit above the elbow). Shortly thereafter, in 1971, the OPTACON was marketed as another tool to allow people who were blind to read text. In that same year, the first Braille Vision Books were produced, which contained one page for Braille next to a page of print.

One cannot discuss the Establishment Period without some mention of the landmark United States Supreme Court decision in Brown versus the Board of Education. The renunciation of the "separate but equal" constitutional concept not only served as a catalyst for the African-American civil rights movement, but it became an inspiration to the disability rights movement that has allowed for the proliferation of AT device creation and use.

To summarize the Establishment Period, it was a time of action on behalf of people with disabilities. World Wars I and II, Korea, and Vietnam had created a new group of Americans with disabilities who were reentering the postwar society with special needs. Advances in medicine were allowing children to live through disease and birth difficulties at a rate unimagined at the turn of the century. People with disabilities were becoming a larger percentage of the United States population, and they had as much of a right to live the American Dream as their nondisabled fellow citizens. Inventions and innovations were helping people use their functional strengths to reduce the impact of their functional weaknesses, and people with disabilities were entering the workforce in record numbers. The disability rights movement was beginning to be recognized as a social and political force. Organizations had been established that pressed for new legislation and policies in education and employment. Assistive technology devices and services were being devised and utilized at an unprecedented rate. It was truly an exciting time, but again to paraphrase a familiar quote, "We hadn't seen anything yet." Beginning in 1973, the disability rights movement was to begin an unprecedented run that continues to this day, a span we refer to as the Empowerment Period.

Empowerment Period: 1973 to Present

Webster's Universal Collegiate Dictionary (1997) defines empower(ment) as "1. giv(ing) official or legal power or authority to. 2. . . . endow(ing) with an ability" (p. 263). Thus, we can describe the Empowerment Period as one which has given, and is giving, people with disabilities and their supporters the ability and legal authority to continue their legitimate pursuit of the American Dream, however they choose to define and operationalize that dream.

The year 1973 was selected because that was the year the Rehabilitation Act was revised to include Section 504, which for the first time made it formal United States policy that discrimination against people with disabilities would not be tolerated. Specifically, Section 504 stated that anyone receiving federal dollars could not discriminate against individuals because of their disabilities. Sadly, this landmark legislation was not implemented until 1977, after a sit-in at the Secretary of State's office several years after its passage. Partially as a result of this activism, disability rights was recognized as a civil rights issue, a distinction that has remained to this day the driving force behind disability advocacy in education, housing, employment, and all other facets of life. Thus, Section 504 is considered as a significant civil rights legislation that ushered in the Empowerment Period.

With regard to assistive technology, Title II of Section 504 referred to auxiliary aids, which must be provided when necessary to ensure that a person with a disability has an equal opportunity to benefit from programs and services provided by a public entity. The law further states that auxiliary aids need not produce the identical result or level of achievement for people with and without disabilities. Rather, such aids simply provide a level playing field in which all people have the same opportunity to succeed. The U.S. Department of Education's Office for Civil Rights (OCR) is the enforcement agency for Section 504 and responds to students and others who question their university's and college's adherence to the auxiliary aid provision. Even though legislation technically allowed a college or university to avoid providing auxiliary aids if such provision caused undue hardships, such instances were rare, because OCR dictated that auxiliary aids could be excluded based on lack of funding.

The year 1974 introduced the development of the closed-circuit television (CCTV) for the electronic magnification of print, and the first compact Braille electronic calculator was developed. In the following year, an early version of the speech synthesizer was developed and the first talking calculator with audio and visual output was introduced. Also in 1975, special education law was enacted with the passage of PL 94-142, later named the Education for Handicapped Children Act (EHA). Education for students with disabilities was now protected in public schools and at publicly supported institutions of higher learning. A period of extraordinary AT development to support educational activities and posteducational employment and living was about to begin.

In 1976, the Kurzweil Reading Machine gave people who were blind the opportunity to access text, but it was so costly that few could afford the technology at the time. During the four years between 1976 and 1979, the Optacon Dissemination project saw that device used with increasing frequency. Grants became available to provide adaptive equipment to classrooms and concurrent training to classroom teachers. VersaBraille was introduced in 1978, followed by the View Scan. The first Braille embosser connected to a microcomputer was introduced in the late 1970s, increasing dramatically the availability of Braille text to children and adults. At the same time, IBM operated its special needs unit, which led the way in developing and adapting technology for people with disabilities.

The EHA was modified in 1985 and made its first provisions for AT. The reauthorization of the law in 1997 went so far as to mandate the consideration of assistive technology for all students with disabilities (see Personal Perspective 1.1). The passage of the Americans with Disabilities Act in 1990 continued the string of legislation passed on behalf of people with disabilities by extending the principles of Section 504 to all sectors of the United States, public and private.

The last law to be discussed here is the Technology-Related Assistance for Individuals with Disabilities Act of 1988 (already introduced as the Tech Act) and its reauthorizations of 1992 and 1998. For the first time, Congress acknowledged the potential of AT to assist persons with disabilities to access the "American

PERSONAL PERSPECTIVE 1.1

Diana Carl is a parent of an assistive technology user. As the Director of Assistive Technology and Preview Services at Region IV Education Service Center (ESC) in Houston, Texas. Diana is the lead facilitator of the Statewide Assistive Technology Network, a collaborative project between the 20 ESCs in Texas and the Texas Education Agency. She is a nationally recognized leader in assistive technology and the education of students with disabilities.

Tell our readers a little bit about your daughter.
My daughter had a cerebral hemorrhage when she was born and was in the hospital for three months in high-intensity care units. We were told by the doctors that the odds were that Dana would have severe and significant disabilities. At that point, she was being fed by tube and they did not anticipate that she would be able to suck a bottle. We were asked to begin to plan our next step and decide whether we would try to care for her at home or place her in an institution. We decided that we would never know if we could care for her unless we tried to take her home. That decision was made 29 years ago. Today, Dana uses a power wheelchair for mobility but when you talk to her, you will find out she does not consider herself "disabled." She does not like to be categorized, since she is very much an individual. She has physical challenges but lives an active and independent lifestyle. Swimming is her passion and her outlet from the wheelchair. Year round she swims about 30 laps four times a week. Many people that we meet, particularly at the health club, say that Dana has been an inspiration to their lives and they often nickname her the "Energizer Bunny."

How has being a parent of a child with a disability influenced your professional life?
Prior to Dana's birth, I worked in the public schools in special education and in the medical center for a prominent medical school. At that time we were called Psychological Associates and we did the testing to determine if the student was eligible for special education services. You would think that I, who was not a novice to the educational system, would have a handle on how to navigate the system for my child with disabilities. What I can tell you is that even having the experience I had as a professional did not prepare me for the experience of having a child with a disability. It is entirely different when it is your own child and you are walking the walk and not talking the talk.

In searching for and investigating methods of therapy for Dana's cerebral palsy, a friend told me about a neuro-developmental treatment (NDT) opportunity. Dana and I spent six weeks for two consecutive summers living in a dorm situation with other parents and children with disabilities, some with severe/profound disabilities. In the mornings the kids received therapy and in the afternoons the therapists were in classes to earn NDT certification. It was a life-changing experience for me to live on a daily basis with these parents and children. I learned about living, loving, and caring for children that previously I had almost seen as unresponsive. Career-wise I soon made a change and became the evaluation specialist at a public school separate campus for students with more severe disabilities. In this position I was supported in learning about and using AT to facilitate student access to curriculum and daily activities. Later it all seemed natural to combine what I had learned as a parent, as an associate school psychologist, and as an assistive technology specialist to take a position in AT at our regional education service center. Today I am the Director of Assistive Technology and Preview Services at Region IV Education Service Center (ESC) and the lead facilitator of the Statewide Assistive Technology Network, which is a collaborative project between the 20 ESCs in Texas and the Texas Education Agency.

You have worked in assistive technology for much of your career. What changes have you seen that can be directly attributed to legislation?
The most profound change has been the impact of the IDEA '97 consideration requirement. Federal law now mandates that in the development of the IEP, each IEP team must consider whether the student needs AT in order to receive FAPE. Thus the responsibility for decision making has shifted from small, expert district AT teams to campus-based IEP teams. As a result, districts have become increasingly aware that IEP team members need knowledge and skills in order to make informed AT decisions and are increasingly seeking professional development opportunities.

What are the most critical issues that will be faced by AT providers in the near future?
Accountability and evaluation of effectiveness are the most critical without a doubt. Educators are increasingly being held accountable to ensure that all students are learning. The performance of students with disabilities must be included in statewide and districtwide assessments. Additionally, if AT is included in the IEP, the effectiveness of its use must be evaluated. Prior to the use of an AT device, the team supporting that student will need to determine how they will know if the trial is successful or not. Then with clearly defined roles and responsibilities, the team members will want to collect implementation data.

Describe the changes you have seen in AT service delivery in the past 20 years.
Of course, the technology has changed tremendously. Our technology today is so much more intelligent, powerful, and compact. For example, look at the differences between the adaptive firmware card and the programming it required to create set-ups and overlays and the present day Intellikeys and Intellitools products that have "smart" overlays. However, what may easily be the greatest difference in service delivery is access to information via the Internet. In 1990, those of us who worked in school districts had to get special permission from administrators to make a long-distance phone call to a manufacturer to get technical assistance. During the 1990s, 800 phone numbers became available and technical assistance was only a phone call away. Today using the Internet, vast amounts of resources and information are instantly available 24/7.

Reprinted with permission from Psycho-Educational Services.

dream" when it passed the Tech Act into law in 1988. The overall purpose of the Tech Act was to provide financial assistance to states to help them develop consumer responsive, cross-age, and cross-disability programs of technology-related assistance (RESNA, 1992). Although assistive technology has been viewed historically as beneficial to individuals with physical and sensory impairments, there has been an increased focus on technology for people with all types of disabilities in recent years (Bryant & Bryant, 1998; Bryant & O'Connell, 1998; Wise & Olson, 1994).

In the mid-1980s, Congress recognized that technological advances were providing an opportunity for Americans with disabilities to realize the potential that the laws were designed to ensure. Thus, the passage of the Tech Act in 1988 reflected:

> Congress' sense that the [Tech] Act promotes values inherent in the ADA. . . . By stating that disability is a natural part of the human experience and in no way diminishes the right of individuals with disabilities to live independently, enjoy self-determination, make choices, contribute to society, pursue meaningful careers, and enjoy full inclusion and integration in the economic, political, social, cultural, and educational mainstream of American society, the [Tech] Act incorporates one of the fundamental concepts of the ADA—that individuals with disabilities are able to pursue the "American dream." (House of Representatives Report 103-208, p. 6)

When Congress passed the 1994 amendments in Public Law 103-218, it purposefully shifted the purposes of the Tech Act from those relating to public awareness of AT benefits to those that focused on systems change and advocacy (Golinker, 1994).

The Tech Act's reauthorization mandated that state Tech Act projects identify and eliminate systemic barriers that impede the timely acquisition and use of AT devices and services. As a result, the Tech Act has profound implications for members of the disability community. Because many children and adults with disabilities can benefit from AT devices and services in school and in the workplace, it is critical that barriers to AT access be eliminated. Tech Act state project efforts work on behalf of individuals with all disabilities to assist in the identification and elimination of AT-related barriers.

FOCUS ON 1.2

You have recently invented a Time Machine that you can use to travel back in time. You have been charged with going back in time to change the face of AT service delivery. During what period would you travel, and what specific action would you take to change the face of AT service delivery? Remember that you will be traveling to a time that has its own political and social climates. How might this affect your decision and the manner with which you would interact with your colleagues and adversaries?

MULTIDISCIPLINARY NATURE OF ASSISTIVE TECHNOLOGY SERVICE PROVISION

It is the nature of assistive technology to be multidisciplinary in that professionals involved in AT come from education, medicine, speech-language pathology, occupational therapy, physical therapy, social work, rehabilitation counseling, and engineering, among other fields. This was evidenced in the previous section as we discussed laws passed to provide training of disability specialists in a variety of disciplines.

Terms such as AT are synonymous with adaptive technology, adaptive aids, auxiliary aids, rehabilitation technology, prostheses, and other such terms that make the field somewhat confusing at times. In addition, there has traditionally been a knowledge gap among professionals; between professionals and consumers; and among professionals, consumers, and vendors. For example, a consumer or family member may hear of an AT device that seems the perfect answer to the person's difficulties. In some instances, professionals may never have heard of the device, or perhaps the reality of the device is not what had been perceived by the consumer or family member. And vendors may be quick to point out the virtues of a device without mentioning potential drawbacks. Added to this may be the "this is what we have, so take it or leave it" mentality, which results from having a library of devices from which people are expected to choose. The reality of AT is that it is a constantly evolving field, with new devices being created or improvements made on existing devices seemingly on a daily basis. A quick tour of the Exhibits Hall at Closing the Gap or CSUN leaves the attendees with their heads spinning from the myriad of devices, all with advantages and potential problems.

Without doubt, knowledgeable leadership and participation in the AT evaluation and implementation processes is critical to successful AT use. Further, interdisciplinary knowledge (i.e., knowledge of how all professionals contribute to the process by bringing specific skills to the table and shared knowledge about devices and services among professionals) promotes dialogue and eventual integration of the devices into the consumer's daily life. Augmentative communication is not strictly the responsibility of speech-language pathologists, nor are positioning and mobility issues restricted to physical and occupational therapists. In the same way, if computer access issues are known only to educators or rehabilitation specialists, the picture is destined to be incomplete.

That said, there is a growing awareness that professionals need to work together and cross disciplinary boundaries for the good of the user. The degree to which that awareness translates to actual practice will dramatically affect the ability to acquire and use AT devices and services in a timely fashion.

SUMMARY

Assistive technology has had a tremendous impact on the lives of individuals with disabilities as demonstrated in this chapter with the numerous developments in the field inspired by influential people who had the insight to see the potential of devices and services. This chapter introduced important concepts, such as AT devices and services, instructional technology, and adaptations, which will be explained in more detail throughout the book. A historical overview of key information during the foundation, establishment, and empowerment periods that influenced developments in AT should provide readers with a sense of the leaders and important events that have shaped AT benefits as we know them today. Finally, the multidisciplinary approach to AT evaluation and intervention—including professionals, families, and users—was emphasized as a critical component of AT service.

DISCUSSION QUESTIONS

1. What is the definition of AT device? Describe the definition's key components and their importance to independent functioning.
2. What are the various AT services? Discuss who might be responsible for making AT service decisions.
3. Create a timeline depicting key events in the history of assistive technology. Divide the timeline according to devices, services, and legislation.
4. Of all the events that occurred in history, create a top ten list of significant happenings across the three periods.
5. Pick a significant person in AT history. Conduct a mock interview with the individual and write it up as part of a mock Internet biography.
6. Assistive technology has a variety of applications for all types of people. Who might benefit from AT use? Why might some people be better candidates for AT use than others?

REFERENCES

Bryant, B. R., & O'Connell, M. (1998). The impact of the collaboration among tech act projects and protection and advocacy systems. *Intervention in School and Clinic, 33*(5), 309–12.

Bryant, B. R., Seay, P. C., O'Connell, M., & Comstock-Galagan, J. (1996). The Texas Assistive Technology Partnership and Advocacy, Incorporated: A cooperative partnership between Texas' tech act state project and its protection and advocacy system. *Technology and Disability, 5,* 275–82.

Bryant, D. P., & Bryant, B. R. (1998). Using assistive technology adaptations to include students with learning disabilities in cooperative learning activities. *Journal of Learning Disabilities, 31*(1), 41–54.

Bryant, W. V. (1996). *In search of freedom: How persons with disabilities have been disenfranchised from the mainstream of American Society.* Springfield, IL: Charles C. Thomas.

Cook, A. M., & Hussey, S. M. (1995). *Assistive technologies: Principles and practices.* St. Louis: Mosby.

Golinker, L. (April, 1994). Memorandum to assistive technology project directors, RE: Review of Tech Act amendments. Professional correspondence.

Hardman, M. L., Drew, C., Egan, W. (1996). *Human exceptionality* (5th ed.). Boston: Allyn and Bacon.

House of Representatives. (1993). House of Representative Report 103-208. Washington, DC: Author.

IBM (International Business Machines). (1991). *Technology and persons with disabilities.* Atlanta: IBM Corporate Support Programs.

McMurtrie, D. C. (1980). Notes on the Early History of Care for Cripples. William R. F. Phillips & J. Rosenberg (Eds.), The origins of modern treatment and education of physically handicapped children (pp. 27–41). New York: ARNO Press. Reprinted from Early History of the Care and Treatment of Cripples, *Johns Hopkins Hospital Bulletin,* Baltimore, 1914, pp. xxv, 57–62.

Pelka, F. (1997). *The disability rights movement.* Santa Barbara, CA: ANC:CLIO.

RESNA. (1992). *Project director's handbook.* Arlington, VA: Author.

Sauberger, D. (1996). *O&M living history: Where did our O&M techniques come from?* Retrieved August 21, 2000, from http://kathyz.home.mindspring.com/history.htm#first

Smith, D. D. (1998). *Introduction to special education* (3rd ed.). Boston: Allyn and Bacon.

U.S. Congress. (1988). U.S. Congress, Public Law 100-406, Technology-Related Assistance for Individuals with Disabilities Act of 1988.

Webster's Universal College Dictionary. (1997). New York: Gramercy Books.

Wiederholt, J. L., & Bryant, B. R. (1987). *Assessing the reading abilities and instructional needs of students.* Austin, TX: Pro-Ed.

Wise, B. W., & Olson, R. K. (1994). Computer speech and the remediation of reading and spelling problems. *Journal of Special Education Technology, 12*(3), 207–20.

CHAPTER TWO

ADAPTATIONS FRAMEWORK FOR CONSIDERING ASSISTIVE TECHNOLOGY

CHAPTER AT A GLANCE

INTRODUCTION TO THE ADAPTATIONS FRAMEWORK
- Personal Perspective 2.1

SETTING-SPECIFIC DEMANDS

PERSON-SPECIFIC CHARACTERISTICS
- Focus on 2.1

ADAPTATIONS
- Focus on 2.2
- Focus on 2.3
- Focus on 2.4

EVALUATION OF EFFECTIVENESS OF ADAPTATIONS
- Focus on 2.5

OBJECTIVES

1. Describe how considering assistive technology is included in the 1997 Amendments to IDEA and the Rehabilitation Act Amendments of 1998.
2. Explain the four components of the Adaptations Framework.

MAKING CONNECTIONS

Review the definitions of assistive technology, and assistive technology devices and services, which were presented in Chapter 1. Identify ways teachers make adaptations for students who qualify for special services under the 1997 Amendments to IDEA. Compare and contrast Section 504 of the Rehabilitation Act Amendments of 1998 and ADA (1990).

INTRODUCTION TO THE ADAPTATIONS FRAMEWORK

According to legislation such as ADA (1990) and IDEA (1997), individuals with disabilities have the right to be able to access environments that are available to all people. Environments include but are not limited to public school classrooms and curriculum, recreational and leisure activities, daily living activities (e.g., public transportation, access to buildings), and vocational and postsecondary settings. Simply, adaptations (or accommodations or modifications as stipulated in IDEA '97) are changes to conditions that facilitate access to those environments. Assistive technology devices can be viewed as examples of adaptations that may be necessary for individuals with disabilities to circumvent disability-related barriers (MacArthur & Haynes, 1995; McGregor & Pachuski, 1996).

The use of AT devices to promote access across environments is evident throughout life. In the classroom, adaptations are a common component of the delivery of special education services for assisting school-aged students to compensate for challenges associated with various disabilities (McGregor & Pachuski, 1996). For example, a student with a severe reading disability who struggles with decoding could use a reading machine to access print. The recognition of the instructional capabilities of assistive technologies has prompted an array of adaptation solutions (e.g., word prediction software, electronic spell checkers) to help students who have academic goals on their Individualized Education Programs (IEPs) and to facilitate progress in the general education or functional life skills curriculum. In the home or other environments where eating occurs, eating utensils can be adapted (e.g., built-up handles) to enable individuals with motor problems to grasp the handle and feed themselves independently. A liquid indicator can be attached to a cup to signal to an individual who is blind the level of liquid in relation to the top of the drinking utensil. Public transportation, such as the city bus, is required to have wheelchair accessibility to provide equal access for individuals who use wheelchairs. Advances in computer-based technology, such as speech recognition and text-to-speech software, have enabled individuals with sensory disabilities, for example, access to computers across environments such as home, school, and work.

As noted in Chapter 1, the rights of individuals with disabilities are protected under law including the need to consider AT devices and services as a means of addressing individual needs and fostering access, success, and independence. The laws protect individuals of all ages across settings. Thus, decision makers can benefit from utilizing a process that assists in the consideration of adaptations, including AT.

Educational Programs

In the field of education, IEPs are developed for all preschool through high school students with disabilities (ages 3 to 21). As stipulated in IDEA '97, the IEP team must "consider" a student's need for AT and services so that the student can receive a free, appropriate public education (FAPE) in the least restrictive environment (LRE) (Bowser & Reed, 1995). According to IDEA '97, AT devices and services are identified as services. IEP teams must "consider" AT to help students compensate for their specific disabilities and to meet the demands and expectations of school environments. Furthermore, "consideration of a child's need for assistive technology must occur on a case-by-case basis in connection with the development of a child's Individualized Education Program (IEP) (p. 1) (Schrag, 1990). For example, for students who are blind or visually impaired, instruction should be provided in Braille and the use of Braille unless the IEP team determines, after an assessment of the student's reading and writing needs presently and in the future, that instruction in Braille or the use of Braille is not appropriate (IDEA, 1997).

IEP teams must have in place a process for determining students' needs for AT on an individual basis. IEP teams must consider ways to help students successfully access the demands or expectations of their educational environments, access the general education classroom, and progress in the curriculum. IEP teams often choose from an array of adaptations or modifications that promote students' learning. Instructional adaptations consist of changes to teaching procedures, curriculum, management, materials and technology, and the physical environment to facilitate learning (Rivera & Smith, 1997). Assistive technology devices and services are certainly viable adaptation options.

IEP team members gather assessment data about the student's needs from the psycho-educational assessment process, and the speech/language and sensory-motor evaluations, if they were conducted. Additionally, technology evaluations must be conducted by specialists to determine the setting demands (i.e., tasks individuals perform in different environments and the requisite abilities needed to perform these tasks) and the needs and strengths of individuals in relation to these demands. AT devices can then be selected based on their features and how the features match the individual's abilities and promote independence. Table 2.1 provides questions for IEP team members to think about when considering the need for AT devices and services.

As a part of the total educational program, the need for AT devices and services for infants and toddlers and secondary level students must also be considered. Individualized Family Service Plans (IFSPs) for children birth through age two and statements of transition service needs and interagency responsibilities for older students can include provisions for AT to meet the student's individual needs. (See Smith, 2000, for a detailed discussion of IEPS, IFSPs, and transition.) For example, a communication device could be identified by the speech/language pathologist as essential for developing language skills and cause-effect responses for a toddler. The communication device then would become a part of the IFSP along with the appropriate support for the family and child to ensure proper use of the device.

For older students, transition service needs and interagency responsibilities, which become a part of the IEP document, are critical for identifying services to

TABLE 2.1 IEP Team Questions to Consider for the Selection of Assistive Technology Devices and Services

1. How can assistive technology devices and services enable the student to receive a free, appropriate public education?
2. How can assistive technology devices and services enable the student to receive an education in the least restrictive environment?
3. How can assistive technology devices and services enable the student to access the general education curriculum and achieve successfully IEP goals and short-term objectives?
4. How do the features of the device match the needs and strengths of the student?
5. How can the use of the devices and services be monitored to ensure successful implementation and benefit to the student?

Source: Adapted from Chambers, A. C. (1997). *Has technology been considered? A guide for IEP teams.* Reston, VA: Council of Administrators of Special Education and the Technology and Media Division of The Council for Exceptional Children.

promote a smooth transition from secondary to postsecondary settings. Therefore, individuals with disabilities, diagnosticians and psychologists, and service providers (e.g., on-campus service provisions, rehabilitation counselors) are challenged to determine appropriate AT devices and services at the secondary level that students can learn to use, which can transfer easily to the postsecondary setting.

Rehabilitation Field

In the rehabilitation field, one of the purposes of the Rehabilitation Act Amendments of 1998 is to empower individuals with disabilities to achieve employment, economic self-sufficiency, independence, and inclusion and integration into society. Assistive technology devices and services are included under the heading "rehabilitation technology," meaning the systematic application of technologies, engineering methodologies, or scientific principles to address the barriers encountered by individuals with disabilities in areas such as education, rehabilitation, employment, transportation, independent living, and recreation (Rehabilitation Act Amendments of 1998). Individuals are assessed for the need of rehabilitation technology devices and services to enable them to develop the capacity to perform in a work environment. Each state develops a plan that includes strategies to be used to address the needs of individuals identified during the assessment process. States must identify how AT devices and services will be provided to individuals at each stage of the rehabilitation process.

An individualized plan for employment must be developed by the vocational rehabilitation counselor and individual with a disability. The plan must include a description of the vocational rehabilitation services necessary to help the individual achieve employment including the use of AT devices and services (Rehabilitation Act Amendments of 1998). Assistive technology devices can facilitate participation in postsecondary and vocational settings and are an integral part of an effective support system used by people with disabilities. Although AT devices are rarely the only support needed, it could be argued that the use of AT devices can assist individuals with disabilities to function more independently (Bryant, Seay, & Bryant, 1999). Thus, AT has widespread application across environments and fields to empower people with disabilities to lead fulfilling lives.

Adaptations Framework

In this chapter, we discuss the Adaptations Framework for considering, selecting, and evaluating the use of adaptations including AT. IDEA '97 requires that the student's needs be examined first as a part of any discussion related to developing plans. Psycho-educational assessments serve as a first step in providing decision makers a wealth of information about an individual's present levels of performance in cognitive, sensory, motor, language, and social domains. This assessment information can help decision makers identify a plan of action, such as an IEP or a transition plan, to address the individual's needs. As the tasks (goals, short-term objectives), such as academic skills, language development, or work-related skills, are identified for the individual to accomplish, decision makers then must consider the individual's need for adaptations, AT being an option, to accomplish the tasks. We propose that the AF be implemented at this point in the decision-making and considerations process.

Professionals need to have a framework for considering adaptations, including AT. There are several choices. For example, in this chapter, our interview with Joy Zabala (Personal Perspective 2.1) features a discussion about the SETT Framework that she and her colleagues have developed and implemented across educational settings for considering an individual's need for AT.

Bryant and Bryant (1998) identified another Adaptations Framework, which is discussed in this chapter, that decision makers can use to examine an individual's needs for appropriate adaptations, including AT. The Adaptations Framework can be used to help professionals, families, and users decide on the type of adaptations that would be most beneficial to enable the individual to become more independent and achieve success with the tasks in any environment. Figure 2.1 shows the context for the Adaptations Framework. Decision makers have options for consideration. They may determine that (1) the individual requires an adaptation, such as AT, to meet his or her needs; (2) the individual requires a different type of adaptation including AT than what is presently being used; (3) the individual does not need an adaptation to meet his or her needs at this time; or (4) further information is required and additional evaluation is necessary, which may include an AT evaluation. In Chapter 3, we discuss AT evaluation, which can be conducted to select appropriate devices if decision makers require further information about matching devices to individual's needs.

PERSONAL PERSPECTIVE 2.1

Joy Zabala is an assistive technology practitioner, professional developer, and consultant in assistive technology and leadership. As an independent practitioner, she provides services to state departments of education, school districts, consumers of assistive technology, and others across the United States and abroad. She also serves as a consultant or advisory board member to several state and federal projects. She is a founding member of the QIAT Consortium and the developer of the SETT Framework.

Your SETT Framework is widely acknowledged as an excellent model for assistive technology service delivery. Describe the SETT Framework briefly for us.
SETT is an acronym for Student, Environments, Tasks, and Tools. Basically, the SETT Framework provides a structure for collaborative groups to work together and think well about the assistive technology devices and services that are needed to provide a student with disabilities access to educational opportunities. When using the SETT Framework, each person shares individual knowledge in order to build the team's collective knowledge of the student, the environments in which the student is expected to function, and the tasks that the student needs to be able to do to be an active learner in those environments. When the team's knowledge about the student, environments, and tasks has been built and analyzed, they are able to consider what system of assistive technology tools (devices and services) are necessary for the student, in identified environments, to do expected tasks.

What prompted you to develop the SETT Framework?
Actually, the development of SETT Framework was needs-based. When assistive technology first emerged, there was great hope that the "right" tools would help most students with disabilities make major strides in their educational programs and their lives. From early on, much effort was made to match the needs of the individual to the features of devices and many seemingly "right" tools were put in place. It quickly became apparent, however, that underutilization and abandonment of assistive technology devices were occurring at an unacceptably high rate. Though great progress was being made by some individuals, many were not benefiting much from the early promise of assistive technology. This was (and is) of great concern to my colleagues, and me and we felt a strong need to address this issue. As I talked with my colleagues and individuals with disabilities and their families about what "worked" and what didn't "work" with assistive technology, it became increasingly clear things "worked" better when tools (devices and services) were based on matches. The matches would consider not only the individual and the tools, but also the factors related to the environments in which the tools were expected to be used and the tasks that those environments required and/or that were very important to the individual. When trying to explain this to a colleague new to assistive technology one day, I wrote the first letters, S, E, T, and T on the board as we talked. He said, "Ah, SETT! Finally! Why didn't you tell me that before?" and the SETT Framework was launched!

How can IEP team members use the framework?
An important feature of the SETT Framework is that it supports the collaborative work by helping IEP team members understand that, while different people bring different

(continued)

knowledge, each person on the team brings critical expert knowledge in some area to the work of the group. When using the SETT Framework, each person shares his or her individual knowledge of the student, the environments, and/or the tasks in order to build the team's collective knowledge. Team members can then use their collective knowledge to consider whether or not assistive technology tools (devices and services) are required by the student, and, if they are, can develop a system of tools that is student-centered, environmentally useful, and task-focused. In other words, they can provide tools that can be used by the student to do expected tasks in a way that is compatible with the student's customary environments. By working through the SETT Framework together, IEP teams not only develop a solid basis for tool selection, but also have a shared vision of when and how the tools are supposed to be used by the student. In my view, this helps the team understand the links between IDEA, the IEP, and assistive technology in educational settings. It also helps all members of the team know when, how, and for what purpose assistive technology is integrated into the student's educational program.

The SETT Framework suggests to examine students as a first step. Describe your rationale for doing so.
The student is the center of the special education process, as required by the Individuals with Disabilities Education Act (IDEA). In order to be most effective, assistive technology processes must be a part of the special education planning process, not a separate process. With that in mind, the SETT Framework first asks this question about the student in a broad way: "What is it that the student needs to be able to do that is difficult or impossible to do at the expected levels of proficiency and independence at this time?" While this may look like a question about tasks, it is really much more general and helps focus on the strengths and challenges facing the student and those living and working with him or her.

In your experience, what has been a significant barrier that has impeded the ability to implement the SETT Framework and how can the barrier be addressed?
Time, of course, is always a problem with everything that involves collaborative thinking, as SETT does. Another is beginning with tools rather than really identifying what the tools will be *for* so that the most promising tools can be selected. One thing that has helped is for people to know a bit about the process *before* coming to the meeting where the SETT Framework will be used. I often send a note to all who will be there explaining that we will be looking at the student's assistive technology needs. I then ask them to spend a few minutes jotting down about five things that, from *their perspective* (student, parent, OT, SLP, teacher, and so on) they think the team needs to know about the student, the student's typical environments, and the tasks that are expected of the student so they can share this with the group. I explain further that we will use the information we gather to help us develop a system of assistive technology tools (devices and services) that will help the student, in those environments, do those tasks. This helps everyone get into the mind-set of what we are about. Also, I think it helps people focus on the collaborative *process* rather than focusing on their preferred solutions. When people arrive at the meeting, I like to have a large chart on the wall with columns for Student, Environments, and Tasks. As people arrive, I provide them with Post-it notes and ask them to prepare fifteen notes (five for student, five for environments, five for tasks) with *one* thing they want to be sure the group knows, then place the notes in the corresponding columns on the wall chart. This way, it is easy to gather a *lot* of information in a very short time. We can then look at what *we* (collectively) know, and discuss what needs to be clarified, removed, or added. This is a quick-start technique that has worked well for some teams and some facilitators.

What student success stories can you offer readers that speak to the helpful nature of SETT to address students' assistive technology needs?
A parent who was not aware of my involvement with SETT recently told me that she had finally had a meeting to discuss assistive technology that really worked well for the school and for her. That is, it resulted in a system of tools that all agreed upon that could really help the student. She explained that they had used a new process, the SETT Framework. Did I know of it? Of course, I was thrilled!

What role do families play in the SETT framework?
Families play a critical role in all planning of the educational program of students with disabilities, including being a part of assistive technology decision making and implementation. The SETT Framework encourages and honors the role of families because it requires the family perspective and expertise, particularly in the area of the Student, but also in the Environments, and the Tasks.

How do school administrators respond to the SETT Framework?
Generally, pretty well, since it is a process that makes sense and focuses on what the student needs to be able to do in order to be an active participant in educational environments, and mastery of the tasks that will lead to improved educational results for students with disabilities.

Reprinted with permission, Psycho-Educational Services.

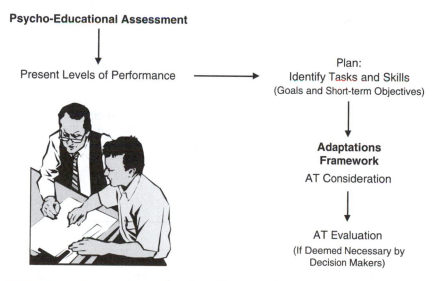

Psycho-Educational Assessment

Present Levels of Performance

Plan:
Identify Tasks and Skills
(Goals and Short-term Objectives)

Adaptations Framework

AT Consideration

AT Evaluation
(If Deemed Necessary by Decision Makers)

FIGURE 2.1   Context for Adaptations Framework

The Adaptations Framework (Bryant & Bryant, 1998) for "considering" whether or not a individual can benefit from adaptations includes examining the setting demands, examining information about the individual's needs and strengths as they relate to the setting demands, selecting appropriate adaptations that may include AT devices, and evaluating the effectiveness of the adaptation to promote access and success. Figure 2.2 provides an example of how the Adaptations Framework works. In this case, toothbrushing has been identified as a task an individual needs to learn how to do. We have to think about the task, the person, and the adaptation solutions, which will help the person complete the task. Only by carefully evaluating each step of the Adaptations Framework can we begin to ensure a good match between the person's needs and the task at hand.

A series of questions can be answered to facilitate decision making as the Adaptations Framework is implemented. As shown in Figure 2.3, the questions are designed to help decision makers think about the setting demands, the person, and the adaptations. IEP teams and other decision makers, such as technology specialists, teachers, and rehabilitation counselors, can use these questions as they discuss appropriate adaptations. Now we will discuss the Adaptations Framework more fully.

SETTING-SPECIFIC DEMANDS

People encounter many settings as they go about their daily business. Classrooms, offices, and grocery stores are all examples of different settings. These settings present specific demands that people must be able to address to be successful in those

Setting-Specific Demands		Person-Specific Characteristics		Adaptations
Task	**Requisite Abilities**	**Functional Capabilities**	**Functional Limitations**	**Simple-to-Complex**
brushing teeth	grasping brush and paste; squeezing paste onto brush; brushing teeth; rinsing mouth	vision; hearing; cognitive ability to complete task	grasping/ fine motor; sequencing difficulties	adapted handle; checklist of steps; electronic brush

⇧   ⇧   ⇧   ⇧   ⇧

Evaluation of Effectiveness

FIGURE 2.2   Example of the Adaptations Framework
Adapted from Bryant & Bryant (1998), p. 51.

Adaptations Framework   **Consideration Questions**

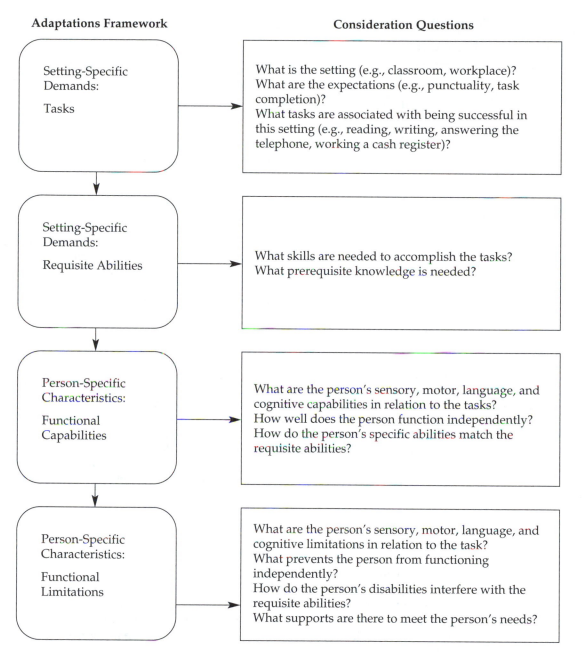

Setting-Specific Demands:

Tasks

What is the setting (e.g., classroom, workplace)? What are the expectations (e.g., punctuality, task completion)? What tasks are associated with being successful in this setting (e.g., reading, writing, answering the telephone, working a cash register)?

Setting-Specific Demands:

Requisite Abilities

What skills are needed to accomplish the tasks? What prerequisite knowledge is needed?

Person-Specific Characteristics:

Functional Capabilities

What are the person's sensory, motor, language, and cognitive capabilities in relation to the tasks? How well does the person function independently? How do the person's specific abilities match the requisite abilities?

Person-Specific Characteristics:

Functional Limitations

What are the person's sensory, motor, language, and cognitive limitations in relation to the task? What prevents the person from functioning independently? How do the person's disabilities interfere with the requisite abilities? What supports are there to meet the person's needs?

FIGURE 2.3   Questions to Facilitate Use of Adaptations Framework
Adapted from Bryant & Bryant (1998), p. 45.

(continued)

FIGURE 2.3   Continued

Adaptations Framework   Consideration Questions

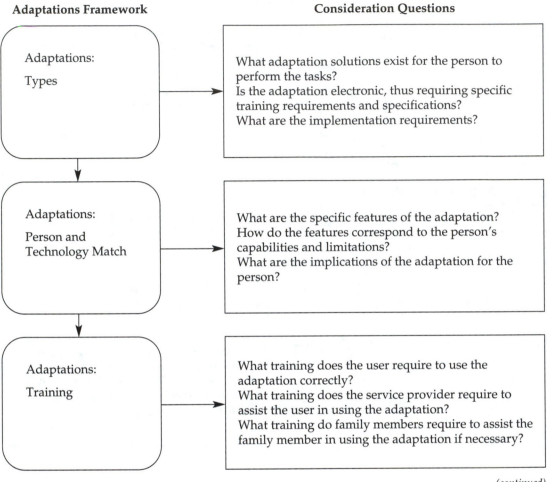

Adaptations: Types	What adaptation solutions exist for the person to perform the tasks? Is the adaptation electronic, thus requiring specific training requirements and specifications? What are the implementation requirements?
Adaptations: Person and Technology Match	What are the specific features of the adaptation? How do the features correspond to the person's capabilities and limitations? What are the implications of the adaptation for the person?
Adaptations: Training	What training does the user require to use the adaptation correctly? What training does the service provider require to assist the user in using the adaptation? What training do family members require to assist the family member in using the adaptation if necessary?

(continued)

settings. Setting demands include (a) tasks people must address, and (b) the requisite abilities or skills people need to perform the tasks successfully (Bryant & Bryant, 1998). For example, in the grocery store (the setting), individuals must be able to select food items (task). To do so, they must be able to read a grocery list or remember what is needed, locate the items in the store, carry them in some fashion, purchase them, and get the items home (requisite abilities).

At the K-12 school and postsecondary level, setting demands are particularly difficult for many students with disabilities. Setting demands include the curriculum that is taught, how information is delivered to and received by students, and how students demonstrate their understanding of the curriculum (Rivera & Smith, 1997). Research findings have informed us about the importance of examining the

FIGURE 2.3   Continued

Adaptations Framework	Consideration Questions

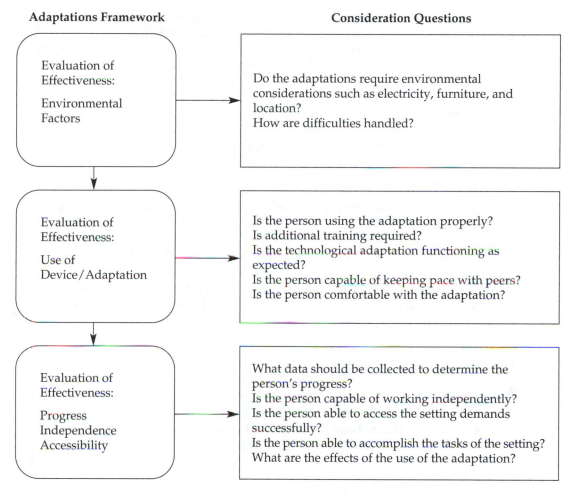

demands of educational settings that students encounter daily (Bryant & Bryant, 1998; Rieth & Evertson, 1988; Schumaker & Deshler, 1984). For instance, in the high school or postsecondary classroom setting, the teacher may expect students to come to class on time, listen to instruction, take notes, read text, and write a report (tasks). To perform these tasks, students must be able to tell time; possess the ability to hear; understand the critical features of the lecture for notetaking purposes; be able to decode and comprehend text; and know how to identify, organize, and produce ideas in written form (requisite abilities for the tasks), respectively. Yet we know that for many students with disabilities, these high school setting demands present challenges that must be addressed.

Tasks

People encounter numerous tasks related to settings on a daily basis. For instance, secondary level students may be expected to comprehend textbook material (Ellis, 1996; Miller, 1996); solve complex mathematical equations; develop a listening, speaking, and reading vocabulary in a foreign language; demonstrate writing proficiency skills, and use notetaking skills (Suritsky & Hughes, 1996). In another setting, a movie theater, people need access to seating and hearing the dialogue. Each task represents a challenge *if* the task clashes with a person's disability-related limitations. Such "functional dissonance" mandates that adaptations be made so that people can accomplish those tasks successfully (Bryant, Seay, & Bryant, 1999).

Requisite Abilities

Requisite abilities are skills that must be demonstrated to accomplish the tasks of the setting demands (Bryant & Rivera, 1995). For instance, the task of "reading the textbook" requires the requisite abilities of seeing print, decoding, comprehending text (including vocabulary), reading fluently, and so forth. The task of communicating with a friend requires the requisite abilities of thinking about the message and articulating the words to send the message. Many people possess these requisite abilities for the tasks; some individuals with disabilities lack the requisite skills that are necessary for meeting specific tasks unless adaptations are implemented.

PERSON-SPECIFIC CHARACTERISTICS

As a part of the Adaptations Framework, decision makers examine person-specific characteristics, the functional capabilities and limitations, as they relate to the setting's tasks. Decision makers should think about possible adaptations including instructional (e. g., extended time to complete assignments, fewer problems to complete) as well as assistive technology, that will enable the individual to perform the task. Figure 2.2 provides examples of questions that can be used for considering person-specific functional capabilities and limitations.

Functional Capabilities

Functional capabilities or strengths refer to cognitive (e.g., reading, writing, reasoning), sensory (e.g., visual, auditory), language (e.g., listening, speaking), and motor (e.g., fine, gross) capabilities that individuals use to perform tasks. Determination of an individual's functional capabilities in relation to setting demands is important for selecting appropriate adaptations. For instance, a student who has a reading disability yet has good listening skills (i.e., functional capability) may benefit from tape-recorded text to access the reading text for class. Similarly, a student's functional capability, such as visual acuity skills, dictates whether preferential seating, a magnification device, and/or Braille materials should be used for accessing and performing the tasks associated with the setting.

Functional Limitations

Functional limitations are disability-related characteristics that could impede an individual's ability to perform the setting demands (tasks). Functional limitations include difficulties with cognitive or academic skills, sensory abilities, language, and motor skills as they relate specifically to the tasks in the settings. For instance, a person who has a mathematical disability (e.g., dyscalculia) may exhibit difficulty with computational or word problem-solving skills (tasks of the setting). Functional limitations typically are documented in a psycho-educational assessment. Decision makers must determine how a person's functional limitations interfere with the ability to perform specific tasks. Following identification of the setting demands (tasks and requisite abilities) and the individual's capabilities and limitations, decision makers can examine possible adaptations.

FOCUS ON 2.1

Develop your own Adaptations Framework chart, which you will add to later in this chapter, by thinking about a particular setting and the tasks associated with that setting. Now consider a person with a disability and identify possible functional capabilities and limitations for this person. This will be your case study. Use the questions in Figure 2.3 (setting-specific demands and person-specific characteristics) to help you think about possible adaptations. Record your answers on your chart.

ADAPTATIONS

As decisions are made about the selection of adaptations, decision makers must consider the setting demands, the needs of the individual, and the features of the adaptations; this is called *setting-person-feature match.* Also, decision makers need to consider if the adaptation is reasonable, is relevant to the setting demands, and is effective. We have already discussed setting demands and person-specific characteristics. In this section, we provide an overview of types of adaptations and discuss selection and training considerations to ensure a good beginning with the setting-person-feature match. Figure 2.3 (adaptations) provides examples of questions that can be considered when selecting adaptations. Also, Chapter 3 provides a thorough discussion of formal AT evaluation, which provides additional information for selecting appropriate AT adaptation solutions.

Types of Adaptations

Adaptations can be discussed according to several dimensions, including nonassistive and assistive technology adaptations, simple to complex adaptations, and features of adaptations.

Nonassistive and Assistive Technology Adaptations.   Adaptations can involve nonassistive technology adaptations and assistive technology adaptations. A nonassistive technology adaptation might involve the use of a reader (i.e., someone who reads the material) for a student whose task is to read the textbook but who has extreme difficulty reading the material because of word recognition and reading fluency problems. In the same way, a person who is required to compose a paper might benefit from the services of a scribe (i.e., someone who transcribes information) to help get words down on paper. Finally, a checklist of steps can help a person remember the steps that are necessary to complete a particular task if assistance is needed in the area of memory and organization. All of these examples illustrate the use of nonassistive technology adaptations to assist individuals with accomplishing the tasks of their environment.

Adaptations become "assistive technology" when they conform to the definition of such technology (see Chapter 1) and help individuals "improve functional capabilities." Thus, if a person with a disability uses a device, it becomes assistive when it is "used to increase, maintain or improve the functional capabilities of individuals with disabilities." Bryant and Rivera (1995) noted that AT, in some instances, is simply technology that becomes assistive when its use satisfies the criteria found in the AT definition. For example, a calculator is "helpful" technology to many people but can be considered AT when used to perform basic calculations by an individual with a math disability.

Simple-to-Complex Adaptations.   Adaptations range on a continuum from simple to complex (McGregor & Pachuski, 1996), depending on features such as user, family, and teacher/caregiver training requirements; ease of implementation and maintenance; and technological features (e.g., hardware platform specifications, electronic capabilities). For example, obtaining a copy of someone's notes from a lecture could be relatively simple because it requires the identification of someone who would be willing to share his or her notes and the use of a copy machine, whereas a multistep behavior management program could be considered a more complex adaptation for a youngster who needs extra structure and teacher intervention.

For AT adaptations, a calculator with large keys might be considered a relatively simple adaptation because limited training is necessary, it is fairly simple to use, maintenance costs are restricted primarily to battery replacement, and the technology features are quite simple. An electronic augmentative communication device, such as Speaking Dynamically™ Pro by Mayer-Johnson (a device that speaks what is displayed on screen), would be an example of a complex AT device. This augmentative communication device requires training for the user, family, and teacher on the technological features such as graphics, buttons, digitized speech, scanning and printing capabilities, word processing abilities, and various access method capabilities. Although these are excellent features in terms of promoting access to the hardware and communication options for the user, the device is complex to operate, at least initially.

Features.   Adaptations can be described in terms of their features, which include purpose of the adaptation, user requirements to use the adaptation, environmental accessibility (e.g., school, work, home), technological components, ease of use, training requirements, and maintenance requirements (e.g., battery replacement, parts placement) (Raskind & Bryant, 1996). Decision makers must carefully analyze the needs of the user and the features of the adaptation so that adaptations are simple enough to use but contain sufficient features to be helpful for the user to be successful with the setting demands (Todis, 1996). Information about adaptations' features can be obtained from vendors, users, and professionals across disciplines (e.g., occupational therapists, speech and language therapists) and organizations that are designed to provide consumer information (e.g., Alliance for Technology Access). Table 2.2 provides questions about adaptations' features for IEP teams to think about as they make decisions about the student's needs for adaptations and appropriate adaptation matches.

FOCUS ON 2.2

Identify several AT adaptations through the Internet, catalogues, or a local AT lab that might possibly be appropriate for your case study. Conduct a feature analysis of the adaptations using the information in the features section and the questions presented in Table 2.2.

Selection of AT Adaptations

There are several considerations for identifying AT adaptation solutions.

Features.   The features of the AT adaptations, as discussed above, must be examined to determine an appropriate match between the setting demands, the person-specific characteristics, and the adaptation features. When selecting AT adaptations, decision makers must determine the types of AT adaptations that would enhance the individual's success and independence (Bowser & Reed, 1995). Features of the AT should promote the individual's independence and ability to function on his or her own across settings. Independence is one of the most promising and crucial aspects of AT. Take, for example, a student who does not have the use of his arms. Previously he could have created term papers only by dictating them to an aide. Now, through the use of a speech-to-text computer system, he can write his own papers independently.

Thus, the features of the adaptation must be matched appropriately to the individual's needs (i.e., strengths and limitations) and to the tasks required in the setting to facilitate independence as much as possible. For example, if the task is to use instructional software to practice a skill and the individual needs an adapted keyboard to be able to access the computer, then a touch screen might be one of

TABLE 2.2   Adaptations Considerations

1. Purpose of the Adaptation
   - What is the intended purpose of the adaptation?
   - Is there a specific target group for whom the device is an adaptation?
   - For what tasks is the adaptation intended to be used (e.g., reading, communication)?
2. Requirements to Use the Adaptation
   - What abilities must the user/student possess to use the adaptation successfully?
3. Environmental Accessibility
   - Is the adaptation transferable across environments?
   - Can the adaptation be transported easily?
   - What are the requirements to use the adaptation in various environments (e.g., electrical, furniture)?
4. Technological Components
   - Does the adaptation involve electrical hardware and software?
   - Is there voice input or speech output capabilities?
   - Does the user/student need to access a keyboard to use the adaptation?
   - Is the adaptation compatible with other technological components?
5. Ease of Use
   - How easy is the adaptation to learn to use?
   - Are there technological components that might take time to learn (e.g., programming)?
   - Does the use of the adaptation promote the individual's independence?
6. Training Requirements
   - How much training is required by the user, family, teacher/caregiver?
   - What kind of follow-up to training might be necessary?
   - Is technical support readily available to troubleshoot when technology problems arise?
7. Maintenance Requirements
   - How durable is the adaptation?
   - How reliable is the adaptation?
   - What regular maintenance is necessary to ensure continued use of the adaptation?
   - Who will do the maintenance?
   - How long will maintenance take to correct problems?
   - What "loaner" options are available?

several possible adaptation solutions decision makers can consider. The touch screen is a possibility because it promotes access by providing a larger area for responding.

When dealing with computer-based AT adaptations, reliability and durability are two critical issues to be considered for successful implementation. Devices that fail or perform sporadically and have parts that break easily will quickly be abandoned unless repair is expedient or "loaners" are readily available (Todis, 1996). In a teacher survey, findings suggested that teachers rate as "very important" the time to program, set up, and customize equipment as well as funds for repair, upgrade, and replacement (McGregor & Pachuski, 1996).

Environments.   Adaptations should be examined across environments for possible barriers to ensure a good setting-person-feature match as individuals move across settings. Environments must be explored to ensure that individuals can use the adaptation as needed. For example, transportability of the adaptation, such as an augmentative communication device (see Chapter 5 for examples), is critical to ensure that the individual can continue to communicate regardless of the environment (e.g., home, school, and community). The transportability of adaptations across environments and tasks, however, raises questions about insuring and replacing them and who bears that responsibility. Physical space may need to be analyzed if it impedes cross-environmental use. For example, if an individual uses a wheelchair, then access to environments (e.g., classroom, corridors, and doorways) must be ensured.

Attitudes and Acceptance.   Because the selection of adaptations requires the collaborative decision making of professionals, families, and users, the attitudes and levels of acceptance by all parties involved can be influential in the sustained use of the adaptation. Attitudes and acceptance are often influenced by a person's comfort level with the adaptation; most people do not feel comfortable initially with new devices and strategies, thus the importance of persistence, training, and support.

Professionals must be involved in the selection process and encouraged to describe their attitudes about the proposed adaptations. Acceptance of the selected adaptations by professionals is critical if the adaptations are to be integrated properly into the environment (e.g., classroom, work).

The implications of technology for people with disabilities and their families are critical. Family members should be active members of any decision-making process (Bryant & Kemp, 1995). Richards (1995) discussed family-related guidelines to be considered when making appropriate setting-person-feature matches. Decision makers must consider family experience and comfort level with technology, their acceptance of the adaptations, and the resources that are necessary to help families integrate AT adaptations into their homes and their community contacts. Families should be aware of the expected outcomes of AT adaptations; these outcomes should reflect the needs of the technology consumers and their families in promoting independence (Parette & Brotherson, 1996). Assistive technology devices should enhance the abilities of the family to help meet the user's needs. Assistive technology services, such as training and funding options, must be provided to families and/or caregivers as they work with the user. Selection of adaptations that are not accepted by family members will contribute to difficulties between home and school and ultimately to the abandonment of the adaptation by the user (Angelo, Jones, & Kokosa, 1995).

Finally, decision makers must consider the user's attitudes and acceptance level of the adaptation (Carney & Dix, 1992). The user's opinions about the types of adaptation options, attitudes about using adaptations, and interest in trying available options must be considered. Decision makers should be sensitive to the user's attitude about whether or not the adaptation will promote his or her independence. Moreover, the motivational level of the user is critical when selecting

AT adaptations (Carney & Dix, 1992; Raskind & Bryant, 2002). No adaptation will work if the user is against it, because the device simply will not be used.

Funding.   Different funding sources are available from which assistance can be provided once the adaptation is selected. Adaptations, such as technological devices, have a wide expense range. Although cost should not be the determining factor when selecting an adaptation, decision makers certainly can explore simple and reasonable, low-cost adaptations as viable options to match the needs of the user. Adaptations do not always have to be high-end "bells and whistles" to be effective for an individual. Locating a funding source can be a problem, but funding alternatives and supplemental funding sources, such as Medicare, insurance, and grants should be explored (Derer, Polsgrove, & Rieth, 1996). Once an AT adaptation has been selected, training for all parties involved is necessary.

FOCUS ON 2.3

Select an AT adaptation for your case study. Based on what you have learned in the Selection of AT Adaptations section, provide a rationale for your choice.

Training for Assistive Technology

Training, which is considered to be an AT service, is critical to ensure that AT adaptations are used and maintained rather than abandoned (Parette, Brotherson, Hourcade, & Bradley, 1996). Not surprising, training in the use of specific AT adaptations is one of the top-ranked issues for the successful implementation of the devices (Wehmeyer, 1999). For instance, Todis (1996) noted that specialists were frustrated by the limited use of adaptations because classroom teachers had difficulty coming up with solutions to problems with technology devices that were not working properly. Unfortunately, Todis (1996) found that devices were left unused and students were left without the support they needed.

The need for training applies to any individual who works with the user, such as classroom teachers, instructional assistants, specialized professionals (e. g., speech/language therapists), family members, and the user (Todis, 1996). Because teachers are usually the first people with whom families discuss school issues, teachers should have a good working knowledge of AT adaptations (Parette, Brotherson, & Huer, 2000). Professional development workshops can provide both low- and high-intensity training, coupled with follow-up support that focuses on practical application and troubleshooting implementation problems (Derer, Polsgrove, & Rieth, 1996). Also, because instructional assistants may be the primary caregivers in different environments, they must be included in workshops so that they too can become competent in the use of AT adaptations (Todis, 1996).

Because of the transportability of AT across environments, including the home, family members must be trained in the use of adaptations (Bryant & Bryant,

1998). For instance, Lemons (2000) found, in a survey of parents whose children used augmentative communication devices, a need to know more about these devices. Specific training procedures should focus on handling, care, and storage of devices to ensure proper treatment of expensive hardware. Also, families should be aware of the outcomes associated with the use of AT devices; these outcomes should reflect the needs of the family in promoting their child's independence. Support services, such as training and funding options, should be available to families as they adjust to the adaptations their children require as part of appropriate educational programming (Bryant & Bryant, 1998).

Training for the user is critical because, without training, the adaptation may not be used consistently or properly, resulting in abandonment. Several topics and procedures can be included in the training, such as:

- providing a rationale for the adaptation
- teaching the vocabulary related to the adaptation
- giving explicit instructions (e. g., modeling, examples, feedback)
- using visual, oral, and written instructions (e. g., videotapes, diagrams) on correct implementation (Anderson-Inman, Knox-Quinn, & Horney, 1996; Day & Edwards, 1996)

Also, users may require training on computer literacy, keyboarding skills, input devices (e.g., speech-to-text software, touch-sensitive mouse, trackball mouse, touch screen), and output devices (refreshable Braille displays, screen readers) (Raskind & Bryant, 1996). Certainly, the quality of the tutorials to teach individuals how to use devices or to serve as a backup after more formal training has occurred is an important training consideration. Finally, evaluation of the use of the adaptation is necessary (see Evaluation of Effectiveness of Adaptations section).

FOCUS ON 2.4

Identify the training you think will be necessary for the AT adaptation you chose for your case study. Talk with a partner and brainstorm a training plan. Share your plan with your peers in class.

EVALUATION OF EFFECTIVENESS OF ADAPTATIONS

Although adaptations have the potential to enhance access to setting demands, promote independence and productivity, and circumvent functional limitations, studies show that almost one-third of the devices are abandoned within the first year of use (Phillips, 1991). This trend is disappointing considering the potential and cost of adaptations. Abandonment occurs because users may not be achieving independence, training was insufficient, or numerous equipment issues (e.g., maintenance, reliability) interfere with their success (Phillips, 1992). Therefore, evaluation of the effectiveness of adaptations including AT is crucial. Figure 2.3 provides examples of questions that can be considered when evaluating the effectiveness of adaptations. Evaluation can include environmental factors, use of the adaptation, and monitoring user progress.

Environmental Factors

Any AT adaptation that involves hardware and software should be examined to determine if the features (e.g., sound, printer, extended keyboard) have specific environmental needs (e.g., space, electricity) (Raskind & Shaw, 1996). Devices that produce sound or require electricity will necessitate environmental accommodations. Devices such as talking calculators, speech synthesizers, and tape recorders, which produce sound, may need to be used in a location of the environment that does not distract others; headphones are an alternative to segregation. Also, the location of electrical outlets will dictate where devices, which require electricity, can be set up; other devices may require batteries—battery-operated versions are often preferable when mobile environments are part of the setting. Finally, professionals, family members, and users should note the versatility of AT devices across environments, such as classroom to dorm room/home, home to community, and class to class, to determine if the device meets their needs across environments (e.g., transporting the device, ability to use device across setting demands).

Use of Adaptations

The use of the adaptation should be evaluated carefully by professionals, family members, and users by examining several factors. First, it should be noted how easy it is for the adaptation to be used and if further training is required. For example, if electronic devices are being implemented, they may overwhelm the family and user, thus limiting the possibility that the device will be used. More training may be required for successful implementation (Lemons, 2000).

Second, the performance (i.e., reliability and durability) of technological adaptations should be monitored carefully (Bowser & Reed, 1995). If the performance of the adaptation necessitates frequent repairs, and thus interferes with the user's success, then the adaptation may need to be reconsidered. Furthermore, the availability of technical support is critical. Users and service providers must have access to support by technology experts when problems are encountered with the AT.

Third, users should note their ability to keep pace with their peers or colleagues to complete the tasks of the setting demands (e.g., taking notes in class). Practice using various types of adaptations (technological in particular) may be needed to maximize their effectiveness. For instance, Anderson-Inman and colleagues (1996) found that secondary school students with learning disabilities expressed a need to develop fluent keyboarding skills so that they could use specialized software for studying purposes. Finally, user fatigue should be monitored to determine if the use of the adaptation proves tiring and thus hinders productivity. Observations of the user in action may also result in optimized patterns of technology usage or the development of new techniques that prove more effective.

Monitoring User Progress

Professionals, family members, and users can evaluate whether the adaptations are beneficial by monitoring the progress of the individual. That is, are the adaptations helping users compensate for specific difficulties (e.g., reading and writing) so that they can meet the demands of the settings? Specifically, is the individual able to perform tasks, master goals and objectives stipulated on plans, and achieve independence? Compared to not using the adaptation, is the individual progressing at a rate commensurate with his or her peers? Is accessibility no longer an issue? These are just some of the questions that can be considered to determine the progress of users with adaptations including AT.

Evaluation of the adaptation needs to be ongoing to determine if the adaptation continues to meet the individual's needs as he or she matures (e.g., a student in the elementary grades will have different needs than a student in a postsecondary setting) and as the setting demands change (public school to workplace setting). As the individual learns more skills and matures, and encounters increasingly complex setting demands, the individual's needs will change. For example, a child with cerebral palsy who receives physical therapy to develop motor skills will probably benefit from different AT adaptations than an adult with cerebral palsy who has developed some motor skills and has adapted to many of his or her environments. Many disability-related technologies (e.g., screen readers) become dated with the evolution of the mainstream technology with which they must work. This factor may actually be more linked to a need to upgrade than to the individual's changing skills, demands, and abilities.

However, as the individual continues to age, his or her AT needs will probably continue to change to reflect the aging process. For school-age children, as their skills increase and as the academic setting demands become more challenging, adaptations at the elementary level (e.g., a pencil grip) may need to be changed to something more appropriate (e.g., a word processing program) to better address the setting-person-feature match.

Evaluation is an integral part of the Adaptations Framework. Reevaluation of any component of the process may be necessary to determine a more appropriate adaptation to satisfy setting demands and user needs and to foster success, independence, and accessibility.

FOCUS ON 2.5

Finally to conclude the Adaptations Framework process, identify an evaluation plan for your case study. Share your ideas with a partner or in a small group.

SUMMARY

Individuals with disabilities are legally entitled to access environments available to everyone. Adaptations including AT are often necessary to promote access to environmental setting demands. Decision makers, including professionals, family members, and users, must consider the need for AT adaptations and are required to do so according to IDEA (1997).

Adaptations are a common component of the delivery of special education services. As decisions are made about the selection of adaptations, decision makers must consider the setting demands, the needs of the individual, and the types of adaptations. Training is crucial to ensure that AT adaptations will be used and maintained rather than abandoned. Training should be made available for all parties involved and be ongoing with follow-up and support. Evaluation of the effectiveness of the adaptations includes environmental factors, use of the adaptation, use of the adaptation over time, and user progress and must be an integral component of the use of any adaptation.

DISCUSSION QUESTIONS

1. What do the 1997 Amendments to IDEA and the Rehabilitation Act Amendments of 1998 say about AT consideration?
2. What are the four components of the Adaptations Framework?
3. Define setting demands and provide examples of tasks and requisite abilities.
4. What are examples of functional capabilities and limitations?
5. Explain nonassistive and assistive technology adaptations, simple to complex adaptations, and features of adaptations.
6. Describe the considerations for selecting AT adaptations.
7. What AT training should be presented to professionals, families, and users?
8. What are the three components of evaluation? Briefly describe each one.

REFERENCES

Anderson-Inman, L., Knox-Quinn, C., & Horney, M. A. (1996). Computer-based study strategies for students with learning disabilities: Individual differences associated with adoption level. *Journal of Learning Disabilities, 29*(5), 461–84.

Angelo, D. H., Jones, S. D., & Kokoska, S. M. (1995). Family perspective on augmentative and alternative communication: Families of young children. *Augmentative and Alternative Communication, 11,* 193–201.

Bowser, G., & Reed, P. (1995). Education TECH points for assistive technology planning. *Journal of Special Education Technology, 12*(4), 325–38.

Bryant, B. R., & Kemp, C. (1995, June). *Assistive technology and the individualized education program.* Paper presented at the Texas Federation CEC annual conference, Fort Worth, TX.

Bryant, B. R., & Rivera, D. P. (1995, November). *Cooperative learning: Teaching in an age of technology.* Paper presented at the Learning Disabilities Association of Texas conference, Austin, TX.

Bryant, B. R., Seay, P. C., & Bryant, D. P. (1999). Assistive technology and adaptive behavior. In R. Schalock (Ed.), *Adaptive behavior and its measurement: Implications for the field of mental retardation* (pp. 81–98). Washington, DC: AAMR.

Bryant, D. P., & Bryant, B. R. (1998). Using assistive technology adaptations to include students with learning disabilities in cooperative learning activities. *Journal of Learning Disabilities, 31*(1), 41–54.

Carnery, J., & Dix, C. (1992). Integrating assistive technology in the classroom and community. In G. Church & S. Glennen (Eds.), *The handbook of assistive technology* (pp. 207–40). San Diego: Singular Publishing Group.

Day, S. L., & Edwards, B. J. (1996). Assistive technology for postsecondary students with learning disabilities. *Journal of Learning Disabilities, 29*(5), 486–92, 503.

Derer, K., Polsgrove, L., & Rieth, H. (1996). A survey of assistive technology applications in schools and recommendations for practice. *Journal of Special Education Technology, 13*(2), 62–80.

Ellis, E. S. (1996). Reading instruction. In D. D. Deshler, E. S. Ellis, & B. K. Lenz (Eds.), *Teaching adolescents with learning disabilities* (2nd ed.; pp. 61–126). Denver: Love Publishing Company.

Individuals with Disabilities Education Act. Pub. L. No. 104-17, 111 STAT.37.

Lemons, C. J. (2000). *Comparison of parent and teacher knowledge and opinions related to augmentative and alternative communication.* Unpublished master's thesis, The University of Texas, Austin.

MacArthur, C. A., & Haynes, J. A. (1995). Student assistant for learning from text (SALT): A hypermedia reading aid. *Journal of Learning Disabilities, 28*(3), 150–59.

McGregor, G., & Pachuski, P. (1996). Assistive technology in schools: Are teachers, ready, able, and supported? *Journal of Special Education Technology, 13*(1), 4–15.

Miller, S. P. (1996). Perspectives on mathematics instruction. In D. D. Deshler, E. S. Ellis, & B. K. Lenz (Eds.), *Teaching adolescents with learning disabilities* (2nd ed., pp. 313–68). Denver: Love Publishing Company.

Parette, H. P., Jr., & Brotherson, M. J. (1996). Family participation in assistive technology assessment for young children with mental retardation and developmental disabilities. *Education and Training in Mental Retardation and Developmental Disabilities, 31*(1), 29–43.

Parette, H. P., Jr., Brotherson, M. J., Hourcade, J. J., & Bradley, R. H. (1996). Family-centered assistive technology assessment. *Intervention in School and Clinic, 32*(2), 104–12.

Parette, H. P., Jr., Brotherson, M. J., & Huer, M. B. (2000). Giving families a voice in augmentative and alternative communication decision making. *Education and Training in Mental Retardation and Developmental Disabilities, 35*(2), 177–90.

Phillips, B. (1991). *Technology abandonment: From the consumer point of view.* Washington, DC: Request Publication.

Phillips, B. (1992). *Perspectives on assistive technology services in vocational rehabilitation: Clients and counselors.* Washington, DC: National Rehabilitation Hospital, Assistive Technology/ Rehabilitation Engineering Program.

Raskind, M., & Bryant, B. R. (2002). *Functional evaluation of assistive technology (FEAT).* Austin, TX: Psycho-Educational Services.

Raskind, M., & Shaw, T. (1996, March). *An overview: Assistive technology for students with learning disabilities.* Council for Learning Disabilities Assistive Technology Symposium, Las Vegas.

Rehabilitation Act Amendments of 1998. Section 504, U.S.C. section 2.

Richards, D. (1995). *Assistive technology: Birth to five years.* Cromwell, CT: ConnSense.

Rieth, H. J., & Evertson, C. (1988). Variables related to the effective instruction of difficult-to-teach children. *Focus on Exceptional Children, 20*(5), 1–8.

Rivera, D. P., & Smith, D. D. (1997). *Teaching students with learning and behavior problems* (3rd ed.). Boston: Allyn and Bacon.

Schrag, J. (1990). *OSEP Policy Letter.* Washington, DC: U.S. Office of Education.

Schumaker, J. B., & Deshler, D. D. (1984). Setting demand variables: A major factor in program planning for the LD adolescent. *Topics in Language Disorders, 4*(2), 22–40.

Smith, D. D. (2000). *Introduction to special education* (4th ed.). Boston: Allyn and Bacon.

Suritsky, S. K., & Hughes, C. A. (1996). Notetaking strategy instruction. In D. D. Deshler, E. S. Ellis, & B. K. Lenz (Eds.), *Teaching adolescents with learning disabilities* (2nd ed.; pp. 267–312). Denver: Love Publishing Company.

Todis, B. (1996). Tools for the task? Perspectives on assistive technology in educational settings. *Journal of Special Education Technology, 13*(2), 49–61.

Wehmeyer, M. L. (1999). Assistive technology and students with mental retardation: Utilization and barriers. *Journal of Special Education Technology, 14*(1), 48–58.

CHAPTER THREE

ASSISTIVE TECHNOLOGY ASSESSMENTS

CHAPTER AT A GLANCE

OVERVIEW OF GENERAL ASSESSMENT ISSUES
- Focus on 3.1

ASSISTIVE TECHNOLOGY ASSESSMENTS
- Focus on 3.2

ASSESSMENT COMPONENTS
- Focus on 3.3

OBJECTIVES

1. Identify the qualities of effective assessments.
2. Determine how tasks, individuals, devices, and contexts work together to influence the nature of AT assessments.
3. Examine the features of an effective AT assessment to ensure that the individual and device combine to provide an effective person-technology match.

MAKING CONNECTIONS

Think about how assessments are used on a regular basis to gather information about people. What types of instruments are administered and by whom? What information is gleaned by such assessments and how are their results used? What kinds of information would be important to obtain concerning AT use? What factors would affect AT use and how might those factors be examined? Who would conduct such assessments? What would be the purpose of such assessments?

In Chapter 2, we introduced the importance of AT assessments to ensure that the devices that are selected and used will match a person's strengths and alleviate disability-related challenges. This chapter explores the evaluation process more in depth by examining a number of assessment-related issues. First, we overview basic issues in assessment that must be considered when any type of evaluation occurs. Then we discuss specific assessment issues as they relate to assistive technology. We complete the chapter by discussing specific components that should be addressed during AT assessments.

OVERVIEW OF GENERAL ASSESSMENT ISSUES

Most assessments are conducted to identify strengths and weaknesses, determine program eligibility, document progress, select interventions, and/or conduct research (Hammill & Bryant, 1998). In reality, AT assessments may be conducted for all these reasons. The purpose of this section is to identify basic assessment concepts that are considered when assessments for these reasons take place. The assessment concepts include reliability, validity, and frame of reference.

Reliability is defined as the consistency with which an assessment instrument (e.g., test, rating scale, observation checklist) measures a particular construct (Hammill, Brown, & Bryant, 1992). During AT assessments, it is important that the evaluation instruments used yield consistent results so that the results obtained today would be the same if the instruments were administered tomorrow or the next day. When unreliable instruments are used, important decisions can be made on obtained data, only to turn out that the data were wrong and subsequent decisions flawed.

Validity occurs when an instrument measures what it intends to measure (Salvia & Ysseldyke, 2000). So when teachers are asked to complete rating scales on a student's reading abilities, the AT evaluation team expects that the results of the scale will be indicative of the student's reading skills. If the rating scale's results indicate that the student is a poor reader but, when asked to read, the student turns out to be an excellent reader, the scale's results are not valid.

Every evaluation has a frame of reference. Norm-referenced tests compare student performance to that of his or her peers (i.e., the test's standardization or normative sample). Criterion-referenced instruments evaluate performance in terms of mastery of specific skills. Nonreferenced tests do neither; instead they provide information about performance intrinsic to the individual. Examples of nonreferenced measures are reading miscue analyses and error analyses of math problems (Rivera & Bryant, 1992).

Three key assessment concepts are of particular relevance to AT assessments. First, the assessments must be ecological. Second, AT assessments should be practical. Finally, the assessments must be ongoing.

Ecological Assessment

Ecological assessment has as its core philosophy the idea that behavior of any type does not occur in a vacuum or in any single location. Thus, ecological assessments consider the person's multiple environments in which behaviors occur. Ecological assessment is particularly applicable to AT assessments because devices are used in a variety of settings and involve a number of significant people (e.g., professionals, peers, family members). As a result, effective assessments consider the various contexts where the device will be used and the people with whom the user will interact.

As an example, consider a seventh-grade student with learning disabilities who is being evaluated for AT adaptations to print access (i.e., reading) problems. In what contexts or settings does the student have to read text? For typical middle-school students, they attend science class in one room, social studies in another, English class in another, and so forth. So the assessment has to consider each classroom environment and each content area teacher. It is critical that each teacher be a part of the assessment process for two reasons. First, each teacher has important information about the demands of the class and his or her expectations (e.g., how much material is read, how information is presented during class time) and the student's abilities and behaviors that have been demonstrated in the classroom. Second, the teacher's input, as well as that from parents, peers, and other professionals, demonstrates a level of involvement in the assessment process that will more likely lead to device use after the technology is determined. Teachers who feel that they are involved in the assessment process, whose input was considered, and who participated in on-site trial use of the device are more likely to "buy into" the device's use and participate in training activities concerning its use.

There are a variety of ways that data can be gathered from teachers. To gain information from teachers concerning their classroom and students' abilities, Raskind and Bryant (2002) have designed a series of rating scales. Figure 3.1 depicts how a rating scale can be used to learn about the setting demands of a particular classroom. As can be seen, teachers provide information about a variety of tasks that are assigned to students or expectations of student participation. Figure 3.2 is a rating scale that is designed to identify, from the teacher's perspective and experience, student strengths and weaknesses in reading and other academic areas. By having each of the student's teachers complete the scale, an ecological perspective can be gained about the student's characteristics and how they match the demands of the academic environment.

Assistive technology team members may wish to create and use their own rating scales. This task is rather easy and can be accomplished by a simple review of various developmental checklists and scope-and-sequence charts. A sample rating scale that looks at spoken language skills is provided in Figure 3.3, which was designed after examining language development texts to identify pertinent skills for examination (Wiederholt & Bryant, 1987). If desired, members of the assessment team can meet with teachers and use the rating scales during an interview as a way to gather data from the teacher. Interviews have the advantage over typical rating scale completion (where the scale is completed by the rater alone) in that the interviewer can probe responses to gather additional information. Regardless of the manner with which data are gathered, the key ingredient is that information is being obtained from a number of people in a variety of settings. This is the importance of ecological assessment.

FEAT

Functional Evaluation
for Assistive Technology

Contextual
Matching Inventory

Name: _____

Examiner Name: _____

Date: _____

Part A. Identification of Specific Settings and Demands

Context (Settings):

1. _____   4. _____

2. _____   5. _____

3. _____   6. _____

Directions: Based on interviews with people in up to six different settings, rate the frequency with which each task is required in each classroom/setting. D = Daily, W = Weekly, M = Monthly, or even less frequently. Write NA if not required.

Task: The individual is expected to . . .	Setting					
	1	**2**	**3**	**4**	**5**	**6**
listen to lectures.						
listen to directions/instructions.						
listen to and/or work with peers/coworkers.						
listen to audiotapes/videotapes/CDs.						
listen to announcements.						
speak to teachers/peers/coworkers.						
make class/workplace presentations.						
communicate during class/workplace discussions.						
read textbooks/handouts/reports/letters.						
read from chalkboard/overhead/and so forth.						
read resource materials (e.g., dictionary, encyclopedia, library books).						
read assignment/instruction sheets.						
read test questions.						
read computer text.						
write test answers.						
write papers (reports, term).						
write stories/essays/poems.						
write homework/work assignments.						
copy from chalkboard/text (words/numbers).						
take notes.						
spell words (in isolation and in continuous text).						
compute.						
solve math word problems.						
use math in applied settings/conditions.						
work with manipulatives.						
use a calculator.						
remember recently presented information that has been heard.						

© Copyright Raskind & Bryant, 2002.
10 9 8 7 6 5 4 3 2 1   06 05 04 03 02

Additional copies of this form (#0273) may be purchased from Psycho-Educational Services
5114 Balcones Woods Dr., #307-163, Austin, TX 78759, 512/335-1591

FIGURE 3.1   Rating Scale Designed to Identify Setting Demands

From M. Raskind & B. Bryant (2002). *Functional evaluation of assistive technology*. Austin, TX: Psycho-Educational Services. Reprinted with permission.

Part A (cont.)	Setting					
	1	2	3	4	5	6
remember recently presented information that has been read.						
remember information learned previously.						
remember sequential information.						
use time-management skills.						
organize work space.						
organize information.						
organize assignments/projects.						
manipulate objects/materials.						
use pencil/pen/marker.						
use keyboard.						
draw/cut/paste/do artwork.						
maintain good posture/positioning.						
attend to task.						
work well with others.						
stay in place.						
cooperate with teachers/peers/coworkers.						

Summary/Remarks _____

_____

_____

_____

Part B. Additional Issues Relating to Contextual Matching

Directions: Based on previous experiences and the situations encountered during the evaluation, write the number (1 to 5, 1 being low, 5 being high) that best corresponds to the anticipated use of the technology in the settings identified in Part A. If the noted use is not applicable, write NA.

Potential Use of the Technology	Setting					
	1	2	3	4	5	6
Compensatory effectiveness						
Compatibility with existing technology						
Social appropriateness						
Ease of integration (considering potential conflict such as noise, time, etc.)						
Space availability						
Appropriateness of space (consider physical environment, such as lighting, noise level, etc.)						
Availability of appropriate furniture						
Availability of supporting equipment						
Availability of required technical support						
Appropriateness of technology for current use						
Appropriateness of technology for use next year						
Appropriateness of technology for use over the next 2 to 5 years						
Appropriateness of technology for use over the next 6 to 10 years						
Ease of portability across contexts/settings						

Summary/Remarks _____

_____

_____

FIGURE 3.1   Continued

| **FEAT**
Functional Evaluation
for Assistive Technology

Checklist of
Strengths and Limitations | Name: _____

Rater: _____

Date: _____ |

Directions: During technology evaluations, specific limitations that may require compensatory intervention must be identified. It is also critical to identify specific strengths that the technology can tap into during compensation. Place a check in the appropriate column (Weak, Average, Strong) that in your opinion best depicts the abilities of the person being rated, when compared to age-mates, in the areas being evaluated.

Listening	Weak	Average	Strong
Differentiates between relevant and irrelevant information			
Hears and understands the spoken word			
Understands basic directions			
Pays attention to speaker for an appropriate timespan			
Comprehends rapid speech			
Distinguishes differences among sounds/words			
Responds appropriately to requests/instructions			
Other (specify)			
OVERALL LISTENING SKILLS			

Speaking	Weak	Average	Strong
Pronounces words clearly and consistently			
Speaks with appropriate vocabulary			
Speaks with appropriate grammar			
Speaks well in everyday situations			
Discusses content that is appropriate to situation			
Can adjust language based on communication partner			
Speaks well, with appropriate tone, pitch, loudness			
Other (specify)			
OVERALL SPEAKING SKILLS			

Reading	Weak	Average	Strong
Has requisite visual abilities			
Reads words accurately			
Understands meaning of individual words			
Reads with speed/fluency			
Is able to maintain place on page			
Understands different sentence structures (e.g., simple, complex)			
Understands the meaning of connected text (i.e., phrases, sentences, paragraphs)			
Other (specify)			
OVERALL READING SKILLS			

Writing	Weak	Average	Strong
Applies capitalization/punctuation rules			
Spells correctly			
Writes neatly with little difficulty			
Uses appropriate grammar			
Uses appropriate vocabulary			
Edits/proofs well			
Writes well conceptually			
Applies sense of audience effectively			

FIGURE 3.2   Rating Scale Designed to Identify Academic Strengths and Weaknesses

From M. Raskind & B. Bryant (2002). *Functional evaluation of assistive technology.* Austin, TX: Psycho-Educational Services. Reprinted with permission.

Writing (cont.)	Weak	Average	Strong
Other (specify)			
OVERALL WRITING SKILLS			
Mathematics	**Weak**	**Average**	**Strong**
Understands basic number concepts			
Calculates basic arithmetic problems			
Knows basic math vocabulary			
Calculates quickly			
Applies math concepts to life situations			
Has a sense of reasonable versus unreasonable answers (i.e., can estimate)			
Other (specify)			
OVERALL MATHEMATICS SKILLS			
Memory	**Weak**	**Average**	**Strong**
Has long-term recall of previously learned information (words/objects/designs/pictures)			
Has short-term recall of recently presented information (words/objects/designs/pictures)			
Follows simple directions in sequence			
Follows complex directions in sequence			
Other (specify)			
OVERALL MEMORY SKILLS			
Organization	**Weak**	**Average**	**Strong**
Understands cause/effect relationships			
Manages personal and work time			
Manages personal and work space			
Makes plans to accomplish tasks			
Organizes ideas into a cohesive whole			
Can understand abstract concepts			
Other (specify)			
OVERALL ORGANIZATION SKILLS			
Physical/Motor	**Weak**	**Average**	**Strong**
Exhibits physical strength/endurance			
Has good posture			
Controls objects (grasps/manipulates)			
Moves about freely			
Has good positioning/orientation			
Other (specify)			
OVERALL PHYSICAL/MOTOR SKILLS			
Behavior	**Weak**	**Average**	**Strong**
Stays on task			
Can work with peers			
Takes care of personal/school property			
Cooperates with people of authority			
Other (specify)			
OVERALL BEHAVIOR SKILLS			
Summary/Remarks			

FIGURE 3.2   Continued

Spoken Language Rating Scale

Rate the individual's spoken language abilities by reading each item on the rating scale and responding to each item using the following descriptors:

1 = Not at all like the student
2 = Not much like the student
3 = Somewhat like the student
4 = Very much like the student

The ability to . . .				
. . . attend to the speaker	1	2	3	4
. . . verbalize complete thoughts	1	2	3	4
. . . name common objects when given a verbal description	1	2	3	4
. . . describe more than one dimension/trait of an object	1	2	3	4
. . . provide concise descriptions of common objects	1	2	3	4
. . . use conventional grammatical word order	1	2	3	4
. . . use prosody (stress, intonation, pitch) to aid meaning	1	2	3	4
. . . use inflectional endings to provide meaning	1	2	3	4
. . . give verbal directions in logical order	1	2	3	4
. . . relate simple personal experiences in proper order	1	2	3	4
. . . adapt language appropriately to different situations	1	2	3	4
. . . pronounce words appropriately for age	1	2	3	4
. . . speak clearly and distinctly	1	2	3	4
. . . participate in conversations appropriately (does not monopolize)	1	2	3	4
. . . identify rhyming words	1	2	3	4
. . . produce rhyming words	1	2	3	4
. . . answer what, where, and who questions (literal comprehension)	1	2	3	4
. . . answer why, how, and what if questions (inferential comprehension)	1	2	3	4
. . . identify multiple meanings of words	1	2	3	4
. . . use compound sentences (uses conjunctions to combine complete thoughts)	1	2	3	4
. . . understand simple prepositions	1	2	3	4
. . . follow simple directions	1	2	3	4
. . . give opposites when requested	1	2	3	4
. . . identify synonyms on request	1	2	3	4
. . . use contractions appropriately	1	2	3	4
. . . talk in sentences of six or more words	1	2	3	4
. . . mark tense appropriately	1	2	3	4
. . . formulate questions to elicit desired response	1	2	3	4

FIGURE 3.3   Checklist of Spoken Language Strengths and Weaknesses

From J. L. Wiederholt and B. R. Bryant (1987). *Assessing the reading abilities and instructional needs of students,* edited by D.D. Hammill. Austin, TX: Pro-Ed. Copyright © 1987 by Pro-Ed, Inc. Reprinted with permission.

Practical Assessment

With respect to AT assessments, we use the term *practical* in its dictionary sense: "pertaining to or concerned with practice or action" (*Webster's Universal College Dictionary*, 1997, p. 620). Thus, ideas presented under ecological assessment are continued by actually using the device in the settings (e.g., the classroom, the workplace) where the student's actions will take place. Practical assessments allow the user to gain experience using the device in natural environments and receive training on the device simultaneously (recall that providing training in the natural environment was introduced as an AT service in Chapter 1). Practical assessment also allows for training on the device to be conducted with various people (e.g., teachers, co-workers, supervisors) in the user's multiple environments, which is another AT service. After a device has been selected and matched to the user, assessment continues in multiple contexts where the device will be used.

Raskind and Bryant (2002) offer a checklist for evaluating device use in multiple environments (Figure 3.4). Assistive technology assessment team members may wish to create their own checklist that most appropriately matches the contexts of the individual. Either way, gathering data across multiple environments, while training people within those environments, can be time well spent during the AT assessment.

A second feature of practical assessment is seeking information and participation from specialists. Think of AT assessment teams in terms of "cafeteria plans." Cafeteria plan is a useful term that describes the availability of a number of options. The insurance industry uses the term to describe plans that have a variety of options (e.g., disability riders, unemployment compensations) that policy holders consider as they purchase the policy, in the same way that one goes through the line at the cafeteria and selects items from among those laid out by servers.

Table 3.1 lists professionals who should be "on call" for membership on the AT assessment team. As is depicted in the table, the user should always be a member of the team. A member of the user's family, if available, should also be a member of the team. An AT specialist, if available, should be a member of every team. If the user is a student, at least one teacher should be a team member. If the student is receiving special education services while also attending classes in general education, then a special educator and a general educator should be team members. We would also suggest that building principals serve on AT assessment teams, if for no other reason than to demonstrate support of the team's actions and provide leadership in AT implementation in the school. Speech-language pathologists should always be key team members when augmentative and alternative communication devices are being considered. Assistive technology considerations involving seating and positioning issues necessitate team inclusion of physical and occupational therapists. When decisions are being made concerning vocational rehabilitation, rehabilitation counselors should be members of the team. We would argue that counselors also should be involved if the user is a student who is transitioning from special education services into rehabilitation services, whether those services

FEAT

Functional Evaluation for Assistive Technology

Individual–Technology Evaluation Scale

Name: _____

Examiner Name: _____

Date: _____

Technology and Setting:

_____

Compensatory Goal/Task: _____

Part A. Individual–Technology Match (Use Individual–Technology Evaluation Worksheets as necessary)

Directions: Circle the number that best corresponds to the level of match for the specified area. If the statement is not appropriate for the evaluation, circle NA. Identify the . . .

effectiveness of the technology in enhancing accuracy/quality.	NA	**Not Effective** 1	2	3	4	**Very Effective** 5
effectiveness of the technology in enhancing speed/efficiency.	NA	**Not Effective** 1	2	3	4	**Very Effective** 5
effectiveness of the technology in enhancing ease.	NA	**Not Effective** 1	2	3	4	**Very Effective** 5
overall effectiveness of the technology in helping the individual compensate for the difficulty.	NA	**Not Effective** 1	2	3	4	**Very Effective** 5
degree to which the person was interested in using the technology.	NA	**Not Interested** 1	2	3	4	**Very Interested** 5
degree to which the individual was proficient in using the technology.	NA	**Not Proficient** 1	2	3	4	**Very Proficient** 5
degree to which the individual was comfortable using the technology.	NA	**Not Comfortable** 1	2	3	4	**Very Comfortable** 5
degree to which the technology "tapped into" (i.e., utilized) the individual's strengths.	NA	**Very Low** 1	2	3	4	**Very High** 5
degree to which the technology fostered the individual's special talents.	NA	**Very Low** 1	2	3	4	**Very High** 5
degree to which the individual sustained attention using the technology.	NA	**Not Attentive** 1	2	3	4	**Very Attentive** 5
extent to which the evaluator needed to support the individual in the use of the technology.	NA	**Much Support Needed** 1	2	3	4	**No Support Needed** 5
extent to which the technology can be utilized by the individual across tasks/functions.	NA	**Very Low** 1	2	3	4	**Very High** 5
individual's ability to learn to use the technology during the evaluation.	NA	**Low Ability** 1	2	3	4	**High Ability** 5
extent to which the individual was able to resolve difficulties when the technology did not work properly.	NA	**Low Ability** 1	2	3	4	**High Ability** 5
individual's reaction when making an error while using the technology.	NA	**Very Negative** 1	2	3	4	**Very Positive** 5

Additional copies of this form (#0277) may be purchased from Psycho-Educational Services
5114 Balcones Woods Dr., #307-163, Austin, TX 78759, 512/335-1591

FIGURE 3.4   Examination of the Person-Technology Match

From M. Raskind & B. Bryant (2002). *Functional evaluation of assistive technology*. Austin, TX: Psycho-Educational Services. Reprinted with permission.

Part A. Individual–Technology Match *(cont.)*

		Not useful				Very Useful
individual's perceived usefulness of the technology.	NA	1	2	3	4	5
		Very Low				**Very High**
perceived cost/benefit ratio.	NA	1	2	3	4	5
BASED ON INFORMATION ABOVE, OVERALL "MATCH" BETWEEN THE INDIVIDUAL AND THE TECHNOLOGY.	NA	**Very Poor** 1	2	3	4	**Very Good** 5

Evidence of performance enhancement (include information used as a basis of comparison—be specific; see *Summary and Recommendations Booklet,* Section IX). _____

_____

_____

_____

Part B. General Technology Literacy

Directions: Based on the findings of the evaluation, circle the number that best corresponds to the individual's level of ability for each specified area. Identify the individual's . . .

		Very Poor			Very Good
overall computer/technological knowledge/literacy.	NA	**Very Poor** 1	2	3	**Very Good** 4
overall ability (i.e., working knowledge) to use computers/technology.	NA	**Very Poor** 1	2	3	**Very Good** 4
keyboarding proficiency (if applicable). SPEED	NA	**Very Slow** 1	2	3	**Very Fast** 4
ACCURACY	NA	**Very Poor** 1	2	3	**Very Good** 4

Part C. Other Considerations

Directions: Based on observations made during the evaluation, respond to each item below with anecdotal remarks.

Posture/Seating: 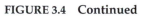 _____

_____

_____

Body orientation: _____

_____

_____

Hand/arm positioning: _____

_____

_____

Range of motion: _____

_____

_____

Visual-height, distance, angle: _____

_____

_____

FIGURE 3.4   Continued

TABLE 3.1   **Members of an AT Assessment Team**

- Student/Client
- Family Members
- Diagnostician
- General Education Teacher
- Occupational Therapist
- Paraprofessional
- Physical Therapist
- Physician
- Psychologist
- Special Education Teacher
- Speech-Language Pathologist
- Others as needed

will be provided in postsecondary or workplace settings. Other members of the AT team should be selected as needed and as appropriate.

Ongoing Assessment

A major purpose of assessment is to document the presence of a disability and determine placement eligibility. Such assessments usually occur one time and the information is secured in the student's cumulative folder for reference and archival purposes (Rivera & Bryant, 1992). Assistive technology assessments, on the other hand, never end. Assessments continue in one form or another indefinitely, because the use of devices is monitored and evaluated continuously to ensure that the decisions of the assessment team were accurate and that the device is being used effectively and as recommended.

Throughout the course of this text, we discuss the benefits of AT in helping a person compensate for functional limitations. For the technology to be effective, it must be matched to the individual; meshed with other devices, services, and individuals; and evaluated constantly to make sure that the technology adaptation is valid; that is, the adaptation is benefiting the individual as hypothesized. Think of AT use as a hypothetical experiment, a testing of a hypothesis, so to speak. In this line of thinking, the AT assessment team hypothesizes that a particular device will benefit the individual in compensating for disability-related or functional limitations (Bryant & Bryant, 1998). The hypothesis is made after a thorough evaluation of the individual and the contexts within which he or she learns, works, and plays. Sometimes the hypothesis proves correct (i.e., the device is helpful), but sometimes the hypothesis proves false (i.e., the device does not result in expected performance gains). The hypothesis must be tested continuously over time, which is a critical yet too often overlooked evaluation component.

FOCUS ON 3.1

You are the parent of a child who has a learning disability in reading. Use what you have learned concerning ecological, practical, and ongoing assessment to construct a list of questions that you feel should be addressed during your child's assessment. To what professionals should the questions be addressed? Once you have come up with the questions, put yourself in the shoes of the professionals on the team. How would you react to the parent's questions? How would you go about finding answers to the questions?

ASSISTIVE TECHNOLOGY ASSESSMENTS

Assistive Technology assessments should incorporate a multidimensional assessment model that recognizes the dynamic interplay of various factors across contexts and over time (see Figure 3.5) (Raskind & Bryant, 2002). As already implied, selecting AT devices requires careful analysis of the interplay among (a) the user's specific strengths, weaknesses, special abilities, prior experience/knowledge, and interests; (b) the specific tasks to be performed (e.g., compensating for a reading, writing, or mobility problem); (c) specific device qualities (e.g., reliability, operational ease, technical support, cost); and (d) the specific contexts of interaction (across settings—school, home, work; and over time—over a semester or a lifetime). Raskind and Bryant provided a framework for systematically determining the most appropriate and potentially effective device considering the four major components described above and depicted in Figure 3.5. Many of the components of the model were described in our adaptations model in Chapter 2. They are reviewed again here with specific reference to AT assessment.

Tasks

As part of living and breathing on planet earth, people perform a myriad of tasks and functions. These pertain to independent functioning, academics, play, work, and so forth. As we noted in Chapter 2, each task has requisite skills (in actuality, smaller tasks) that lead to the completion of the larger task (Bryant & Bryant, 1998). Part of an ecological assessment is identifying what tasks are to be performed, in what settings or contexts the tasks are performed, and who are significant players (e.g., co-workers, job coaches, teachers) in those settings. Documentation of these tasks provides a contextual mapping of the person's life and activities.

Context

Context is an important consideration when conducting AT assessments (Raskind & Bryant, 2002). The specific contexts of interaction (across school, home, and work settings; and over time whether it's over a semester or a lifetime) are examined as the

TASKS The specific tasks/functions to be performed (e.g., reading, writing, remembering) and the requisite skills associated with the tasks	**INDIVIDUAL** The individual's specific strengths, weaknesses, special abilities, prior experience/ knowledge, and interests
DEVICE The specific device (e.g., reliability, operational ease, technical support, cost)	**CONTEXT** The specific contexts of interaction (across settings such as school, home, work; and over time such as over a semester or a lifetime)

FIGURE 3.5   Examination of Technologies, Individuals, Tasks, and Contexts

From M. Raskind & B. Bryant (2002). *Functional evaluation of assistive technology.* Austin, TX: Psycho-Educational Services. Reprinted with permission.

assessment team examines how an AT device fits into a person's daily routine. For example, if a boy uses a wheelchair, all the various places he goes, along with his mobility needs, are considered. How are his classrooms configured? What does his home look like? What accessibility issues must be considered? Clearly, numerous questions must be asked. If a young girl uses an augmentative communication device, what must be programmed into the device to meet her communication needs? Who are her communication partners? How can the device fit in with her practicing the drums? These questions relate to the contexts within which she travels; that is, where she lives. When these and other questions are considered, the person-technology match comes into a clearer focus.

Individual

The individual who will use the device is central to the assessment (Raskind & Bryant, 2002). The person's specific strengths and functional limitations in a variety of areas (e.g., sensory, affect, cognitive, motor), prior experiences, and interests all must be examined by the assessment team. An examination of the individual's cumulative records will yield considerable information in all of these areas. For example, juniors in high school who have been receiving special education services since third grade have been tested and retested dozens of times over the course of their academic life, and there is a wealth of anecdotal data that has been collected in their school folders over the years. Before conducting additional assessments, these records should be thoroughly reviewed and data should be extracted. If "holes" appear (e.g., there is a lack of data on sensory and motor skills) and the need for additional data gathering is identified, then additional testing should take place.

Testing can include gathering quantitative and qualitative data. Quantitative data consist of norm-referenced test scores that compare a person's assessment performance to that of a peer group; intelligence test scores are perfect examples. Criterion referenced tests also yield quantitative data in that they identify areas of mastery; for example, students demonstrate mastery of double-digit addition when they achieve a preset criterion (e.g., 9 of 10 items correct) on a test. Checklists of observed behavior also can yield quantitative data, depending on how the checklist is scored. Qualitative data are not reported as numeric comparisons nor in terms of achieved mastery. Rather, they are data that can be accumulated through anecdotal observations, interviews, document review, and rating scales that yield descriptive information. Qualitative information can also be obtained by watching examinees and recording their actions (e.g., body tension, facial strain, grimaces) during testing. Additional information can be gleaned through error analyses of missed test items. For instance, a student's response of 51 for a subtraction item "94 – 45 = ?" may result in the clinical observation that he does not apply regrouping knowledge and instead always subtracts the smaller number from the larger number. All data are helpful in assessment because they provide information that is valuable in identifying strengths and functional limitations. Very often in AT assessments, the strengths and weaknesses relating to use of a device appear self-evident.

In summary, effective assessments yield quantitative and qualitative information that, together, provide information that is useful in making adaptation decisions. Neither source of information is sufficient in and of itself. It should be remembered that the more data that are gathered, the more reliable will be the decisions that are made based on available data.

Device

Assistive technology teams have a wide selection of devices from which to choose (Raskind & Bryant, 2002). That is a good thing, because it allows team members to begin the assessment process with a corpus of potential technologies that can be considered during the assessment process. Unfortunately, not all AT devices are created equal, and it is necessary for the devices themselves to be evaluated. Raskind and Bryant (2002) have created a rating scale that can be used to examine certain types of devices. Assistive technology team members should create their own checklists for each type of device they prescribe (e.g., wheelchairs, augmentative communication devices, input/output devices for information technology). Through personal experiences, literature reviews, or interviews with users, AT assessment team members can complete evaluations on a variety of devices and consider those evaluations when making decisions.

Care should be taken not to become enamored with a specific device before the evaluation takes place. More than one parent or practitioner has come away from a product demonstration workshop with the feeling, "Now, *that* is what my child [student] needs!" Sadly, not all devices that appear spectacular during demonstrations meet expectations when purchased. Each device must be evaluated according to specific criteria. Usually those criteria relate to reliability (i.e., consistency of use), validity (i.e., does the device do what it is intended to do?), technical support (e.g., does the toll-free tech support number have a human being on the other end, and is the local sales representative capable of providing on-the-spot technical assistance?), and cost (what is the cost-benefit ratio?). Regarding cost, we have often heard two sides disagree over a particular device because of the device's price tag. In all cases, the bottom line should be whether the device meets the needs of the user. If two devices are equally reliable, yield valid results, and the vendors offer equal technical support, we would follow the lead of generic prescription drugs and select the less expensive device. But that should be the decision of the assessment team based on the information at hand.

FOCUS ON 3.2

Jon, a junior in high school, wakes up in his bedroom. He showers and returns to his room to get dressed. He goes into the kitchen for breakfast, returns to the bathroom to brush his teeth, and walks to the end of the street to take the bus to school. He gets on the bus and sits next to his friend and they talk throughout their 30-minute ride to school. Jon gets off the bus and goes to homeroom. When the bell rings, he goes to science class, then math class. The bell rings and he sits down in Junior Row with his friends for a ten-minute break. Gym class is next, followed by computer programming. The bell rings and he rejoins his friends on Junior Row for lunch. He grimaces as he eats his bologna sandwich. After lunch Jon goes to content mastery class to do his homework with the help of the special education teacher. The next class is history, which is followed by band. After school, he stays for concert band practice. He then goes five blocks to an ice cream shop, where he works after school. Because it's Friday, many of his friends come in as customers, and they pick him up after work to go see a late movie. A late night stop at the local burger place is followed by a return home. Still hungry, Jon picks through the refrigerator and makes a bedtime snack (sandwich—no bologna this time). Then he proceeds to the living room and watches the late movie before returning to the bathroom and then to his bedroom; getting into bed caps off another day in the life of Jon, Junior Guy. Space doesn't permit listing all of the tasks that Jon worked on throughout the course of the day. But needless to say it has been a busy day consisting of more than 100 or so tasks. By the way, Jon has spastic cerebral palsy and dyslexia. Now consider your own day. Document your activities and generate questions that must be addressed by the AT assessment team.

ASSESSMENT COMPONENTS

Once it is time to actually conduct assessment, it is important to look at a variety of issues. What are the contexts that have to be considered? What are the user's strengths and weaknesses? What to-date experiences does the person have with technology? What technology should be considered and is it a quality device? What is the match between the technology and potential user? These questions form the basis for the remainder of this chapter.

Considerations of Various Contexts

As already stated, it is important to look at the various contexts within which the device will be used. To do so, one can identify the various contexts within which the individual works and plays and then examine requisite skills needed to accomplish expected tasks. The evaluator identifies the frequency (i.e., daily, weekly, or monthly/less frequently) with which each task is accomplished in the different settings examined.

One might also wish to anticipate the potential usefulness of an AT device across the settings identified in the previous paragraph. Areas examined in this part of the scale might be the device's compensatory effectiveness, compatibility, social appropriateness, portability, support requirements, and potential appropriateness over time (Raskind & Bryant, 2002). Once the technology is identified and implemented, one would then want to examine the extent to which the technology application has generalized across the settings identified earlier.

Considerations of Strengths and Weaknesses

It is important to determine the individual's strengths and weaknesses across a variety of academic and cognitive tasks (e.g., listening, memory, organization, physical/motor). A person who knows the individual's behaviors could rate the individual's abilities in the areas of interest. It would be beneficial for more than one rater to complete the scale in order to gain an ecological perspective.

Information from the scale can be used to identify potential areas of difficulty that may be circumvented by AT. Also, the examination can help identify areas of strength upon which a device can capitalize to bypass a specific difficulty (Bryant, Seay, & Bryant, 1999; Bryant & Bryant, 1998). This is particularly important when setting demands and requisite abilities are identified for the student and the strengths and weaknesses must be considered (see Chapter 3).

Considerations of Technology Experience

It may be helpful to identify the individual's prior experience with AT devices. An assessment team member has a conversation with the individual being evaluated. Based on the discussion, the examiner rates the individual's expertise in using specific devices. This could be accomplished by identifying various devices that have potential to compensate for difficulties in the areas of spoken language, reading, memory, mobility, organization, and so forth.

Consideration of Technology Characteristics

A factor that is too often overlooked in an AT evaluation is the device itself. As we stated, people can become smitten with what a particular device is supposed to do but fail to look at such qualities as the technology's dependability, the vendor's technical support record, and so forth. It is important to examine the specific device being used in the assessment in such areas as reliability, efficacy of purpose, compatibility, screen presentation, operational ease, and technical support. We agree with Raskind and Bryant, who noted that technology that is not trustworthy is best left in the showroom.

Considerations of the Person-Technology Match

Every AT assessment should examine the interplay between the individual and the device while performing specific tasks and/or compensating for specific difficulties. A series of questions might be asked relating to compensatory effectiveness, interest, ease of use, comfort, operational ease/proficiency, and behavioral responses (Raskind & Bryant, 2002). Raskind and Bryant provide some guidance as to topics of the scale, which should examine the device's ability to enhance accuracy/quality, speed/efficiency, and ease; the technology's ability to tap into the individual's strengths and special talents; the extent to which the individual is able to resolve difficulties if the technology does not work properly or if he or she makes an error when using the technology; and so forth. Of particular interest is whether the individual perceives the technology to be of value and whether the person is interested in using the technology. The effectiveness of technology becomes a moot point if the person is disinterested or is indifferent. In addition, the person-technology match should include a comparison of the individual's performance with and without the device. Because the purpose of the AT device is to improve performance, it is critical that such improvement, or lack of improvement, be documented.

FOCUS ON 3.3

You are the Assistive Technology Assessment Team Leader. You have to conduct an AT evaluation for Jon, the student discussed in Focus on 3.2. Given what you have learned about the assessment process, generate a list of 10 questions that should be considered during an ecological and practical AT assessment. Then identify what ongoing assessments should be conducted to ensure that Jon's needs are being met by the device(s) that was (were) selected.

SUMMARY

Assessment plays an important role when dealing with individuals with disabilities. Ecological assessments account for the varying influences that affect a person's life, whether those influences are in school, at home, or among peers and colleagues. Practical assessments are authentic in that they deal with the reality of a person's situation. That is, practical assessments deal with real life, daily circumstances a person encounters; thus, they are a natural extension of ecological assessments. Ongoing assessments acknowledge that decisions made during assessments are actually hypotheses that must be examined over time. Assessment team members gather data about a person and make decisions based on those data. If the decisions are made based on reliable and valid practices and instruments, the decisions are *probably* right, but may not be entirely accurate. Ongoing AT assessments follow along with the person using the device to make sure that the decisions were indeed accurate and that the device is fulfilling its purpose to the desired extent. But there are times when the hypothesis is wrong and the device is not doing what it was intended to do and the individual is not benefiting from the person-technology match as intended. Without ongoing assessments, the hypothesis goes untested; and the potential benefits of AT devices and services may not be fully realized.

In this chapter, we also presented Raskind & Bryant's (2002) model for AT assessments that considers four critical considerations: tasks to be performed, the individual performing the task, the device that will be used to perform the task, and the contexts within which the device will be used. By considering each of these considerations, it is more likely that a valid person-technology match will be made.

Finally, we expanded the discussion on the assessment model by presenting specific components that should be considered during assessments. We asked the following questions:

What are the contexts that have to be considered?
What are the user's strengths and weaknesses?
What to-date experiences does the person have with technology?
What technology should be considered and is it a quality device?
What is the match between the technology and potential user?

By discussing these questions, we provided the basis for an ecological, practical, and ongoing assessment that can lead the way for effective AT implementation.

REFERENCES

Bryant, B. R., Seay, P. C., & Bryant, D. P. (1999). Using assistive technology to help people with mental retardation compensate for adaptive behavior deficits. In R. Schalock (Ed.), *Issues in adaptive behavior assessment*. Washington, DC: AAMR.

Bryant, D. P., & Bryant, B. R. (1998). Using assistive technology adaptations to include students with learning disabilities in cooperative learning activities. *Journal of Learning Disabilities, 31*(1), 41–54.

Hammill, D., Brown, L., & Bryant, B. R. (1992). *A consumer's guide to tests in print* (2nd ed.). Austin, TX: Pro-Ed.

Hammill, D. D., & Bryant, B. R. (1998). *Learning disability diagnostic inventory.* Austin, TX: Pro-Ed.

Raskind, M., & Bryant, B. R. (2002). *Functional evaluation for assistive technology.* Austin, TX: Psycho-Educational Services.

Rivera, D. M., & Bryant, B. R. (1992). Mathematics instruction for students with special needs. *Intervention in School and Clinic, 28*(2), 71–86.

Salvia , J., & Ysseldyke, J. (2000). *Assessment.* Boston: Houghton-Mifflin.

Webster's Universal College Dictionary. (1997). New York: Gramercy Books.

Wiederholt, J. L., & Bryant, B. R. (1987). *Assessing reading abilities and instructional needs of students.* Austin, TX: Pro-Ed.

CHAPTER FOUR

ASSISTIVE TECHNOLOGY DEVICES TO ENHANCE MOBILITY FOR INDIVIDUALS WITH PHYSICAL IMPAIRMENTS

CHAPTER AT A GLANCE

INTRODUCTION TO MOBILITY ADAPTATIONS
- Focus on 4.1
- Personal Perspective 4.1
- Focus on 4.2

BASIC DESIGN CONSIDERATIONS
- Focus on 4.3

SEATING AND POSITIONING ISSUES
- Personal Perspective 4.2
- Focus on 4.4

OBJECTIVES

1. Describe how wheelchairs and other wheeled mobility units help individuals develop mobility.
2. Describe the components of a standard wheelchair.
3. Explain seating and positioning issues.

MAKING CONNECTIONS

Think about how you maneuver through the course of a day. Where do you go? How do you get there? What obstacles do you sometimes encounter? How do you overcome those obstacles? What might be different types of mobility impairments? What obstacles might be present for those with mobility impairments? How do they face those challenges? How might those obstacles be overcome with and without mobility adaptations?

In Chapter 3, we presented a day in the life of a junior in high school. In that brief scenario, Jon moved from room to room in his home, used the bus to go to school, went from one classroom to another, went to work, and then socialized with his friends before returning home for the evening. Throughout the course of his day, Jon had the freedom of movement to transition from one location to another. The description of Jon's day might have been a bit different had he used a wheelchair to move about his environments. The purpose of this chapter is to examine issues related to mobility and to identify how people with mobility impairments function by using a variety of mobility-related AT devices. We begin by introducing mobility adaptations and the devices that help people with physical disabilities compensate for their mobility challenges. We then overview basic seating and positioning design considerations that are particularly relevant to mobility. Information is then presented on specific types of wheelchairs, including manual and power chairs. It is important to note that we do not discuss mobility issues for people who have sensory or cognitive impairments. Mobility issues for individuals with these conditions are discussed in the chapter that deals with independent living.

INTRODUCTION TO MOBILITY ADAPTATIONS

The rationale for AT adaptations is that the skills for accomplishing tasks of various settings may not be present because of disability-related functional limitations; when these limitations are present, adaptations are made. Hence, if people are unable to move about because of a physical or health condition, we must find a way to use their strengths to help them develop mobility. This section of the chapter examines why and how this is done using wheelchairs and other wheeled mobility units.

Reasons for Wheeled Mobility Adaptations

More than three quarters of a million Americans use wheelchairs on a daily basis (Wilson, 1992). Most wheelchair users do so because they cannot walk, but many people use wheelchairs because they have heart problems or other concerns that make walking difficult or impractical. Wilson divided users into three categories: those who have lost function in their lower limbs, those who have unstable posture, and those with general physical problems.

Lower-limb dysfunction can result from many conditions. One of the most common causes of lower-limb problems is spinal-cord injury, which occurs predominately in males ages 16 to 30 (Hardman, Drew, & Egan, 1996). About 10,000 spinal-cord injuries occur each year, about half of which are the result of automobile accidents. Traumatic brain injury (TBI) also can cause acquired mobility impairments. According to Karp (1999), about 373,000 Americans sustain TBI each year, and about one-fourth of those exhibit lifelong functional limitations, including limitations associated with mobility. Other causes of lower-limb problems include arthritis, cerebral palsy, polio and post-polio syndrome, muscular dystrophy, stroke and brain trauma, amputation, amyotrophic lateral sclerosis (ALS, sometimes referred to as Lou Gehrig's disease), Friedreich's ataxia, multiple sclerosis, and myasthenia gravis, to name a few (Karp, 1999; Wilson, 1992).

Brain trauma and cerebral palsy can cause unstable posture severe enough to result in a loss of walking ability, even with the help of walkers or crutches. Spinal cancer can also cause postural instability that necessitates mobility adaptations. In these instances, some functional use of lower limbs exists, but mobility is so impaired that wheelchairs or other units are needed for moving about. At times, people with health impairments will use wheelchairs or some other wheeled mobility device to conserve energy. A colleague told us of a story where a lay person was quite surprised to see an individual in a wheelchair stand and walk, but such an observation is not uncommon.

General physical problems affecting the lower limbs can result from a number of conditions. For example, people break their legs or have surgeries that result in temporary use of a wheelchair. For some, obesity limits their ability to walk; for them, the condition may have concomitant conditions (e.g., shortness of breath, stress) so profound that wheelchair use is mandatory. Older people sometimes fall and sustain leg injuries that require temporary mobility adaptations. Older individuals may experience knee and hip joint problems resulting in arthritis and rheumatism.

Each condition presents its own challenges to the user and those who are responsible for making mobility adaptations. For instance, people with arthritis may benefit from raised seats on their wheelchairs so as to make transfers from the chair to bed or auto easier; larger wheels to make it easier to self-propel; or brake extensions to make it easier to lock the wheels. Also, people with muscular dystrophy have special needs for their mobility devices. If excessive spinal curvature exists, lumbar support will likely be required, as will full-length armrests to support the curvature. Because muscular dystrophy is often diagnosed at a young age, the chair should have seat and armrest growth capabilities so that the chair can be used as the child grows up (Batavia, 1998). These are but two examples of special considerations that are made depending upon the wheelchair user's specific physical attributes.

Types of Wheeled Mobility Units

There are different mobility units available to consumers to serve a variety of purposes (Lewis, 1993). Here, we discuss the most common: wheelchairs and motorized carts.

Wheelchairs have been used in this country at least as far back as the 1860s during the Civil War, and there is some evidence that their use dates back to the 17th century (Wilson, 1992). A variety of wheelchairs currently exist and are discussed in terms of manual and power wheelchairs.

Manual wheelchairs are propelled by the user. Some users prefer a rigid frame wheelchair because its fewer parts result in a lighter-weight chair that is easier to maneuver. The rigid chair is energy-efficient in that it is easier to push, a benefit not lost among long-term users. Folding frame chairs, although heavier and less energy-efficient, are still preferred by many users because they are likely to fit into most vehicles (Karp, 1999). Flexible frames also tend to absorb the typical bumps and vibrations that occur in daily use. With both rigid and folding frame chairs, large driving wheels are located at the back, with the smaller caster to the front. Footrests are provided with both models.

In 1983, *Sports 'N Spokes*, a magazine published by the Veteran's Administration, began classifying lightweight chairs (i.e., chairs weighing about 30 pounds or less; Wilson, 1992) as belonging to one of four categories: everyday wheelchairs, sport wheelchairs, junior wheelchairs, and racing wheelchairs.

Everyday wheelchairs, as the name implies, refer to lighter chairs that are used for day-to-day activities. These wheelchairs have a rigid frame, thus they are easier to push.

Sport wheelchairs (see Figure 4.1) are specially designed to allow the user to play in such sports as tennis, basketball, hockey, and rugby (Karp, 1999). These chairs have rigid frames that afford greater agility and responsiveness (see Personal Perspective 4.1). Wheel cambers align the top of the wheel inward, expanding the wheelbase outward for stability, thus minimizing the chances of the athlete tipping over during competition. Hockey and rugby players, by the nature of their sports, often collide with one another, so metal guards are included in the chair's base to avoid damage to the chairs and occupants.

As the name suggests, *junior wheelchairs* (Figure 4.2) are designed for children and young teens. Junior wheelchairs are lighter in weight because they are relatively small; they may have rigid or flexible frames.

The *racing wheelchair* is a special sports chair designed with speed in mind. Many racing chairs have a single wheel in the front of the chair, and all are made with new alloys that provide stability yet reduction in the chair's weight.

FOCUS ON 4.1

For several years, marathon, 10K, and 5K racing have been popular athletic events for people who use wheelchairs. Find a wheelchair racer and interview the athlete. How did he or she become interested in the sport? How long has the person been racing? What are the person's most interesting, most exciting experiences? What kind of support group is available to wheelchair athletes? Does the person compete in other sports? These are but a few of the questions that you can ask to gain information about this growing sport. Find out how one might go about gaining additional information about wheelchair racing. What Internet sites are available? (Some are listed in the appendix.) Are there wheelchair racing support groups or clubs in the city in which you live? Take some time to learn about wheelchair athletics and what it means to its participants.

Powered, or motorized, wheelchairs (see Figure 4.3) are those that have external power supplies (i.e., they are not manually powered by the occupant). Powered chairs satisfy the needs of wheelchair users who have insufficient strength or phys-

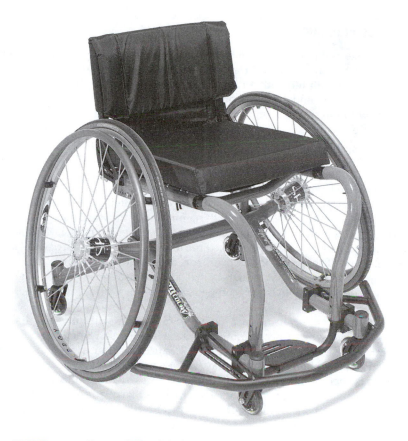

FIGURE 4.1   Sports Wheelchair
Reprinted with permission of Sunrise Medical.

ical capabilities to manually operate their own chairs and thus would otherwise have to be assisted by others (Angelo, 1997).

Powered chairs come with a variety of options. Users must decide whether to purchase chairs with front-wheel drive (they may provide better traction with changing surfaces, but these chairs may not be sufficiently stable if a tilt system is needed), rear wheel drive (they may offer a sense of better control, but tipping is a risk—many users equip these chairs with anti-tip devices), or mid-wheel drive (a relatively new option that offers a reduced turning radius and good traction). Not surprisingly, users may not want to select the mid-wheel drive option if they lack good upper body balance (Karp, 1999).

PERSONAL PERSPECTIVE 4.1

Michael Haynes is the supervisor of the Wheelchair Fitness Program at St. David's Rehabilitation Center in Austin, Texas. He has twenty years of personal and professional experience in dealing with life with a disability. His expertise is in the field of kinesiology, recreational therapy, and adaptive fitness and wheelchair sports. Mike teaches youths and adults with physical disabilities how to recreate and adapt activities to enjoy life to the fullest. He competes in wheelchair sports including basketball, handcycling, tennis, triathlons, road racing, football, and softball. He also coordinates and enjoys outdoor adventure programs including snow skiing, water skiing, SCUBA diving, and hunting.

How did you first get involved in wheelchair athletics?
I had become independent with all my activities of daily living and was back at UT studying accounting, but there was still something missing in my life. I had always been active in sports and was looking to fill the void in my life. I met a guy at a Mexican food place and over a couple of margaritas he talked me into coming out to play wheelchair basketball. I met some of the guys on the team and realized that they were real athletes who trained hard and competed at local, national, and international events. When I saw that there was an opportunity to travel, compete, and see the world, I was hooked.

What recreational opportunities are available for people with physical disabilities?
Twenty years ago when I became injured, there were just a few sports that had been developed. WW II veterans developed wheelchair basketball when they got back from the war, and the revolution began. Today, the sky is the limit.

There is a sport for everyone. Traditional sports like tennis, softball, and football were adapted just enough to meet our needs. Other sports like quad rugby changed the whole aspect of the game and started to develop to meet the specific needs of various disabilities. The unique thing about wheelchair sports is that there is a place for everyone. There are recreational teams for those who just want to play and there are highly competitive teams that strive to be the world's best at the Paralympics.

For the last twenty years, disabled athletes have been pushing the limits of their disabilities by developing assistive technology. This came in the form of adaptive sports equipment and included sit skis for snow skiing, can-ski for water skiing, downhill mountain bikes, and hand cycles. Athletes have climbed mountains, sailed across oceans, and completed Ironman Triathlon distances.

You're an accomplished tennis player. Describe the levels of competition that exist.
Open division is a professional division that is sponsored by the International Tennis Federation (ITF). There is an international circuit with tournaments all over the world that pay prize money by the round. Players must be registered with the ITF and all the rules of regular tennis apply. Players must maintain a ranking of at least top 100 in the world to compete in most tournaments. Players represent their respective countries in World Team Cup and Paralympic competitions.

In *recreational divisions*, the player's skill level determines what division he or she competes in. Sometimes skill level is determined by a combination of sports skill and disability function. In other words, no matter how good some players get, their functional ability may limit them from rising to the professional level. All recreational level players compete for national rankings except novice division.

A: players trying to make it to the pro level, but not in the top 100.
B: recreational players who have been playing for years.
C: first- or second-year recreational players or more functionally disabled.
Novice: beginning players, no national ranking in this division.

These are the men's and women's divisions. We also have quadriplegic divisions for people with limited function in all four extremities including Quad Open, Quad A, and Quad B. We have a national circuit with more than 50 tournaments across the nation culminating in the U.S. Open in California at the end of the year.

You tell a great story about your first whitewater rafting experience. Share your experience with our readers.
My buddy Wes Harley and I went north one summer for the Colorado Triple Crown Wheelchair Tennis Circuit, which included tournaments in Boulder and individual and team competitions in Grand Junction. Between tournaments we camped out in the Rocky Mountain National Park.

We were traveling by ourselves so this meant that we were on our own as far as camp setup. You can't imagine what a spectacle two guys in wheelchairs are while putting up a tent. We were such a sight that people set up chairs so that they could watch the whole ordeal unfold. They didn't offer to help us out of the awkward situation, they just wanted to watch.

The following day we decided to be adventurous and go whitewater rafting down the Arkansas River out of Buena Vista, Colorado. We drove to the town early in the morning to make sure that we could take a half-day trip through the Brown Canyon. When we arrived at the booming metropolis of Buena Vista we soon realized that the outfitters had probably never even seen a person in a wheelchair, much less taken someone down the river at 3700 cubic feet per second.

These two Texas boys were not about to let anyone tell us we could not do something. So we quickly devised a plan that would ensure our trip. We would lie! We went into Buffalo Joe's River Trips and told them that we had paddled down half the rivers of North America. We told them exactly how to set up our seating system and where we would ride. All that said, we were off to the river in no time.

Once we had gone down a couple of miles on the river, the scraggly river guy who was guiding our vessel down the canyons turned to us and said, "So, I hear you guys have done a lot of rivers across the states. What's your favorite?" We were busted. I turned to Wes and said, "Should we tell him?" We went on to tell him that we had never done whitewater rafting before. We just did not want to be told that they would not or could not take us down the river.

Sometimes you just have to act confident and tell people what they want to hear to do what you want in life.

Are there additional risks that a person with a physical disability takes in athletics? If so, how are those risks minimized?
Yes, people with spinal-cord injuries have more brittle bones and risk fractures because of non-weight-bearing. Skin breakdown is another concern for people with sensation deficits. We minimize these risks by strapping the limbs down to the chair; you stay with the chair if you flip or fall over. We also use high-tech cushions to prevent skin breakdown from the shearing of playing sports in a wheelchair.

What advances in wheelchairs have benefited wheelchair athletes?
The invention of the sports chair in the early 1980s revolutionized wheelchair sports. It allowed wheelchair users to compete to the best of their ability and push the limits of traditional wheelchair sports. New sports were added every year with minimal adaptations to the new rigid frame wheelchair. Today, wheelchairs are so specialized that each sport has its own chair that meets the needs and demands of the individual sport. They come in three, four, five, and six wheels. There is also a big demand for sports equipment like handcycles, downhill mountain bikes, water skis, snow skis, and the list goes on and on.

Reproduced with permission from Psycho-Educational Services.

Some professionals prefer manual chairs to powered chairs for their consumers who have sufficient strength to operate a manual chair. But others argue that powered chairs offer users the option of conserving their strength for other activities. Chair use by young children is another issue regarding manual versus powered chairs. For years, younger children were denied powered chairs for safety reasons. With improved control systems, however, powered chairs are now seen as a viable mobility option for children as young as 2 years of age. The freedom power chairs give children to explore their surroundings makes this an exciting option for older toddlers.

It is important to note that some parents of young children find it difficult to deal with their child's use of a wheelchair. We have heard more than once the story of a mother whose dream it is for her child to walk. To her, accepting wheelchair use is an admission of defeat. Only after seeing the child use the chair as a freedom of movement tool can she recognize fully its value. Still, it is a difficult adjustment that is an important consideration for wheelchair prescribers and other professional caregivers.

Motorized carts, or scooters as they are also called, tend to be used by people who have better sitting and transfer skills (i.e., moving in and out of the chair) than those who use powered wheelchairs. In addition, because motorized carts use a steering wheel, scooter users must have good use of their upper limbs. Often, scooter users have some ambulatory skills. Motorized carts offer advantages to powered wheelchairs because carts tend to be much lighter and are narrower; thus, they may provide mobility in aisles that otherwise inhibit wheelchair use. Additionally, people who have temporary conditions that inhibit mobility may prefer scooters over wheelchairs because they "look" less like a disability vehicle. When compared to manual wheelchairs, scooters and powered chairs have decided disadvantages when they break down (i.e., it is much more difficult to transport broken powered units than manual units) or when they are used in areas that are less accessible (e.g., curb cuts are not available, stairs are not supplemented with ramps).

Scooter boards are cushioned strips of wood that have small wheels that are designed to be used on smooth surfaces. The scooter board varies in length, depending on the size of the rider. It may be the same length as the user for full support or may be shorter to allow the rider to exert additional body control. Scooter boards help to develop head and trunk control and upper body and arm strength.

FIGURE 4.2   Junior Wheelchair
Reprinted with permission, Psycho-Educational Services.

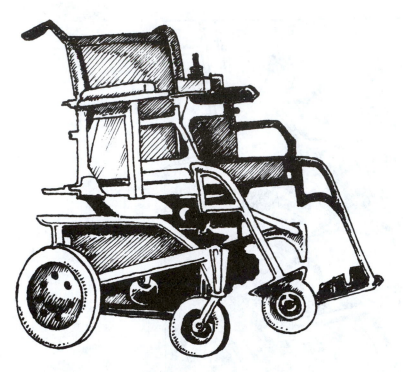

FIGURE 4.3   Powered Wheelchair
Reprinted with permission, Psycho-Educational Services.

Switch-operated power scooter boards are available for use. When manual boards are used in the prone position, the rider uses his or her arms to reach to the ground and propel the board. Or the board can attach to a rope that can be pulled by someone other than the rider.

When used while lying in the supine position (i.e., with the rider lying on his or her back), the user uses feet for self-propulsion. Finally, scooter boards can be used in the sitting position, with propulsion accomplished using the feet, whereby the hands are freed up for grasping.

Several upright mobility units exist for people who prefer to be standing as they move about and who have some use of their legs. These weight-bearing devices allow people to look at others face to face and allow for more vertical movement. *Walkers* have rigid frames that may or may not be folded when not used. Some walkers have postural supports and/or wheels, while others do not.

Gait trainers (see Figure 4.4) are used by people, usually children, who may have balance and/or muscle control problems. Users of gait trainers propel the

FIGURE 4.4   Gait Trainer
Reprinted with permission, Psycho-Educational Services.

device with their feet. Gait trainers often come with different supports (e.g., chest laterals, leg abductors and prompts, forearm supports), and most are equipped with seats that allow the user to rest when tired or when the user wants to relax. Adjustments are available to vary the physical supports.

Mobile standers (see Figure 4.5) are a third type of upright mobility unit that can be used by people with limited or no use of trunk or leg muscles. Users are supported with pads and the units are adjustable in height, width, and tilt angles. Users may use their arms to move the unit's wheels. The devices may be equipped with adjusters that reduce weight-bearing capacity, which is important for users who have unstable hips or those who cannot extend their legs fully.

FIGURE 4.5   Mobile Stander
Reprinted with permission, Psycho-Educational Services.

FOCUS ON 4.2

It is difficult for some parents of young children to accept the fact that their children will have to use a wheelchair. Yes, their children have had difficulties moving about, but there has always been hope that the therapy being received will result in their children's being able to walk. This is not the case in this instance. Consider the thoughts going through their minds. What might they be thinking? How will they reconcile their expectations with the reality that their child will be using a wheelchair, perhaps for his or her entire life? It might be helpful to interview a parent who went through this experience to find out what thoughts transpired as this situation was encountered. Or perhaps you can find a disability support group online and conduct an interview with a parent. How have the person's thoughts changed, or not changed, over time? Did anyone support the parent as the child was being fitted for his or her chair? What might that parent say to another parent encountering the same situation?

BASIC DESIGN CONSIDERATIONS

Wilson (1992) described the components of a standard wheelchair (see Figure 4.6). Each chair consists of a seat, a seatback, armrests, controls, front riggings, wheels and rear tires, casters, handrims, and other features. Each is briefly discussed in this section.

Seats

Seat types sent from manufacturers are hammock or sling, both of which are quite flexible. Seats may be solid to provide postural support. In this instance, the seat can be removed so that the chair can be folded, or the solid seat can be specially installed to fold with the chair. When the user's body offers particular challenges, seats are specially fabricated to conform to the user's seating needs. This occurrence is discussed later in this chapter.

It is generally accepted that seats should be as narrow as possible without making contact that causes pressure sores. Wheelchair seats usually range in size from 10 to 30 inches and are available in 2-inch increments. Although larger seats are available, their size makes the chair more difficult to fold for transport.

Seat depth refers to how long the seat is from front to back. A seat that is too shallow (i.e., short) results in the user's legs extending too far in front of the seat. When this occurs, too much pressure is placed on the body's soft tissues and pressure sores can develop. In addition, shallow seats inhibit proper foot contact with the footrests. Seats that are too deep inhibit blood flow unless the users slump backward on their chairs or extend their legs outward. Either position is detrimental to comfort, and slumping that results from rotating the pelvis backward can lead to spinal degeneration (Karp, 1999).

Seat height is usually 19½ to 20½ inches, depending on the height of the user. The height of the seat is obviously affected by the size of the cushion. At times the

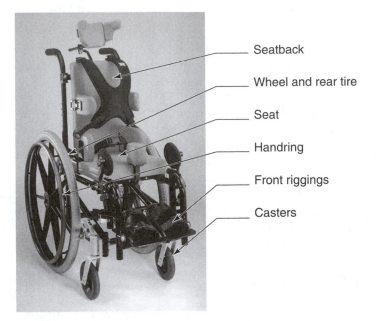

Seatback

Wheel and rear tire

Seat

Handring

Front riggings

Casters

FIGURE 4.6   Components of a Wheelchair
Photo courtesy of Adaptive Engineering Lab, Inc.

height will be altered to make the user feel more stable. That is, by tilting the seat slightly to the back and establishing contact between the user's back and the chair back, the user feels more secure than might be if the posture is forward leaning.

Seatbacks

For years, seatbacks had to be flexible so that they could fold with the chair for storage purposes. Unfortunately, these flexible seatbacks were unable to provide lumbar support, lateral trunk stability, and accommodation to unique positioning needs (Karp, 1999). With the introduction of rigid frame wheelchairs, seatbacks now provide much better support because they pivot downward against the seat rather than closing sideways. New technology also has allowed for the inclusion of back supports on traditional folding chairs.

Like seats, seatbacks should be fitted to accommodate the size of the user. Backs that are too short cause problems when the upper part of the back hangs over and causes discomfort or sores. The height of the device should allow for firm support without restricting motion.

Armrests

Almost all powered wheelchairs have armrests, but manual wheelchairs may or may not have armrests, depending on the needs and desires of the consumer. There are a number of factors to consider concerning armrests. Karp (1999) offered the following benefits of armrests:

- Armrests can help prevent spinal problems. When you put the weight of your arms on the armrest, you relieve some of the load on your spine.
- Armrests may be important for transfers into and out of the chair.
- Armrests are helpful for shifting your weight in the chair, a crucial habit for the prevention of pressure sores.
- If you have limited upper body balance, your safety may depend on having the added stability armrests provide (p. 259).

Some people prefer not to include armrests on their chairs because they are simply not needed. Others choose to have flip-up or swing-away armrests installed because they only need armrests some of the time. When not needed, the armrests are pivoted out of the way. Still other wheelchair users choose to have removable armrests that can be easily taken off and put on the chair as needed. Finally, some users choose to have permanent armrests. Some power wheelchair users choose to use sculpted armrests that fit the arms for joystick ease or use. In some instances, straps can be used to keep the arm securely placed in the mold.

Controls

Church and Glennen (1992) discuss a variety of control methods that can be employed by a power chair user. By far the most common control is a hand-controlled joystick, similar to the device used in video games. This application of the joystick allows the user to propel his or her chair in a particular direction. Proportional-drive joysticks allow the user to control the speed and direction of the chair's movement. Microswitch joysticks, on the other hand, offer only on-off alternatives.

Remote joysticks are employed by some wheelchair users who require head-stick or chin controls. Typically, these types of joysticks offer the same advantages as their proportional-drive counterparts, with the obvious difference being their mode of operation. Less common are controls that are operated by sip and puff or another type of switch. The main point to consider is that power chairs can be propelled by any number of controls, thereby making power chairs a viable alternative for many potential users.

Front Riggings

Front rigging is a generic term that is used when discussing foot and leg rests. Batavia (1998) notes four purposes of riggings:

1. They prevent the users' feet from dragging on the floor as they ride.
2. They support the back of the base of the thigh from pressure sores that result from contact at the front edge of the seat.

3. They allow the knee joint to bend at the preferred angle.
4. They provide the ankle joint with the proper dorsiflexion (i.e., the ankle flexes at the required angle).

Like armrests, footplates can be fixed or detached. Also like armrests, footplates can pivot to allow for easier entry to and exit from the wheelchair or allow for easier access to work tables. In addition, front riggings can be adjusted to allow for straight leg use (i.e., parallel to the ground). Such a configuration allows for comfort for those whose legs are in a cast or who have knee problems (Wilson, 1992).

Wheels and Rear Tires

Wheelchairs usually include two 20- to 26-inch rear spoke or molded wheels that support the tires (standard wheelchair wheels are 24 inches in diameter). Spoke wheels are lighter than molded wheels but require more maintenance. In contrast, molded wheels are more durable. As the size of the wheel increases, maneuverability tends to decrease.

Tires are pneumatic, solid, or airless. Pneumatic tires are air-filled. They can be smooth or treaded, depending on the terrain of the ground that is traversed. Smoother areas, such as inside buildings or on sidewalks, can be traversed easily with smooth tires. Different tire treads are available for rough or semi-rough terrains. Pneumatic tires are the most shock-absorbing type of tire; thus, they tend to prolong the life of a chair by reducing shock to its systems. Pneumatic tires also make riding more comfortable.

Solid tires have the advantage of lower maintenance and are firmer than pneumatic tires. Because pneumatic tire blowouts can occur in a work environment that has sharp edges (e.g., broken glass, sharp metal) on the floor, solid tires may be the preferred choice for some locations.

Airless, solid-insert tires offer similar advantages to traditional solid tires. Their shock absorption is superior to standard solid tires but considerably less than pneumatic tires.

Casters

Casters are small front (usually) wheels that allow the wheelchair to be steered. Although casters can be of any size, they range in size from 2 to 8 inches, with typical sizes being 5 or 8 inches in diameter. Larger casters provide better shock absorption, but smaller casters offer a smaller turning radius and less "fluttering" (i.e., shaking back and forth). The increased maneuverability of smaller wheels should be considered against the inconveniences that are presented by obstacles such as small potholes. Wider, ball-shaped casters improve rolling resistance and allow wheelchairs to be used on sand. Like rear wheel tires, caster tires can be solid or pneumatic or a hybrid of the two.

Handrims

Handrims are usually circular tubes that attach to the driving wheels to allow for control of the chair. Many tubes are made of steel and allow the user to push the chair and keep the hands clean. Some users who have grasping problems find knobs or other projections helpful when they are attached to the tubes. These attachments allow the user to propel the drive wheels using the palms or the meaty portion of the hand.

Other Features

Seat belts, parking locks, anti-tipping devices, and trays are just a few of other helpful tools that can be a part of a rider's wheelchair. Each of these, and the many other features available for wheelchair users, allow for added safety, comfort, and support. Of particular value are specialized seating and positioning systems, which are described in the next section.

FOCUS ON 4.3

Go to a medical supply store that sells wheelchairs. Inquire about the cost of features listed in this section. How much do they cost? How are the features fitted for the user? Is there a person at the store who is qualified to fit the features to the individual? If not, what services are available for fitting customized features? Also, does the store help the user with identifying funding sources?

SEATING AND POSITIONING ISSUES

People who use wheelchairs come in a variety of shapes and sizes. To help wheelchair users best fit into the chair, seating and positioning specialists work to create the best seating system for the rider.

Anyone who has had to sit or lie in one position for an extended period of time knows how uncomfortable the experience can be. (See Personal Perspective 4.2 for a general discussion of positioning issues.) Seating systems include several wheelchair components such as seat cushions, seat inserts, back inserts, lateral trunk supports, hip guides, pommels, anterior trunk supports, and head supports (Batavia, 1998). Positioning describes the process of supporting a person's posture at a particular point in time using these seating system components. Thus, positioning is an important mobility consideration because people who use wheelchairs stay in their chair for much of the day. It is important to place people in positions from which they can comfortably participate in their daily activities. By paying careful attention to a person's positioning needs, factors can be reduced that may lead to muscle tightness, abnormal postures, and/or restricted movement associated

PERSONAL PERSPECTIVE 4.2

Jamie Judd-Wall has been a leader in the field of assistive technology for over a decade. She is the founder and director of Technology and Inclusion, a not-for-profit, 501(c)(3) tax-exempt organization based in Austin, Texas. Jamie has pioneered training programs such as PECS with TECH, worked with many companies to develop assistive technology products such as the new "Sound Commands" voice recognition software, and has served as guest editor for publications such as DREAMMS, in addition to her work on Technology and Inclusion's newsletter. Jamie is a frequent presenter at conferences and annually hosts several conferences and training workshops in Austin.

We have heard you talk about the importance of positioning when considering AT. Why is positioning such a critical factor for some people with disabilities?
Positioning is a critical factor for everyone. Simply put, if you are uncomfortable, you can't focus on the task. For people with disabilities there are many aspects of positioning that play a part in their performance. Some people are not able to change their positions and so rely on others for their physical comfort. Some others are just not aware of their position and they don't realize that they are uncomfortable or that their work is being affected until after the decline in performance has begun.

What can teachers look for to ensure that a student is positioned correctly in classroom environments?
Teachers should be sure that certain critical supports are in place for every student.

1. Are their hips securely placed in the chair so that the upper body has a good base of support? Is foot support available? We don't all keep our feet on the ground all the time but chairs that are too tall to allow for solid foot support encourage poor positioning. Imagine sitting on a stool without ever being able to put your feet on something—that's the effect of the lack of foot support.
2. Is there good back support? Again, we don't lean back all the time, but when the student leans into the chairback, is it in the right location to help support his or her spine in a "working" posture?
3. Various positions: Most people spend their day sitting, standing, and walking. A few folks have reason to lie down, but for most folks you lose focus on the task at hand when you recline. So reclining is a break-time posture rather than a work-time posture.
4. Benefits of good positioning: Good positioning helps you focus on the task, it supports organs, muscles, and joints for proper functioning, and it extends peak performance. Poor positioning at a minimum is uncomfortable and at its worst results in deformities that become lifelong disabilities.

Describe muscle tone as it relates to positioning.

Muscle tone is a more important positioning factor when it is abnormal, too high, or too low. Low muscle tone means that someone's muscles are too "soft" to assist the person in maintaining proper positioning, like the child who can't hold up his or her head. High muscle tone means that the muscles are too "rigid or stiff" to assist in maintaining proper positioning, like the child who can't bend to sit down. Our hope in using positioning devices is that we can bring the person's tone closer to normal so that he or she can have more control over movements and perform tasks more independently and with less effort.

How do reflexes affect positioning?

Reflexes take control of your body away from you, like when you hear a loud noise unexpectedly—you have a physical reaction that is out of your control. People who have very strong reflexes move their body in certain ways that are out of their control (without positioning aids and therapy). When your body is out of your control, you can't do the things that you want to do. For some people this means that every little noise makes them jump, for others this means that they can't bring their hand to their mouth to eat.

What are some of the devices that are used to aid in positioning?

There is a wide range of items to help in maintaining a proper position. Sometimes it is a box or rolled-up towel placed in a strategic location, at other times it is a custom-made seat, one that is made specifically to match the curves in a person's spine so that they can sit without pain or discomfort. Designing proper seating and positioning systems for people with severe physical challenges is a specialty service provided by highly trained therapists.

You do a lot with switches. Describe the importance of positioning with regard to switch use.

Using a switch is a part of the chain of events set in place by positioning. If the person's ability to use the body to work and perform other tasks is affected by position, then using a switch is one of the tasks that is affected. For some folks this is a minor difficulty in reaching a switch on their wheelchair tray, a little hard to do in one position but easy if their hips are properly placed in their seat. But when people aren't properly positioned and need to use their hands to hold themselves up so they can't reach for the switch at all, that means that they can't perform any of the tasks asked of them. Sadly, this is often interpreted as a lack of ability or understanding when it is actually the result of poor positioning.

Positioning plays a critical role in food digestion. Can you describe how the two are related?

There are many things that affect digestion; positioning is one of them. Think of yourself after a big holiday meal—you want to get up and stretch, stand up, walk a little bit; that gives your body space to let your organs work properly. Imagine how uncomfortable it would be if you had to remain in your chair at the dining table for hours without being able to make those simple movements. That is the relationship between positioning and digestion. Movement encourages digestion; sitting all the time inhibits it. For some people who are in their wheelchairs for long periods of time, extended sitting, lack of stretching, and lack of weight-bearing positions inhibit their digestive process. Standing lets gravity help your body process food; weight bearing sends certain signals to your internal organs about what they need to do. Moving, especially standing and stretching type movements, helps your body move food through your system.

Here's your chance to tell our readers the one thing you think is most important for them to know about positioning. What would that be?

Everybody strives to maintain a normal posture and have normal tone. When you don't see that happening, there is always a reason. Kids who are fussy and inattentive often don't have enough positioning support to focus and work. If you would be uncomfortable assuming the position of a person in a wheelchair, they are probably uncomfortable too.

Reprinted with permission from Psycho-Educational Services.

with bone malformation, discomfort, and reduced functional abilities. Proper positioning does more than help a person achieve functionality, however; it is an absolute necessity for the person's physical welfare throughout the lifespan. Comfortable positioning is important for people to be able to pay attention, move their heads so that they can see and hear what is happening in their vicinity, shift their weight or change positions for comfort's sake, breathe easily, and manipulate objects or operate switches. Also, proper positioning in youth may set the stage for the maintenance of abilities later in life.

Positioning not only provides comfort, but it also can reduce further malformations. For instance, for a child with a developing scoliosis (i.e., a lateral curvature of the spine), positioning systems can help control the scoliosis and reduce continual degeneration. In Table 4.1, Batavia (1998) provides a number of positioning questions to consider for wheelchair users and caregivers.

To conclude, positioning ensures comfort and function (i.e., promotes maximum use of the body that helps a person to be ready to perform activities) while promoting access to a variety of environments and allowing for a positive self-image.

TABLE 4.1   Questions to Consider for Wheelchair Positioning

YES	NO	NA	CONSIDERATION
____	____	____	1. Are postural supports properly installed on the frame?
____	____	____	2. Is the seat depth acceptable?
____	____	____	3. Is the seat width acceptable?
____	____	____	4. Is the back height acceptable based on the user's activity level?
____	____	____	5. Is the foot height level acceptable?
____	____	____	6. In the frontal plane, in the pelvic level, are the shoulders and eyes horizontal, and is the nose vertical?
____	____	____	7. In the sagittal plane, is the pelvis in a neutral tilt and the shoulders and head balanced?
____	____	____	8. Are the rear wheels positioned properly with respect to the user's arms?
____	____	____	9. Are straps and seatbelts positioned properly?
____	____	____	10. Does the chest harness provide proper clearance around the neck?
____	____	____	11. Is the pommel positioned distally, between the knees, rather than proximally, into the groin?
____	____	____	12. Do lateral trunk supports allow for acceptable clearance of the axillary region so that there is no pressure to the brachial praxis?
____	____	____	13. Is there sufficient space between the lap board and the abdomen to allow for clothing comfort and respiration?
____	____	____	14. Is the frame stable when the user is in the wheelchair?

Adapted with permission from Batavia, M. (1998). *The wheelchair evaluation: A practical guide.* Boston: Butterworth-Heinemann.

When used in conjunction with each other, positioning and mobility allow people freedom to move about comfortably in their multiple environments.

FOCUS ON 4.4

Contact an occupational therapist who specializes in wheelchair positioning. Ask questions about the job. What got him or her interested in this line of work? With what ages does the therapist prefer to work and why? What specialized training has the person received and from where? How does he or she keep abreast of the latest developments? What equipment has been recently made available on the market? How has positioning changed in the years the therapist has worked in wheelchair positioning? What would be the person's advice to anyone considering this line of work? Think of some more questions on your own to get a good feel for what a wheelchair positioning expert does. In addition, ask if you might be able to watch the person as he or she works with a wheelchair user on positioning issues.

SUMMARY

In this chapter, we provided an overview of mobility issues for people with physical disabilities and mobility needs. We first introduced mobility adaptations by discussing various physical impairments and their attributes. We also presented a number of devices that are available to people with mobility needs. Manual and electronic wheelchairs were presented, along with a variety of other wheeled mobility units that are available (e.g., scooter boards, sport wheelchairs). We then presented information on the various design features (e.g., wheelchair backs, wheels) available for wheelchair users. Finally, we discussed briefly a number of positioning issues for people who use wheelchairs. These issues are especially important to allow the wheelchair user to move about with comfort and efficiency.

DISCUSSION QUESTIONS

1. What various wheelchairs are available to people with mobility needs? How would one go about selecting the best wheelchair? What design features should be considered?
2. With whom would you consult when purchasing a wheelchair? What questions might you ask? How would you determine whether the answers to your questions were accurate? Where might you go to obtain more information about wheelchairs?
3. You are an athlete who is interested in wheelchair racing. What concerns might you have about taking up the sport? Where would you find information on wheelchair racing? What exercise regimen would you have to adhere to? What specialized equipment would you want to acquire?

4. Wheelchair positioning is a specialized area. Why might someone be inclined to be an occupational therapist and specialize in wheelchair positioning? How would you go about your training to become an occupational therapist? What might be the pluses and minuses of the profession as it applies to wheelchair positioning? Where might you work?

REFERENCES

Angelo, J. (1997). *Assistive technology for rehabilitation therapists.* Philadelphia: E. A. Davis.

Batavia, M. (1998). *The wheelchair evaluation: A practical guide.* Boston: Butterworth Heinemann.

Church, G., & Glennen, S. (1992). *The handbook of assistive technology.* San Diego: Singular.

Hardman, M. L., Drew, C. J., & Egan, M. W. (1996). *Human exceptionality* (5th ed.). Boston: Allyn and Bacon.

Karp, G. (1999). *Life on wheels: For the active wheelchair user.* Cambridge: O'Reilly.

Lewis, R. B. (1993). *Special education technology.* Pacific Grove, CA: Brooks/Cole.

Wilson, A. B. (1992). *Wheelchairs: A prescription guide.* New York: Demos.

CHAPTER FIVE

ASSISTIVE TECHNOLOGY DEVICES TO ENHANCE SPEECH COMMUNICATION

CHAPTER AT A GLANCE

NATURE OF SPOKEN LANGUAGE
- Focus on 5.1

INTRODUCTION TO AUGMENTATIVE AND ALTERNATIVE COMMUNICATION SYSTEMS
- Focus on 5.2
- Focus on 5.3

SELECTION TECHNIQUES FOR AIDED COMMUNICATION SYSTEMS

OVERVIEW OF NONELECTRONIC SYSTEMS AND ELECTRONIC DEVICES
- Focus on 5.4

OBJECTIVES

1. Identify the components of language and their role in language development.
2. Determine the purpose of alternative and augmentative communication, specifically with regard to unaided and aided communication.
3. Examine the components of an augmentative and alternative communication system and how they combine to provide individuals with severe speech problems the opportunities to communicate on a daily basis across environments.

MAKING CONNECTIONS

Think about how often you communicate throughout the day. How do you communicate? With whom do you speak? What are the topics of conversation? Are the conversations formal or informal? What are the purposes for your communications? What skills do you have to possess to communicate effectively? What if you did not possess those skills? How might you communicate otherwise?

From the time you woke up this morning, you probably have communicated with dozens of people, depending upon the time of day it is when you are reading this. The purpose and form of each communicative act probably differed in some way. But, more or less, your day has been made easier because of your ability to communicate ideas to someone. The purpose of this chapter is to examine the communicative act, particularly for those who have disability-related communication problems that require the use of AT. We do so by (a) overviewing spoken language communication; (b) introducing the nature of augmentative communication; and (c) describing various devices that enhance communication.

NATURE OF SPOKEN LANGUAGE

Hegde (1991) noted that language has become so important in modern societies that it has become an essential component for "social survival" (p. 3). Such an observation illustrates the need for humans to communicate, that is, to be a part of the social phenomenon we call life. Young children, especially those with significantly impaired or delayed language skills, need a great deal of stimulation and modeling in order to develop language skills. Likewise, mature language users need continuous feedback and stimulation to improve their communication capabilities. The same approaches used in the development and maintenance of oral language apply to learning to use and maintain alternative and augmentative communication ("aug com") systems.

When we typically discuss a person's oral language skills, we do so in its most basic form by talking about listening and speaking (Sternberg, 1994). We can then discuss more in-depth language skills by talking about semantics, syntax, phonology, and pragmatics. Although considered and discussed separately, the components of language are intertwined and interact with one another to allow for effective and efficient communication. Listening, for example, involves more than simply "hearing" sounds and tones—it involves obtaining meaning from what is heard. In order to gain meaning from what is heard, a person must have a listening vocabulary (i.e., a corpus of words that are meaningful), syntactic sense (i.e., the ability to make sense of perceived word order), phonological awareness (i.e., the ability to discriminate among speech sounds so that *ship* isn't heard as *chip*), and a pragmatic sense to place what is heard in the proper context. In the same vein, speaking involves more than simply grunting out meaningless sounds and involves the same attributes (e.g., semantics, syntax, pragmatics) as listening, except that it does so in an expressive manner.

Put simply, when examining language from a perspective of augmentative and alternative communication, we examine listening and speaking skills while considering semantics, pragmatics, and other language features so that we can be better able to prescribe devices that enhance a person's ability to communicate by utilizing his or her communicative attributes (Myers, 1987). Each language component is described briefly in this section.

Listening

As we stated, listening, as a construct, involves more than simply "hearing" sounds and tones—it involves obtaining meaning from what is heard. So listening refers to a person's ability to gain meaning from the spoken word. As we examine a person's listening skills, we examine the kinds of words and language structures to which a person can respond. That is, we are concerned with the number of words, types of words (nouns, verbs, adjectives), and types of syntactic structures that are possessed by a person as he or she listens to others.

Speaking

When we consider a person's speaking skills, we examine production (i.e., the number of words uttered), types of words used, and types of sentence structures that a person employs. At times, people do not have the neurological capabilities to voice words, even though they may be able to put sentences together in their minds. Imagine the frustration of having something to say yet not being able to speak the words coherently. The thoughts exist, words are well chosen, and the words are sequenced in the proper word order. But because of problems that might involve muscles within the oral mechanism, the mouth simply is unable to produce the ideas generated by the mind.

Speaking skills are often augmented by nonverbal modes of communication. Gesture, eye gaze, facial expression, and body language often convey messages just as effectively as speech. As a result, a person may be naturally inclined to use gestures, which may indicate that sign language may be used as one mode of communication if a situation warrants. Interest in books and pictures may indicate that picture communication could be an effective means of augmenting a person's speech.

Semantics

Semantics refers to the meaningful aspects of language and involves words (i.e., vocabulary), chunks of words (i.e., phrases, clauses), and continuous text (i.e., sentences, paragraphs). With regard to aug com devices, semantics is important because devices can include only those words that are meaningful to the user in order to engage in meaningful dialogue. At the same time, communication partners (i.e., those who communicate with the aug com user) must select words in the user's meaning vocabulary.

Syntax

Syntax refers to the system of language that strings words together in a way that makes sense. In its most basic terms, syntax involves word order, or putting words together to make the communicator's message clear. For example, the statement "The red big apple was juicy" simply doesn't sound as correct as "The big red apple was juicy," but the statement "Juicy the red was apple big" makes no sense at all. This nonsense is simply a lack of syntactic sense, which is an important consideration when examining a person's language skills prior to prescribing an aug com device.

Morphology

Morphology is the examination of the smallest units of speech that have meaning (i.e., morphemes). Unbound morphemes are those that stand alone meaningfully. For example, *girl* is an unbound morpheme because it has meaning by itself. On the other hand, *s* is a bound morpheme because it must be attached to an unbound morpheme to have any meaning. When attached to *girl* to form *girls*, the bound morpheme *s* means more than one girl. With regard to aug com, morphemes are important because they are critical to semantic proficiency.

Phonology

Phonology deals with the sound system of language. Because most aug com users have weak or no phonological skills, their devices are meant to produce phonemes and string them together to communicate meaningfully with their communication partners.

Pragmatics

Pragmatics is the use of language to achieve a specific purpose. Young children, using only single words, can request objects (e.g., "drink" to request a glass of milk), request actions (e.g., "eat" to request lunch), indicate choices (e.g., "juice" to request apple juice), or label (e.g., "kittie" to identify a cat). People learn to use language for other functions, such as accepting/affirming or denying/refusing (e.g., responding "yes" or "no" when asked whether the individual wants to go out to eat), greeting (e.g., stating "Hello, my name is Donald, you?" to provide a name while asking for another's), commenting (e.g., saying "big" when responding about a dog's size), asking questions (e.g., "Tommy?" for "Where's Tommy?"), or providing information (e.g., "hungry" when indicating a desire for some food).

Summary

Language skills, both receptive and expressive, are best developed in authentic, language-rich environments. Homes, classrooms, and/or work environments provide the best opportunities for language development and reinforcement because they are the naturalistic environments within which people work and play. Syntactic, semantic, and pragmatic skills can be modeled, taught, and learned in these environments through normal activities, whether training is being conducted by a therapist or reinforced by teachers, family members, coworkers, and so forth.

FOCUS ON 5.1

Consider your morning activities. List the communication activities you engage in during those activities. Classify them according to listening and speaking, and consider a few typical utterances in terms of semantics, syntax, morphology, phonology, and pragmatics. Now take a moment to see how those activities would be influenced if you were unable to speak. How might you communicate? How would your world be affected?

INTRODUCTION TO AUGMENTATIVE AND ALTERNATIVE COMMUNICATION SYSTEMS

Augmentative and alternative communication (AAC) has been described as "an area of clinical practice that attempts to compensate (either temporarily or permanently) for the impairment and disability patterns of individuals with expressive disorders (i.e., the severely speech-language and writing impaired)" (AHSA, 1989, cited in Angelo, 1997, p. 160). An AAC system refers to an individual's complete functional communication system that includes a communicative technique, a symbol set or system, and communication/interaction behavior. Each of these AAC components will be discussed later.

There are no specific guidelines for the use of AAC systems. Rather, they are generally considered when speech is inadequate for a person to communicate effectively, especially when receptive language exceeds expressive skills.

The use of AAC systems does not mean that a person will not develop speech, or that the system will be the only means to communicate. The word "augmentative" indicates that the system is meant to add to existing abilities. In many instances, speech may be a person's primary means of communication, and the AAC system supplements vocalizations when speech is not understood by a particular communication partner. For others, AAC systems may be the primary means of communication. In either case, it is important to begin the use of AAC as early as possible.

When first asked to consider aug com devices, some people express concern that AAC system use will interfere with speech development. On the contrary, the use of AAC systems may enhance speech and language development by relieving the pressure and frustration that comes with ineffective communications and social interactions with others. This question has been addressed for many years, and the prevailing opinion is that the use of AAC systems does not inhibit speech development (Freedom Center, 1996).

The selection, development, and implementation of AAC systems should result from recommendations by a team of professionals and those who interact with the user. A speech-language pathologist with a background in AAC use will usually assume a leadership role in AAC system evaluation team meetings (Angelo, 1997). Because it is important that AAC systems and strategies be used across the user's environments, all people who interact with the user as communication partners should learn how to use the system to communicate effectively with the user. To the extent possible, key communication partners should be members of the evaluation and implementation team and, at the very least, be trained with the system to become effective communication partners. Of course, the user should always be a team member and no decisions should be made without his or her advice and consent. Without such consent, there is no guarantee that the device will be used.

One result of a lack of training in the use of AAC systems is the limitation of interactions that might occur. Some AAC users respond rather than initiate dialogue, especially if the user has been taught symbol vocabulary by eliciting responses to nonmeaningful or contrived questions. In all instances, training should occur in naturalistic settings during meaningful conversations that reflect authentic communicative experiences. Initiating and responding to conversational speech should be a focus of instruction because these are important pragmatic skills for language users.

The person interacting with an AAC system user needs to learn new communication skills. Effective skills include communication partners who are appropriately positioned, pause to allow responses, ask easily understood open-ended questions, confirm statements made by the AAC user, and provide elaborations when needed.

FOCUS ON 5.2

Think about the role of communication partners. What traits do you find pleasing and annoying in your communication partners? What attributes make for effective communication partners? How might these traits inhibit effective communication when conversing with individuals who have severe speech problems? How might these problems be overcome?

Musselwhite and St. Louis (1988) noted that there are three functions of an AAC system:

1. An alternative communication system, substituting to some extent for a vocal mode. This may be a temporary use for a client who is learning to use vocal communication. The goal here is to transmit information though nonvocal means.
2. A supplement to vocal communication for the client who has difficulty with formulation or intelligibility, but who has some usable speech. The term "augmentative" is often used to describe this function.
3. A facilitator of communication, with emphasis on speech intelligibility, output and organization of language, and/or general communication skills (p. 105).

Lloyd, Fuller, and Arvidson (1997) discuss AAC systems as being divided into two broad categories: aided and unaided. Each category is discussed here.

Unaided Communication

Unaided communication refers to a communication system that does not involve the use of external equipment or devices (Shane & Sauer, 1986); rather, unaided communicators use their body parts, usually their arms and hands, to "speak" (Musselwhite & St. Louis, 1988). Because this text deals with AT, and unaided communication systems by their nature are not assistive technologies, we will not devote a lot of space to discussing unaided systems. Yet no discussion of AAC would be complete without at least a brief overview of unaided communication systems. Here we present three types of unaided communication systems: sign languages, educational sign systems, and gestural language codes.

Sign Languages.   Almost everyone is familiar with sign language systems that are used by people who are deaf. The same systems have been used effectively with some people who have severe communication problems that have nothing to do with deafness (Alvares & Sternberg, 1994).

The most common sign language system in the United States and Canada is the American Sign Language (ASL), or Ameslan as it is sometimes called. It has been speculated that ASL was brought to the North American continent by Thomas Gallaudet and Laurent Clerc, who adapted the Old French signing system for their use in American educational settings. Others (Woodward, 1978) argue that ASL is a hybrid language that combined French signing with other signing systems that were in use for years in America prior to Gallaudet and Clerc's efforts. Either way, ASL has been adopted by the "Deaf Community" as its unofficial language, and it has also been used effectively with others who have severe communication challenges. It is important to note that ASL has its own syntax that is different than English. For instance, Musselwhite and St. Louis noted that the English sentence "'They have already eaten their dinner would be signed in ASL as 'THEY FINISH EAT NIGHT' or 'FINISH EAT NIGHT THEY'" (p. 121). This is not to say that ASL is an ungrammatical language. On the contrary, ASL is a grammatically different language that possesses its own rules of grammar.

Educational Sign Systems.   According to Musselwhite and St. Louis (1988), educational sign systems were developed to create a better grammatical correspondence between sign language and regular English. The most common system is Signing Exact English, which was developed as a result of a 1969 meeting among parents, teachers, and deaf adults to help students learn the syntax and vocabulary they will encounter as they read. The sign system is composed of about 4,000 signs that include about 70 common English prefixes, suffixes, and inflectional endings.

Gestural Language Codes.   Although finger spelling is often associated with sign language, it is really its own gestural code. The most common finger spelling system is called the American Manual Alphabet (see Figure 5.1). Obviously, a person who uses finger spelling must have good motor control of one hand, must be able to spell, and must have good visual skills to recognize what is being spelled.

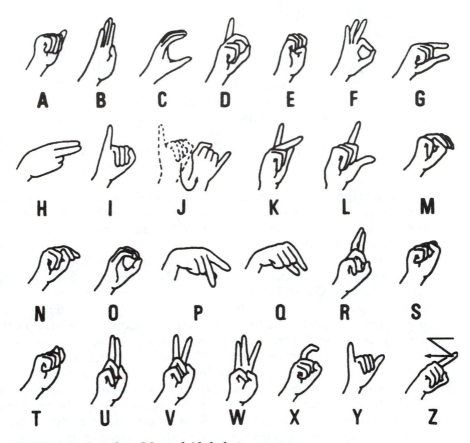

FIGURE 5.1   American Manual Alphabet

A second popular gestural code is cued speech. Cued speech involves hand shapes, hand placements, and nonmanual signals to produce a visible code to help supplement speech reading, sometimes called *lip reading*. Thus, cued speech could be considered a visible partner of speaking. Because cues are used in conjunction with speech reading, cues differentiate phonemes that look similar on the lips. Utterances are cued by dividing what is to be said into consonant-vowel pairs. These pairs are formed by combining the consonant's hand shape with the hand's vowel. Because all cues accompany speech, a cued speech reader sees a multidimensional visual cue (i.e., hand shape, placement, and mouth configuration) for each unique sound of the utterance.

Aided Communication

In contrast to unaided communication systems, aided systems use equipment and/or devices to provide people with the ability to communicate (Brett & Provenzo,

1995). In this section, we provide a brief introduction to symbol systems that form the basis of aided systems, nonelectronic systems, and electronic systems.

Symbols play a similar role as spoken words by representing ideas and concepts. For example, when you hear the word "play" you think of playing a game and create a mental image to represent the concept. When this mental image is displayed as a picture, the idea of "playing" can be conveyed from one person to another. According to the Freedom Center (1996), symbols can vary in (a) level of abstraction, (b) style, and (c) size.

Levels of Abstraction. Abstractions in this case occur on a continuum from simple to complex. Simple abstractions are first and presentations continue through complex stimuli. The simplest abstraction is represented by life-sized models or miniatures. Photos (e.g., soup can labels, magazine pictures) also can be used to represent objects. Next on the continuum are exacting colored drawings that contain considerable detail.

Line drawings, next on the continuum, are more detailed than conventional "stick figures." Multiple-meaning icons (i.e., pictures that lend different meanings in different contexts) are considerably more abstract. For example, a picture of the sun can represent "hot," "circular," "yellow," "happy," or whatever concept is selected as being reasonable. Printed words, either single words or phrases, also can be used without pictures to represent concepts and ideas. Spelling, for those who can spell functionally, allows for the highest level of flexibility because it can convey just about any message desired by the communicator.

For the most part, abstract symbols are the most flexible because they provide an unlimited variety of sequences that can be used to generate thousands of messages. Spelling is also versatile because it allows communicators to access all words in their writing vocabulary.

Style. Pictures can vary in detail, outline, color, and/or background color. The features of pictures are important because they "belong" to the MC system user. Their selection should be made based on functional use, personal preferences, and the capability of the communicator to deal with the abstraction continuum discussed in the previous section. To reiterate, because the MC system belongs to the user, that user should be integrally involved in decisions about the style of the pictures that are part of the system. Continuous evaluations are made to determine the effectiveness of the user's style choices.

Size. In general, larger pictures are easier to use than smaller pictures in terms of vision, cognition, and motor ability. Larger pictures are easier to see, recognize, and point to. The size, spacing, and positioning of pictures is specifically determined for each user's needs. For many young children, full-page-size pictures are preferred when they first use communication boards; some children adapt quickly to smaller (i.e., 1-inch or 2-inch) drawings.

Although it is convenient to fit more small pictures on a page or display, it is critical that the size of the pictures accommodates the user's visual and motor needs. With younger children, it is usually advisable to use pictures no smaller than 2 inches in size. As children grow, or with adult users, size becomes less of a concern and is overshadowed by the need to provide more communication options that come with having more pictures on the board.

FOCUS ON 5.3

Think about the factors that should be considered when selecting the various features (e.g., levels of abstraction, size) of AAC symbol systems. Then conduct an Internet search using the keywords "augmentative communication." Look for discussions about the factors. Which considerations did you identify that are found in the Internet discussions? Which ones did you come up with that were not mentioned? How could you validate your considerations?

SELECTION TECHNIQUES FOR AIDED COMMUNICATION SYSTEMS

The selection technique is chosen according to the user's motor strengths and needs. For example, a person who can point will likely use direct selection, whereas a person who has severe motor limitations may prefer scanning with some kind of switch (Shane & Sauer, 1986). Each technique is described briefly here.

Direct Selection

Direct selection systems require some form of directional movement as a means of pointing. The user directly selects the desired item (e.g., object, picture, word) by one of three typical selection techniques: finger-pointing, head-pointing, or eye gaze-pointing. Electronic direct selection devices usually use a keyboard or membrane board that allows the individual to make selections by pressing the pictured item on the display. An example of such a system is provided in Figure 5.2. Here, direct selection is represented in a homemade eye-gaze display. The student user responds to an addition problem (e.g., "How much is 2 + 2?") by gazing at his or her response. The communication partner, in this case a teacher, follows the student's gaze to identify what number was selected as an answer.

Direct selection systems are preferable to scanning systems for some immature users because they are relatively efficient and easy to learn (Freedom Center, 1996). If the user struggles with pointing, it is best to reduce the amount of physical effort during communication by limiting the selection on the display to only a few larger items.

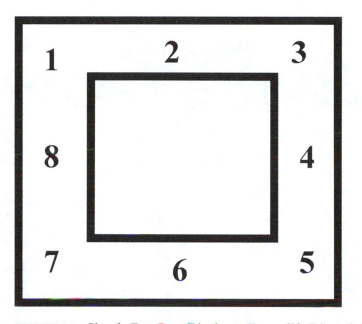

FIGURE 5.2   Simple Eye-Gaze Display to Exemplify Direct Selection

Scanning

With scanning systems, the user selects his or her choice when the scanner gets to the desired icon in a row or column. With nonelectronic systems, the communication partner points to items individually until the user responds with a facial, motor, or vocal response (Heward, 2000). The pictures or other abstractions are displayed on small communication boards or books, and the communication partner scans through the choices by pointing with finger, stylus, or penlight.

Electronic scanning systems contain items that are displayed on the face of the device. Individual lights or highlights scan the choices and the user activates a switch to select the desired item. The users develop rhythm and timing skills to activate the switch at the precise moment the desired item is highlighted. One of the more sophisticated devices is the Vanguard, which is pictured in Figure 5.3. The Vanguard can be operated with the keyboard, infrared head-pointer, or switch-activated scan.

Auditory scanning is used if the user's visual skills are insufficient to use visual displays. The names of the items are spoken one at a time to the user, who responds when the desired item is heard. Typically, categories are spoken first, followed by items within the identified category. For example, the communication partner could select the following categories: food, sport, and work. The communication partner states a category (e.g., food), and the user makes his or her selection by nodding or blinking. Next, the partner names the items within the specified category (e.g., meat,

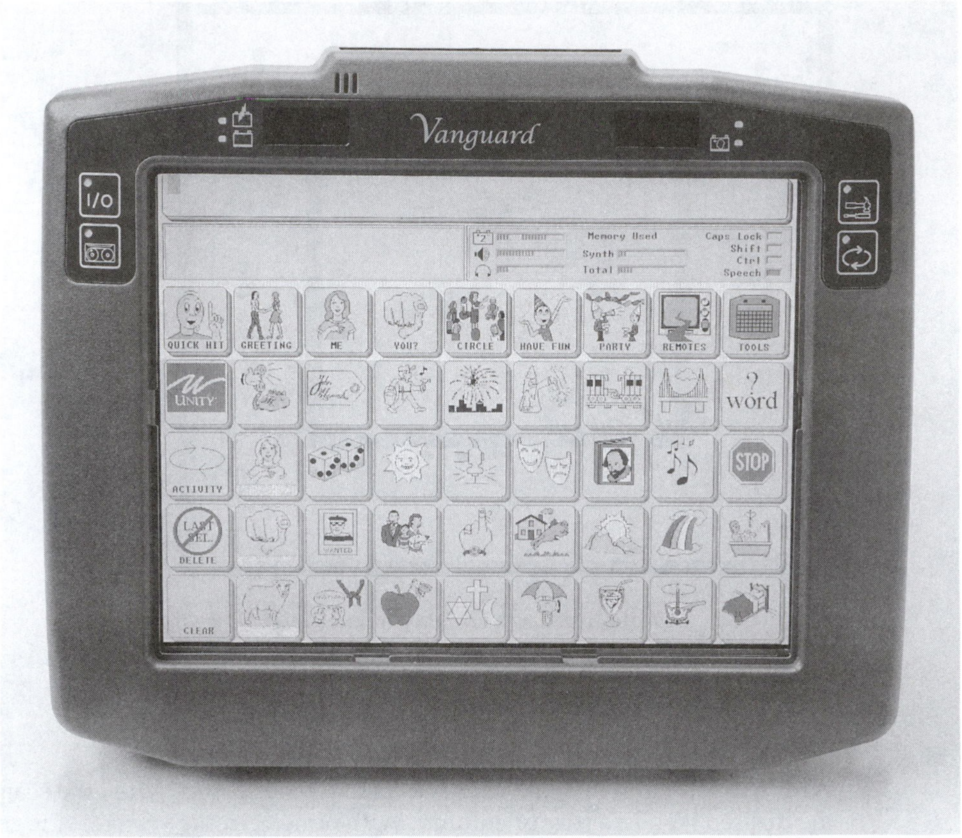

FIGURE 5.3   Vanguard Electronic Scanning System
Photo courtesy of Prentke Romich Company, Wooster, OH.

vegetable), and the process continues until the user communicates his or her intent. Such a scanning technique can occur in row-column, linear, or rotary configurations.

Row-column.   Items arranged in a grid are highlighted row by row, and the user responds when the desired row is indicated. The items within that row are then offered item by item (column) from left to right. The user again responds when the desired item is indicated.

Linear.   Linear devices indicate items one by one. In a grid display, the device would individually highlight each item on the top row then move to the items on the next row one by one. The user waits until the desired item is highlighted and then selects his or her choice.

Rotary.   A rotary device looks somewhat like a clock, with items appearing on the outer edge of the device, and a pointer (similar to a second hand) moves around the circle. When the pointer reaches the desired item, the user makes his or her selection.

OVERVIEW OF NONELECTRONIC SYSTEMS AND ELECTRONIC DEVICES

Aug com devices come in a variety of shapes and forms. One of the easiest ways to differentiate and discuss devices is by categorizing them as nonelectronic systems and electronic devices. Each category is described in this section.

Nonelectronic Systems

Nonelectronic systems are often the first systems used with individuals who have severe speech problems because they are flexible and relatively inexpensive. As would be expected, nonelectronic systems use picture displays that are customized for the user's needs and desires. Here, we briefly introduce communication boards, mini-boards, communication books, and eye gaze displays. Before discussing the various types of devices, however, it is important to mention how vocabulary is selected for use on the different displays.

Selecting vocabulary for specific activities is accomplished by examining each activity and writing out the words and phrases that might be needed. A display for going fishing, for example, might include "bait the hook," "cast for me, please," and "I have a nibble." The challenge is to select words and phrases that the user will be able to apply to situations as they arise.

Nonelectronic Communication Boards.   Communication boards are traditional augmentative communication systems that are convenient enough to be placed on wheelchair lap trays. Communication boards contain a single display of vocabulary words and phrases. The size, number, and position of pictures depend on the user's motor and visual skills and the size of his or her vocabulary. Because the board serves as the user's primary means of communication, it contains as many words and phrases as can fit onto the device. Figure 5.4 depicts a conversation taking place between communication partners using a nonelectronic communication board.

Nonelectronic Mini-Boards.   Mini-boards have become popular displays of vocabulary words and phrases that fit specific settings or activities. For example, a recreation mini-board will contain pictures that relate to play activities. Mini-boards are used most effectively when vocabulary displays for all activities are prepared ahead of time for different activities and allow the user to select the most appropriate vocabulary for his or her daily activities.

Communication Books.   Books are excellent vehicles to help provide access to a large vocabulary compilation. Communication categories (e.g., play, work, daily

FIGURE 5.4   Nonelectric Communication Board
Photo courtesy of Mayer-Johnson, Inc.

living) or activities (e.g., dining, dating, working) can be found as book chapters that are accessed dynamically as the communication situation warrants. In reality, a communication book is a collection of mini-boards that occurs as chapters and pages within the text. A sample communication book is depicted in Figure 5.5.

Eye Gaze Displays.   Eye gaze displays usually are composed of clear material like Plexiglas. Pictures of objects are placed along the border of the display so that the communication partner can follow the user's gaze to an item on the display (see Figure 5.6). Eye gaze displays can be made to serve as mini-boards for use in daily activities. When used in this manner, the communication partner identifies the needed display and positions it properly for the user's benefit.

FOCUS ON 5.4

Create your own communication book. Consider first the person who would use the book. Then select a communication context that would likely be encountered by that person. Script a conversation that would take place between communication partners in the identified context. Then look through magazines to find pictures that could be used to represent vocabulary and phrases that would be used during the conversation. Cut out the pictures and paste them onto a communication book.

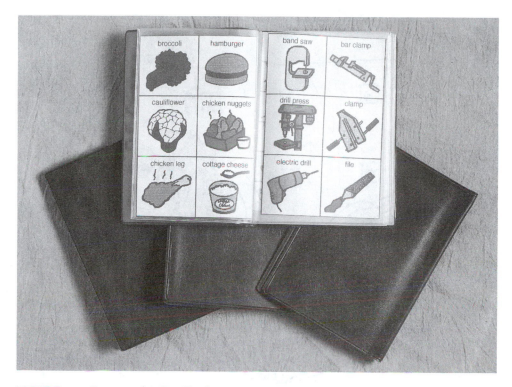

FIGURE 5.5   Communication Book
Photo courtesy of Mayer-Johnson, Inc.

Then share your work with others and attempt to carry on a conversation using your book. What situations do you presume will be encountered as a result of the conversation? When the conversation is completed, were your presumptions correct or incorrect? What situations did you encounter that were unexpected?

Electronic Devices

Electronic devices are obviously going to be more expensive than nonelectronic devices and involve unique considerations in their selection (Alvares & Sternberg, 1994). In this section, we provide information concerning (a) advantages and disadvantages of electronic systems, (b) the types of electronic devices that are available, and (c) key features of electronic systems.

Advantages and Disadvantages of Electronic Systems.   There are several advantages to the selection of electronic communication devices. For the most part, these advantages involve increased independence and options of speech output. Although very young children may not be able to operate an electronic device without assistance, adults are usually capable of independent use. When children are

FIGURE 5.6   Eye Gaze Display
Reprinted with permission, Psycho-Educational Services.

able to communicate successfully without assistance, they learn self-control and independence. Electronic devices can allow independence that nonelectronic systems cannot provide by independent operation of a scanning device with a switch. Nonelectronic systems require considerable assistance from the communication partner.

Until fairly recently, speech output has been available only to older children and adults, because there have been too few examples of such technology for young children (Freedom Center, 1996). Now, however, most experts promote the use of speech output devices for young children to mirror speech and language development.

When a young child speaks for the first time, parents respond quickly to reinforce language use. The child learns quickly to communicate verbally and experiences the power and success that speech provides. Speech output devices can provide similar experiences. Consider, for example, the child who activates the message "I love you, Daddy." Such a statement will likely result in an immediate response from the child's father, particularly when such a statement had not been heard prior to the acquisition of the device. Thus, electronic systems have positive attributes that make their use extremely beneficial, even for very young children. Yet disadvantages are also present. These disadvantages involve cost, maintenance, and portability.

Electronic communication systems range in price from about $300 to $7000. Numerous excellent systems cost about $1000, but these prices are beyond the means of many families. Although funding is available to help defray expenses, many times funding streams are difficult to identify and access, particularly for families with little experience in dealing with the paperwork and routines that are involved with accessing external funds.

All communication systems, especially electronic systems, require periodic maintenance. Battery charging and vocabulary programming are but two of the more common maintenance procedures that must be worked into a daily or weekly routine. The responsibility for maintenance must be clearly delegated.

The added weight and size of electronic communication systems can add difficulty to making the equipment readily accessible to the user. Because active people change positions and locations frequently, it can be difficult for a system to follow them from place to place. Thus, portability is another legitimate concern. In most cases, the advantages of electronic communication devices outweigh the disadvantages. But such decisions must be made on a case-by-case basis.

Types of Electronic Devices.   It is helpful to distinguish the various devices by the kind of input technique they provide. We have already briefly discussed direct selection and scanning. In this section, we reintroduce these features with specific reference to electronic AAC systems. We then introduce three additional features: type of voice, voice quality, and amount of vocabulary.

Direct Selection.   Membrane keyboards allow devices to be customized for each child's needs with respect to the number, size, and spacing of pictures or other items. An overlay may have a single item or dozens of items. Some membranes require more activation pressure than others, and young children may sometimes find it difficult to apply enough pressure to activate the board.

Some devices offer optical pointing. A small pointing device is positioned on the user's head, and the communicator points to items on the device by moving the head from side to side or up and down.

Some systems are operated by nonscanning switches. For example, a portable tape recorder with a continuous loop tape can be activated by a switch. With this approach the message is recorded and played repeatedly. Because the tape is a continuous loop, it repeats the message as long as the user continues to activate the switch. Some speech output devices allow the user to speak a single message each time a switch is depressed. These devices use numerous switches, each one responsible for playing a particular message. This is a type of direct selection, because the user selects the switch used for each message.

Scanning. Several MC systems are operated by a single switch, using step, inverse, or automatic scanning techniques. As we discussed earlier, users begin with simple scanning techniques and progress to more complex techniques as their abilities allow.

Type of Voice. The two major categories of voices used in electronic systems are synthesized speech and digitized speech (Church & Glennen, 1992). Synthesized speech is produced electronically and is programmed by some form of text-to-speech procedure. Digitized speech is essentially recorded human speech and is recorded using a microphone, usually one built into the device.

Quality of Voice. Voice quality varies a great deal, ranging from robotic sounds to voices that are relatively smooth, flexible, and easy to understand. Digitized speech is influenced by the quality of the recording and playback. Early devices used robotic sounds that did not approximate the human voice. Now a variety of male and female voices are available, and the user can select the voice that he or she associates with.

Amount of Vocabulary. The number of words that can be used on a device varies according to the device's memory. Many devices provide a large range of memory options, while others provide very few. It is better to have too much memory than too little, because people tend to stretch memory as their own vocabulary and skills develop.

SUMMARY

This chapter provided a very brief introduction to AAC systems. First, we acquainted the reader with the components of language, including listening and speaking and semantics, syntax, morphology, phonology, and pragmatics. We then defined AAC systems and discussed aided and unaided communication. Unaided communication systems discussed included sign languages, educational sign systems, and gestural language codes. We then introduced the two common selection techniques used with aided communication systems: direct selection and scanning. We concluded the chapter by discussing the differences between nonelectronic and electric systems.

Because of the importance of communication, the value of AAC systems for those who need them cannot be overstated. Nor can the need for trained and dedicated professionals to work in and support the field of AAC. To that end, we conclude our discussion of AAC systems with information presented in Figure 5.7. The Rules of Commitment located here are guidelines for all to consider when working with people who require specialized speech services. But the rules are also of value to those who are seeking professionals to provide AAC services.

Compliance with the following rules will distinguish those who hold in the highest regard the interests of the individual who relies on AAC.

Rule 1: Be committed to the most effective communication system for the individual being served.
The AAC assessment may be the single most important event in the life of a person who relies on AAC. Where that person goes in life will be influenced by communication effectiveness.

Rule 2: Be committed to following your professional code of ethics.
All members of the team must not only agree, but be motivated to provide the system and services that result in the highest level of personal achievement. In addition, the team must be working toward helping the child develop communicative competence that results in a spontaneous, interactive exchange of information, feelings, and thoughts. Parents should be asking team members how their educational plan and recommendations are going to help their child communicate effectively.

Rule 3: Be committed to involving the consumer and family in the service delivery process.
Children and parents have rights to assistive technology under the Individuals with Disabilities Education Act (IDEA). Family involvement in the Individualized Education Plan (IEP) process should be motivated by what is best for the child. Parents may need to remind team members that the reason for all these procedures is because of their child. A Consumer-Centered Service Delivery model places the team members and processes in proper perspective. The consumer and family are the focal point and parents may even decide to request outside supports. Each person on the team has a contributing role in achieving the identified outcomes. Outcomes are influenced by the environment. Defining the roles and responsibilities of the individual team members in this model can have a positive influence on Rule 4.

Rule 4: Be committed to achieving the maximum outcomes for the individual.
Stakeholders are those with an interest in the outcomes of the process. Stakeholders in the AAC service delivery process include the service delivery team and others, including administrators, funding agencies, and so on. Parents need to realize that because of different roles and responsibilities, some stakeholders are vested in achieving different outcomes. Clinicians and therapists tend to be more concerned with outcomes related to clinical results and functional status, whereas administrators and funding agencies will be more concerned with best use of staff time and cost effectiveness for service delivery. Consumers and family members have concerns connected to quality of life and satisfaction issues. Acknowledging differing interests can help teams reach a better understanding of contrasting positions and swifter resolutions to any disagreements.

FIGURE 5.7   AAC Rules of Commitment

Reprinted with permission from AAC Institute (http://www.aacinstitute.org).

(continued)

FIGURE 5.7   Continued

Rule 5: Be committed to advocating for language.
If the team agrees on the central goal of AAC as being the highest possible personal achievement, then language becomes the focus of assessment and intervention. Unfortunately, many AAC strategies and programs focus on modifying behaviors, such as providing for classroom vocabulary, rather than real communication. The technology is used to promote responses to environmental cues and the child is limited to activating scripted messages. Little language learning is possible when no provisions are made to explore and create self-generated utterances. Parents need to ask questions about the ability of the language representation method and technology to facilitate language acquisition and growth and not just foster routine behaviors and compliance to tasks. A sure sign of a behavior focus to therapy is the prevalence of nouns, colors, and other words that would be considered extended vocabulary. The mastery of basic core vocabulary words should precede the introduction of vocabulary specific to daily activities and academic subjects.

Rule 6: Understand the merits of ALL language representation methods.
The three commonly used language representation methods are single-meaning pictures, spelling, and semantic compaction. The outcomes an individual who relies on AAC is able to achieve depends heavily on the language representation method(s) being used. Ease of use at first encounter may not be most effective in the long run.
    Single-meaning pictures involve the use of graphic or line drawn symbols to represent single word vocabulary or messages (phrases, sentences, and paragraphs). Reading skills are generally not required for using this method. However, recognition of symbols (especially abstract concepts) is facilitated by the presence of words associated with the symbols. These words, however, are useless and possibly distracting for anyone who cannot read. By the very nature of the system, a large vocabulary also requires a large symbol set. Consequently, having quick access to any symbol can become an issue for augmented communicators needing more than just a very limited number of words or messages.
    Spelling, sometimes referred to as traditional orthography, involves the use of the alphabet. Generally, spelling and reading skills are required. Although the symbol set is small, spelling letter by letter is a slow and inefficient AAC strategy. Acceleration techniques such as abbreviation systems and word prediction are commonly used with spelling to reduce the number of keystrokes. However, disadvantages in increasing the memory and reading demands for these acceleration techniques can outweigh any advantages. Research has shown that word prediction is no faster than spelling.
    Semantic compaction or "Minspeak" involves the use of a relatively small set of multi-meaning icons that do not require spelling and reading skills. The specific meaning of each icon is a function of the context in which it is used. Minspeak is perhaps the most commonly used AAC language representation method, because of its ability to handle both vocabulary and rules of grammar and support the notion of a core and extended vocabulary.

Rule 7: Support the language representation method(s) for core and extended vocabulary access that best serve the interest of the individual.
Vocabulary selection and organization has been one of the most widely researched topics in AAC. Access to a vocabulary based on the notion of core and extended categories is

FIGURE 5.7 Continued

more important than vocabulary frequency lists to support vocabulary selection. The vast majority (approximately 85 percent) of what we say in daily situations consists of a few hundred core words. Most of these core words are determiners, verbs, adjectives, prepositions, indefinite pronouns, and the like. They are not familiar nouns typically associated with given activities or situations. Rather, situation-specific nouns would be considered extended, or fringe, vocabulary.

Rule 8: Advocate for the AAC system that supports the chosen language representation method(s).
Most individuals reaching the goal of AAC are using multiple language representation methods with the AAC system. Observation of their achievement indicates the use of semantic compaction for core vocabulary access and spelling for extended vocabulary words. Single-meaning pictures appear to have limited use for when the individual only requires access to a small core vocabulary set or for access to extended vocabulary when the individual cannot spell.

Rule 9: Be committed to using language activity monitoring to support clinical intervention.
The most useful and beneficial information on which to base decisions regarding educational and clinical AAC services is analyzed performance data (language samples taken from natural settings). This is done by using automated language activity monitoring, a procedure that is relatively new to the field of AAC. Tools to facilitate the collection and analysis of language samples for individuals who use AAC devices are just now being developed. Use of language activity monitoring will provide team members with detailed information from spontaneous language samples to measure changes in communicative performance. An objective, realistic record of how the child is using technology in different settings will soon be possible. Easy comparisons between vocabulary use, amount of communication, and methods used can be made over time and across activities.

Rule 10: If unable to adhere to any of these guidelines, be truthful about it to the individual, family, and advocates.
If parents are in doubt regarding the commitment of a team member, they must feel empowered to question the continued participation of that member on the team. Not every professional will have the same level of commitment, motivation, and willingness to learn new technologies and strategies. Rule 10 provides an opportunity for any team member to express discomfort with what is being expected of him or her. It also provides for disclosure of being "between a rock and a hard place" relative to making recommendations that may be contrary to administrative directives, such as "Don't write that into the IEP, or the school will have to buy it."

DISCUSSION QUESTIONS

1. How might you go about identifying strengths and weaknesses across language components? Of what value would your findings be when considering whether AAC systems would be beneficial?
2. How might you approach parents of a young child and discuss the need for an AAC system and the benefits such systems offer? If the parent were to question whether AAC systems might actually stunt language growth, how might you respond?
3. Earlier you were asked to examine the characteristics of an effective communication partner. How might these characteristics be developed and implemented in your own routines? What special challenges might be encountered when communicating with a person who uses an AAC system?
4. Many people with severe speech problems also have motor difficulties. How might these motor problems interfere with the use of AAC systems, and how can those systems be adapted to foster effective communication?
5. Imagine that it is the year 2100. Describe the perfect AAC system and how it would be incorporated into the life of a person with severe motor, cognitive, and speech problems.

REFERENCES

Alvares, R., & Sternberg, L. (1994). Communication and language development. In L. Sternberg (Ed.), *Individuals with profound disabilities* (3rd ed.; p. 193–229). Austin, TX: Pro-Ed.

Angelo, J. (1997). *Assistive technology for rehabilitation therapists.* Philadelphia: E. A. Davis.

ASHA. (1986). *Augmentative communication: An introduction.* Rockville, MD: Author.

Brett, A., & Provenzo, Jr., E. F. (1995). *Adaptive technology for special human needs.* Albany: State University of New York Press.

Church, G., & Glennen, S. (1992). *The handbook of assistive technology.* San Diego: Singular.

Freedom Center. (1996). *Training program in assistive technology.* Unpublished manuscript.

Hegde, M. N. (1991). *Introduction to communication disorders.* Austin, TX: Pro-Ed.

Heward, W. L. (2000). *Exceptional children* (6th ed.). Upper Saddle River, NJ: Prentice-Hall.

Lloyd, L. L., Fuller, D. R., & Arvidson, H. H. (1997). *Augmentative and alternative communication: A handbook of principles and practices.* Boston: Allyn and Bacon.

Musselwhite, C. R., & St. Louis, K. W. (1988). *Communication programming for persons with severe handicaps.* Austin. TX: Pro-Ed.

Myers, P. (1987). The nature and structure of language. In D. Hammill (Ed.), *Assessing the abilities and instructional needs of students* (pp. 49–64). Austin, TX: Pro-Ed.

Shane, H. C., & Sauer, M. (1986). *Augmentative and alternative communication.* Austin, TX: Pro-Ed.

Sternberg, L. (1994). Definitions, characteristics, and conceptual framework. In L. Sternberg (Ed.), *Individuals with profound disabilities* (3rd ed.; pp. 3–20). Austin, TX: Pro-Ed.

Woodward, J. (1978). Historical bases of American Sign Language. In P. Siple (Ed.), *Understanding language through sign language research* (pp. 333–47). New York: Academic Press.

CHAPTER SIX

ASSISTIVE TECHNOLOGY DEVICES TO ENHANCE ACCESS TO INFORMATION

CHAPTER AT A GLANCE

INTRODUCTION TO INFORMATION ACCESS

COMPUTER ACCESS
- Focus on 6.1

TELECOMMUNICATION
- Focus on 6.2

LISTENING AND PRINT ACCESS
- Personal Perspective 6.1
- Focus on 6.3

OBJECTIVES

1. Describe the features of input and output devices and explain considerations for selecting the devices to meet individual needs.

2. Explain the telecommunication issues encountered by individuals with disabilities and the possible solutions for these issues.

3. Describe assistive technology adaptations to promote access to information presented orally and in print.

MAKING CONNECTIONS

Think about the technology tools you access on a regular basis, such as computers, fax machines, answering machines, Internet, newspapers, calculators, and so forth. These tools provide you with a variety of information on a daily basis, enrich your life, keep you informed, help you communicate, and provide information for decision-making purposes. Now, identify ways in which your life would be changed if access to these devices was not possible.

This chapter was written by Diane Pedrotty Bryant with Ae-Hwa Kim.

INTRODUCTION TO INFORMATION ACCESS

We live in a technological society where the ability to access information in multiple formats, such as print, computers, and the Internet, is critical to becoming and remaining an informed citizen. Beginning in the early years, children need to learn how to use the devices that provide access to our information-rich society. This knowledge of devices needs to be reinforced by educators and families as children mature. As adults, individuals with disabilities must continue to be able to access the devices that promote independence, keep them informed, and enable them to contribute to and participate in society. There are many ways individuals can access information, including computers, telecommunication, listening, and print material. Each of these has unique features and requires individuals to possess specific requisite abilities to be able to access them. The purpose of this chapter is to present information about how individuals can access information that is conveyed through computers, telecommunications, orally, and in print.

COMPUTER ACCESS

Conventional computer access involves using the hard drive, a standard keyboard, and a mouse to input information, and a monitor for information output. For individuals with different types of disabilities—such as physical, cognitive, sensory, and communicative—standard input and/or output devices may require modification to promote access and independence. There are many types of computer adaptations that can be identified depending on the individual needs of users, and their purposes for using computers.

Input Devices

Standard Keyboards.   The keyboard that comes with a computer is often called the standard keyboard. When considering adaptations for keyboards to best suit the needs of the user, sometimes starting with standard keyboard adaptations may make sense because they are a simple solution to a possible access issue. Access utilities software can help to facilitate the use of standard keyboards. Access utility software provides visual or auditory cues, and simplifies keyboard operation for individuals who need to increase or decrease keystrokes, who cannot depress more than one key simultaneously, or who may unintentionally strike keys. For example, Easy Access by Macintosh offers modification features that enable individuals to adjust their keyboard to meet their needs. AccessDOS for MS-DOS and Access Pack for Windows offer keyboard modifications for IBM and IBM-compatible systems (Alliance for Technology Access, 1996).

Changing the keyboard layout is another adaptation that can be used to facilitate access. The standard keyboard consists of a format, called QWERTY, that was designed many years ago when typewriters were common. The layout of the manual typewriter, and subsequent keyboard, was intended to reduce the jamming of keys that were used frequently. Another keyboard layout, Dvorak, has gained acceptance because the most frequently used keys are on the home row. This layout supposedly limits fatigue for users. Also, there are Dvorak layouts for people who type with only one hand. Finally, alphabetically arranged keys is another type of keyboard layout, which makes sense for individuals who use communication boards with a similar layout. Questions to consider for assessing the needs of the user and determining a good match with the features of standard keyboards are listed in Table 6.1 (Cook & Hussey, 1995; Alliance for Technology Access, 1996).

Keyboard Additions.   For individuals who can use standard keyboards but need adaptations, keyguards and moisture guards are available to augment the keyboard. For example, users who have difficulty with fine motor skills and thus have difficulty selecting keys accurately may benefit from the use of a keyguard. Keyguards provide more separation between keys for easier input and limit the accidental pressing of keys. Moisture guards are another type of keyboard addition, which can protect the keyboard from spillage and other types of moisture. Finally, using labels to color-code specific keys or to provide a tactile cue can help individuals who might benefit from visual or tactile input (Alliance for Technology Access,

TABLE 6.1   Questions for Decision Makers to Consider for Access to Information Adaptations

STANDARD KEYBOARDS AND KEYBOARD ADDITIONS

- What size keyboard would be most beneficial to meet the needs of the user?
- What size keys would be most beneficial to meet the needs of the user?
- How much pressure will be required to depress the keys?
- How much space between keys would be most beneficial to meet the needs of the user?
- What adaptations are needed to use two keys simultaneously (e.g., shift and key for capital)?
- Will the user need visual or tactile cues?
- Is moisture in the keyboard area a potential problem?
- Can the user reach and target the keys?
- Can keys be released quickly enough to avoid "key repeat" (repetition of depressed key character: kkkkkkkkkkkk)?

VOICE RECOGNITION SYSTEMS

- Is the individual capable of articulating speech with consistent vocalization?
- Is there an adequate range of vocabulary in the system?
- Will the voice recognition system be affected by background noise?

1996). Keyguards can be purchased from a variety of vendors including Don Johnston, Inc., IntelliTools, and TASH International, Inc. Global Computer Supplies carries moisture guards. Questions to consider for determining possible keyboard additions are listed in Table 6.1 (Alliance for Technology Access, 1996; Cook & Hussey, 1995).

Joysticks, Trackballs, Touch Screens, and Interface Devices.   There are a variety of alternative keyboard input devices including joysticks, trackballs, touch screens, and interface devices. Joysticks are a popular input device for game machines, such as Nintendo, and are found on wheelchairs to promote mobility; thus, they are readily available. Some joysticks can be plugged into the mouse port and others require special software for the computer to accept them. Individuals who might benefit from using joysticks should be evaluated to determine if they possess the cognitive ability to control multi-directional movement and the strength that is needed to operate some joysticks.

Trackballs, which replace the mouse and work with keyboards, are alternatives to the conventional mouse and consist of a stationary platform with a movable ball. Some trackballs include the ability to drag and click-lock to minimize hand movements and a chording ability to access keyboard features easily.

A touch screen (see Figure 6.1) is a device that is placed on the computer monitor and permits direct selection by merely touching the screen. The touch screen is appropriate for individuals who require a simple input device. Depending on the touch screen, it can be used with switch software or on-screen keyboards (Alliance for Technology Access, 1996).

Interface devices provide the use of switches, alternate keyboards, and other input devices, such as joysticks and speech synthesizers, to access the keyboard and keyboard functions (Alliance for Technology Access, 1996). Interface devices can make communication boards accessible by a switch or alternate keyboard, connect a switch to a computer with scanning options, and permit multiple input devices to be connected, such as several switches, that can activate keyboard functions. (See Chapter 9 for additional information about switches and scanning.)

Pointing Devices.   Pointing devices, which can be used for direct selection access, are an option for individuals who need an alternative to the mouse and keyboard to input information into the computer because of limited or lack of functional movement of their arms and hands (see Figure 6.2). Pointing devices also can be used to access switches, which can activate a variety of devices including computers, toys, and environmental control units. Pointing devices, including mouthsticks, handpointers, and headpointers, have different access options including wires, remote control, and switch control. Both mouthsticks and headpointers require head and neck movements; oral-motor control is an additional requirement to use a mouthstick effectively (Cook & Hussey, 1995). The slant and position of the keyboard must be considered so the user can reach the keyboard comfortably. Also, games initially with large target surfaces that are easier to access can be used to teach the individual how to use the pointing device (Angelo, 1997).

FIGURE 6.1   Touch Screen
Photo courtesy of Psycho-Educational Services.

Alternate Keyboards.   For users who cannot access a standard keyboard even with access utilities software and keyboard additions, an alternate keyboard might be an appropriate option. Alternate keyboards consist of keys or switches that replace or add to the traditional keyboard. Keyboards are reduced or enlarged to address access issues by individuals with motor problems, physical disabilities, and so forth (Church & Glennen, 1992). Alternate keyboards include mini-keyboards, on-screen keyboards, and programmable keyboards. Mini-keyboards are characterized by a small surface that requires less range of motion and touch to access the keys. Users may find this type of keyboard less tiring and may be able to benefit from a smaller access area. Individuals who use headpointers, for example, might be able to benefit from these features. Tash International, Inc. makes a WinMini keyboard that plugs directly into an IBM computer. This alternate keyboard includes functions

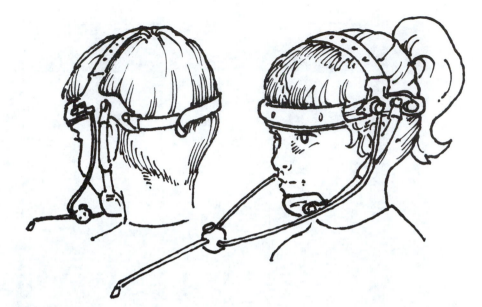

FIGURE 6.2   Pointing Devices
Reprinted with permission, Psycho-Educational Services.

for both the mouse and keyboard including adjustments for response rate, key repeat rate, mouse tracking speed, and auditory feedback. The keyboard layout comes in two versions: frequency-of-use and QWERTY.

On-screen keyboards provide access for individuals who need to bypass the physical demands of conventional computer input, such as the standard keyboard. Input device options, such as a trackball, touchscreen, or mouse, can be used depending on the individual's needs to select words or letters directly on the screen. Some alternate keyboards have scanning options (Alliance for Technology Access, 1996). The on-screen keyboards offer a variety of options depending on the cognitive level of the user and the skills being taught. For instance, the Discover: Screen (see Figure 6.3) by Don Johnston, Inc. features pictures, word banks, and a full keyboard so students can enter text and participate in classroom writing projects. Discover:Screen can be used with any word processing, decoding, or spelling program that requires text entry. For example, pictures are displayed on the screen for symbolic writing for students who cannot read; word banks are available for completing phrases and constructing sentences. Discover:Screen also offers speech feedback so students can monitor their selections.

Programmable keyboards are enlarged keyboards with wide-spaced keys that connect to the computer and allow easier access for individuals with limited motor control. Programmable keyboards can be used across environments, such as different classrooms, and some can be mounted to laptop computers as well. The Discover:Board (Don Johnston, Inc.) and Intellikeys (Intellitools®) are two programmable keyboards. The Discover:Board (see Figure 6.4) is a large, all-in-one key-

FIGURE 6.3   Discover: Screen
Copyright © Don Johnston Incoporated, Volo, IL. Used by permission.

board that enables students to use reading and writing software programs available for other students. IntelliKeys® comes with six standard overlays that are ready to use with any word processing program or software that has keyboard input. Standard overlays consist of large, well-spaced keys in bright colors so students can locate letters and numbers easily. Settings can be customized with a special set-up overlay to control the response or repeat rate for students who press unwanted keys or keep their finger on a key too long. Also, IntelliKeys® is a flexible switch interface that works with a wide variety of switch software. Intellitools® offers an Access Pac that includes products for teachers to create and individualize curriculum including Intellikeys®, Overlay Maker®, IntelliPics®, and an auditory feedback component, IntelliTalk II®. See Chapter 9 for additional information about switches, scanning methods, and on-screen keyboards.

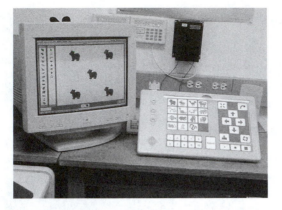

FIGURE 6.4   Discover:Board
Copyright © Don Johnston Incorporated, Volo, IL. Used by permission.

Voice Recognition.   For individuals who have physical disabilities and have difficulty accessing the keyboard, voice or speech recognition systems are a good alternate input device. Also, voice recognition may be helpful for some individuals with learning disabilities whose oral language exceeds their written language abilities (King & Rental, 1981). Voice recognition can be used to navigate wheelchairs and operate environmental control units.

Voice recognition systems allow the user to operate the computer by speaking to it. There are two basic systems. The *speaker-dependent system* means that the individual trains the system to recognize his or her voice. The more the voice recognition system is used, the better able it is to understand what the user is saying. The main problem with this system is that sometimes the system does not recognize the speaker's voice because the speaker may have different intonation or pitch, or background noise may interfere with reception. The *speaker-independent system* recognizes a variety of speech patterns from different people without training. Unfortunately, sometimes the vocabulary set that is a part of the software is relatively limited (Cook & Hussey, 1995). Voice recognition systems operate with personal computers and include speech recognition hardware (internal board), software, headphones, and a microphone. The individual dictates into the microphone and the speech is converted into text onto the computer screen.

There are two basic types of systems: discrete and continuous speech. Discrete voice recognition systems (e.g., Dragon Dictate, 1994) require a pause of approximately $\frac{1}{10}$ second between words. The spoken word appears on the screen. If the word is incorrect, the user can choose the correct word from a menu of similar-sounding words that appear on the screen (this feature is not present in all systems). Keyboard editing and control commands (e.g., "delete word") can be done with the voice alone. Continuous voice recognition systems (e.g., Dragon Naturally Speaking®, 2000; Dragon Systems, Inc.) allow the user to dictate without pausing between words. For example, Dragon NaturallySpeaking® provides support for letter writing, e-mail work, and Internet browsing. Errors can be corrected by voice or keyboard commands. Questions to consider for assessing the needs of the user and determining a good match with the features of voice recognition systems are listed in Table 6.1 (Cook & Hussey, 1995).

Output Devices

Screen Magnification. Screen magnification refers to enlarged character display on the monitor and includes hardware and software options (Church & Glennen, 1992). For individuals with low vision, screen magnification sometimes can be a simple adaptation to promote access to print displayed on the monitor. Regarding hardware options, monitors come in different sizes. Using a large screen monitor (17 inches, for example) is one way to create a larger visual display for easier print access.

Probably the simplest adaptation is to enlarge the print displayed on the screen through the word processing software program: type size (18 point). Large point size may be able to provide sufficient magnification for some individuals depending on their acuity. Specially designed software also can be purchased that offers magnification solutions for individuals with low vision. For instance, ZoomText Xtra 7.03 (Ai Squared) software (Windows platforms) consists of two product levels. Level 1 is an advanced screen magnifier, and Level 2 includes both a fully integrated magnifier and screen reader. Level 1 includes up to 16X magnification, color filtering for contrast, cursor enhancement to locate the cursor quickly, and quick zooming in and out. Level 2 includes screen reading (see next section for information about screen reading) that speaks all on-screen text (speech synthesizer included), including menus, dialog boxes, and controls. There are also speech settings for adjusting voice, rate, and pitch. Level 2 includes DocReader™, which is a full-screen environment for reading text from any Windows application. DocReader™ reads documents, including web pages and e-mail.

MAGic 6.2 (Henter-Joyce, Inc.) screen magnification software contains color support (up to 32-bit) and an extensive array of list boxes for Microsoft® Office (Windows 95/98, Windows NT®, Windows 2000). These list boxes help the individual to call up lists of frames, links, document reformatting, hyper-links, and more. MAGic 6.2 screen magnification software is designed to be used with the JAWS® (Job Access with Speech; Henter-Joyce) screen reading software for Windows® (JAW) screen reader software (see below).

Speech Synthesis/Screen Reading. Screen reading software makes possible electronic spoken language output that involves a synthetic or computerized voice output system (i.e., speech synthesizer). This voice output system can consist of an internal board, which includes a chip or circuit board inserted into the computer or external hardware device, which is a portable external device that connects to the computer and comes with a speaker. Most computers today come with speakers to amplify sound. Thus, speech synthesis is helpful for individuals who are blind or who have low vision, who have a mild hearing loss, or who have difficulties with written language, both reading and writing, and can benefit from auditory feedback.

Many software programs now include both visual and auditory feedback. For example, word prediction programs (see Chapter 7, writing section) may include speech output, which reads back a letter, word, line, sentence, paragraph, or "screen" at a time. For some students, hearing what they wrote may help them catch errors in grammar, spelling, and punctuation that might otherwise go undetected. Also, the user can be alerted to problems regarding the coherence and semantic integrity of the document (Bryant & Bryant, in press).

There are three techniques for producing speech on computers. First, text-to-speech synthesis involves converting letters and letter combinations to speech sounds. The speech sounds rather robotic. Second, digitized speech involves a person recording words into the system, thus producing human-sounding speech (Church & Glennen, 1992). Finally, Linear Predictive Coding (LPC) is also digitized speech but requires a lot more memory than the text-to-speech technique (Lewis, 1993). When selecting speech synthesis as a solution to promote access, decision-makers and users should consider audio output and intelligibility. Audio output is affected by the quality of speakers and amplifiers. Although technology continues to improve so that large-sized equipment does not always mean better-sounding quality, it is still true that speakers and amplifiers have a certain size and weight that may affect portability and cost. Intelligibility is another consideration. Speech synthesis features a variety of voices, both male and female, and techniques for producing speech (e.g., digitized speech). Individuals must consider not only the quality of audio output but also the intelligibility of speech. If an individual relies on speech synthesis for expressive language (e.g., communication boards) or for a work environment, then the quality of speech may be particularly important. In most cases the speed, pitch, and tone of voice can be set to accommodate individual preferences. The voice quality of speech synthesizers varies considerably from more "human" to more "mechanical" sounding. In some instances, more mechanical-sounding voices may actually be more intelligible to experienced users; plus they allow for faster rates of production.

As a stand-alone speech synthesizer, DECtalk® (Force Computers), which is one example, is text-to-speech technology that transforms text into natural-sounding, intelligible speech. It pronounces single characters, words, phrases, and proper names. DECtalk speech is featured in personalized voices. Also, DECtalk Express (Blazie Engineering) is a portable, external synthesizer that plugs into a computer's serial port. DECtalk Express is used with screen reader software and can be used with PC, laptop, notebook, palmtop, and Macintosh computers.

There are a variety of screen reading programs on the market. For instance, JAWS (Job Access with Speech; Henter-Joyce) is a speech synthesis program for Windows 95/98/ME or Windows NT/2000 operating system. JAWS consists of an integrated voice synthesizer and the computer's sound card to output the content using speakers or refreshable Braille displays. JAWS works with e-mail, word processing programs, spreadsheets, and web browsers. Screen Reader (Text HELP!®) is another screen reading program with a utility tool bar that allows the individual's PC to read text in any Windows-based application. Screen Reader is capable of reading e-mail, web pages, or documents aloud. OutSPOKEN (ALVA Access Group, Inc.) is a screen reader that allows individuals with visual impairments to easily control applications in the Windows and Macintosh environment. Hence, outSPOKEN provides individuals with visual impairments access to Windows and Macintosh environments. There are two configurations: outSPOKEN Solo, which is a speech-only package, and outSPOKEN Ensemble, which is designed for users with a Braille display and an optional speech synthesizer. Finally, eReader (Center for Applied Special Technology; CAST) is screen reading software for both the Macintosh and Window platforms that provides voice output for content from any electronic source (e.g., web page, word processing). eReader consists of spoken output, visual highlighting, and document navigation. eReader promotes access to electronic text and supports literacy development. Whether it is work- or school-related, tasks that require access to text on screen can be readily accessible for individuals with disabilities to enable people of all ages to interact with current electronic technology.

Printers.   Printers are a conventional device to output text and other forms of print. A computer's printer type size can be altered to enlarge it for more accessible reading. For individuals who read Braille, computer-generated text is transformed into embossed Braille output through the use of a translation program (Alliance for Technology Access, 1996). For example, VersaPoint Duo (Blazie Engineering) is an embosser with speech. It includes two-sided printing, reduced noise levels, and built-in speech that permits the setting of configurations (see Figure 6.5). Next, we will focus on access issues and solutions related to telecommunication.

FIGURE 6.5   VersaPoint Duo
Photo courtesy of Blazie Engineering.

Select either input or output devices and conduct an online search to locate examples of devices that promote access at the input or output level. Prepare a list of your devices, identify the features, and provide specific examples of individuals with disabilities who might benefit most from your device selections.

TELECOMMUNICATION

Telephones

Access to telephone communication is crucial not only to enhance independence and access information but also as a safety device. For individuals with hearing and speech impairments, the Americans with Disabilities Act of 1990 mandated that all states provide public access services or relay services for individuals who are deaf or hard of hearing, or who have speech disabilities. For individuals who are deaf, the text telephone (TTY) is the most common mode of telecommunication services. The TTY, which was formerly called the telecommunication device (TDD), is a device that enables people to send and receive phone calls. A telecommunication relay service (TRS) is required by law in all states and is a free service. The TRS consists of the operator at the relay center reading the typed message from the sender to the person who is receiving the phone call, so the message goes from written to voice form via the operator. The person receiving the message can respond conventionally, then the operator types the message and sends it to the sender whose TTY translates the message (Smith, 2000). Although the telecommunication system provides phone access for people who are deaf, it certainly is not private. Recent developments in technology, for example the voice carry over (VCO), enable individuals to use their voice to communicate their message and still have access to the use of the TTY to receive the printed message.

Internet Access

Access to the Internet and the World Wide Web (WWW) is imperative in today's society. Services such as e-mail, e-commerce, electronic-based research, and telecommunication are important tools in daily living activities at home, school, and work across all age groups. As more schools and libraries become wired and businesses rely on the Internet, all individuals will need access to this great resource if they are to compete and interact successfully in today's market. Internet access is becoming increasingly an issue as more people with a variety of needs seek to use this great resource. Particularly, accessibility issues focus on the ability to see the graphics, to hear audio features, to navigate complex and unorganized sites, and to use adaptive technology.

As stipulated in the 1998 Rehabilitation Act Amendments, Federal agencies have to make their electronic and information technology accessible to people with disabilities. Section 508 was enacted to eliminate barriers in information technology, to make available new opportunities for people with disabilities, and to encourage development of technologies that will help achieve these goals. The law applies to all federal agencies when they develop, procure, maintain, or use electronic and information technology (Section 508, 29 U.S.C. 794d). See Appendix B for information about Section 508.

Universal design features focus on the importance of ensuring accessibility. Universal design means that the instructional activities are accessible and the learning goals are achievable by all people regardless of their ability to read, write, hear, see, speak, comprehend, move, and remember. For example, if an activity is designed it should be accessible for individuals with sensory impairments, cognitive impairments, and communication difficulties. WWW page design can include universal design features with some thoughtful planning prior to development. In the area of basic page design, consistent layout, contrasting backgrounds, use of HTML, and large buttons are all examples of ways to make the page accessible to a variety of individual needs. Graphical features also should be considered. Alternative text information should be available for all graphics to indicate that a graphic is present. Providing captions for video and scripting audio can address multimedia features that may be inaccessible for individuals with sensory disabilities. Also, the use of tables and figures, which may be difficult for screen reading software to read accurately, should be used on a limited basis (University of Washington, 1997). Certainly, access to online courses and electronic communication is an area that warrants consideration by instructors when they design their courses and course assignments. Again, web-accessibility issues must be addressed to ensure that all students have equal access to course content. All students must be able to utilize this instructional tool effectively.

"Bobby" (CAST) is a web-based tool that examines pages for accessibility for people with disabilities. Questions about the free service can be directed to bobby@cast.org. Once a site is examined and depending on the findings, the designer can receive an official seal of approval for prominent display on the web page. Also, DO-IT (Disabilities, Opportunities, Internetnetworking, and Technology) at the University of Washington provides a list of Internet resources for accessible web design (http://weber.u.washington.edu/~doit/). Finally, the National Center for Accessible Media (NCAM) provides examples of accessible web pages (http://www.boston.com/wgbh/pages/ncam/currentprojects/webaccess.html). The final section of this chapter focuses on listening and print access issues and devices.

FOCUS ON 6.2

This focus provides several choices for practicing what was discussed in the telecommunications section. The first choice includes reviewing the information found on the web design accessible tools (e.g., "Bobby") pages, locating a web page with information that can be used for educational purposes in a classroom, and deciding if that web page is accessible for individuals who have sensory or motor disabilities. The second choice is to interview an individual who is deaf and learn about the telecommunications issues and possible solutions for that individual. The third choice is to interview an adult with a sensory or motor impairment and learn about AT adaptations that are used in a work setting. The final choice is to interview an instructional technologist about universal access issues in designing web-based platforms. Share your findings in class.

LISTENING AND PRINT ACCESS

In this section, we provide a personal perspective by Tony McGregor, who talks about life growing up as a person who is deaf, the challenges he has encountered, and his suggestions for educators (see Personal Perspective 6.1).

Listening Aids

Hearing Aids.   As we all know, hearing aids are small battery-operated devices that amplify sound. Hearing aids can help individuals with hearing loss access oral communication; in some cases, hearing acuity can become within the normal range. Hearing aids are designed to be worn behind the ear, in the ear, and in the canal (Smith, 2000). Hearing aids amplify all sound within an environment; therefore, they work best in quieter environments where background noise is minimal. Hearing aids do not necessarily improve the clarity of sounds, and sometimes hearing aids produce noise, such as acoustic feedback.

Personal Frequency-Modulated Transmission Device.   A frequency-modulated (FM) transmission device or auditory trainer enables students with hearing impairments to listen to their teacher via a student receiver or hearing aid. FM transmission devices consist of two basic components, a wireless transmitter with a microphone and a receiver with a headset or earphone. The speaker (teacher, for example) "wears" the transmitter unit (about 2×3 inches), which is easily clipped to a belt or shirt pocket, and the user wears the receiver unit (also about 2×3 inches). The microphone is only about 1½ inches long and is easily clipped to clothing (e.g., tie, lapel). The transmission device allows teachers to move about the classroom and maintain communication with students who have hearing impairments without also having to have full face view for lip-reading (Smith, 2000).

Tape Recorders.   Probably taking notes is the most common example of a tape recorder being used an AT listening aid. Tape recording a class lecture or a discussion in a work session enables the user to focus on the speaker and content and not the arduous task of listening, identifying the salient features, and writing them down all in a relatively short period of time. For individuals who have difficulty taking notes, writing, and identifying critical information quickly, the tape recorder

PERSONAL PERSPECTIVE 6.1

A lifelong Texan, Tony L. McGregor was born in Garland on November 18, 1958. He became deaf at approximately 18 months of age from hereditary causes. Tony was heavily encouraged to pursue art during his boyhood and studied drawing and painting in both private and "mainstreamed" public schools. He attended studio art classes at Gallaudet University in Washington, D.C., and later transferred to the University of Texas at Austin, where he received a Bachelor of Fine Arts with honors. Tony also obtained a certificate in Engineering Design Graphics at Austin Community College in Austin, Texas, and then later worked, sequentially, as a technical illustrator, computer graphics designer, and CAD/CAM graphics coordinator in three different corporations located in both Austin and San Antonio, Texas. For the last four years, Tony has worked as a Resident Artist-in-Education at the Austin Museum of Art working with children of all ages who are deaf or hard of hearing and who go to various schools in the Austin metropolitan area.

In addition, Tony earned a Texas state teacher certification in art education and a Masters in Education in Multicultural Special Education at the University of Texas at Austin. Currently, he is a doctoral candidate majoring in Multicultural Special Education with an emphasis in art education at the University of Texas, Austin. His dissertation topic focuses on the life of a deaf Navajo rug weaver living in the Four Corners area.

What types of assistive technology devices and services do you think are important for individuals who are D/deaf to be able to access information in their daily lives?
Teletype Devices for the Deaf (TTY or TDD), signaling systems (the telephone ring signaler, the door knock or door bell signaler, a baby cry signaler, and so on), the smoke alarm device with strobe light, a TV with closed-captions, and many other AT devices are important for individuals who are deaf so they can access information and warnings. In most medical, educational, legal, and general settings, American Sign Language/Signed English Interpreting services and statewide relay service (telephone) are primary services where individuals who are deaf have access to information.

How can service providers (educators, speech-language therapists, and the like) assist school-age students who are deaf in accessing information in an educational setting?
Service providers (educators, speech-language therapists, and so on) can assist students who are deaf in accessing information by setting up a K–12 curriculum that will promote greater understanding of what's out in the real world for deaf people and include children's books that will explain how deaf people perform different routines in their daily lives. Educators also can invite deaf people as guest speakers to talk about their use of AT devices and services. It is best to start educating children about AT devices and services at the earliest age possible because most children who are deaf (90% or more) have hearing parents and are educated in public school settings. Many families, including hearing parents, are not aware of what is available for deaf people, and the service providers can provide information in this area.

How can service providers work more effectively with families in promoting the use of assistive technology to facilitate independence?
Service providers can help promote the use of AT to facilitate independence through (1) family involvement in school, (2) shared resources of AT devices and services in the local

(continued)

community, and (3) home visits to explain to families where they can purchase AT devices, how to operate the devices, and where to obtain AT services.

What are your experiences with assistive technology? How have your experiences changed as you have gotten older?

I recall when I first obtained a large antique text telephone (TTY) machine at the age of 12. How my family learned about TTY was that my first Deaf teacher, who graduated from Gallaudet University in Washington, DC, told us about it. There were no deaf teachers in my school before that and they never told us anything about AT technology. That was the 1970s. Deaf members in my family were surprised about these AT devices.

I can see many changes in the appearances of TTYs as well as the costs over the years. TTYs have became smaller and cheaper. There is a larger availability of AT devices and more choices are provided. AT services are widely available in large cities. Laws such as the Closed Captioned TV Act of 1993 (requiring TVs to be closed-captioned) and the Telecommunications Act of 1996 (requiring computers to be accessible to people with disabilities and Instant Messaging, or IM, to be provided) have benefited the American Deaf community.

The newest AT service is Video Relay Interpreting (VRI). In this service, deaf people use video capabilities through the computer to communicate with Relay agents who use ASL. Deaf people will need computers if they want to use this type of service. Most deaf people use regular relay service, where TTYs relay information to an operator, who will relay the message to the person who can hear.

What are some challenges in your life as someone who is deaf in accessing information in the community, school, recreational and social activities, work, and so forth?

Deafness made me a strong and aggressive person. I wanted the same things or opportunities that hearing children had. When I faced struggles, I found ways to overcome them. The only obstacle I remember in high school was that the school district and day school for the deaf would not let me go to a magnet high school that emphasized the arts. Interpreting costs for classes at a magnet high school was one of the problems for the administration. That was the biggest reason why I decided not to finish high school and to move on to Gallaudet University.

There were other obstacles, but I never did give up. Costs of ASL/Signed English interpreting in some situations continue to be a challenge in my life as a Deaf person or employee. At the university, I am grateful that I usually do not have problems of obtaining an interpreter for my classes and teaching assistant work. Most of the interpreters at the university are among the best.

For a long time, there were no pay TDDs on campus and it was rather difficult to make phone calls from campus. Not until a few years ago when a group of Deaf students on campus got together with the leadership of Walter Kelley, a doctoral student at the university, did we finally have the pay TDDs placed in different buildings on campus after a battle with the university administration.

Here is your chance to tell our readers anything else that you think is important for them to know about AT.

I think it is extremely important that all children with disabilities, including those who are deaf, be computer literate because most AT technology devices require knowledge of computer technology. Educators should help prepare them for the future.

Reproduced with permission from Psycho-Educational Services.

can be a simple adaptation of the notetaking process. The advantage to tape record-ing material is that the individual can review the content at a later date by listening to tapes as many times as necessary to comprehend the material. Of course, the individual still needs to possess the ability to listen and identify the critical infor-mation. Also, it is time-consuming to listen to lectures and discussions several times; thus, the user must take into consideration the time factor when choosing to use a tape recorder as an assistive device.

Notetakers. Depending on the needs of the individual, there are a variety of note-taking devices from which people can choose to help them take notes efficiently and effectively. For example, abbreviation expansion is a tool that can be used with a word processing program. Users can create their own abbreviations for frequently used words, phrases, or standard pieces of text, thus saving keystrokes. For exam-ple, a student in a science class who has to frequently type out "photosynthesis" in taking notes might create the abbreviation "ph." The user types in the abbreviation (e.g., "ph"), presses the spacebar on the keyboard (or depending on the particular program, points and clicks), and the abbreviation is expanded (e.g., "photosynthe-sis"). Abbreviations are recorded easily by executing a few simple commands and may be saved from one writing session to another. Abbreviation expansion is an important part of many word processing programs and is available as "memory resident add-on" programs, operating simultaneously with the word processing program (Bryant & Bryant, in press).

The Braille 'n Speak (Blazie Engineering; see Figure 6.6) is another notetaking tool that can be used by individuals with visual impairments. It operates using refre-shable Braille cells, which are an alternative format to the embossed paper used with conventional Braille. The individual inputs information in Braille and the information is stored electronically, which can be transferred to a computer for edit-ing purposes or read back by screen reading software. Voice output is also included in Braille note takers.

Print Aids

Magnification Aids. Magnification aids focus on size, spacing, and contrast. Magnification aids range from simple to more complex and include optical aids, nonoptical aids, and electronic aids (Cook & Hussey, 1995). Because more than 90 percent of people with visual impairments have some degree of usable vision, optical aids can be used to promote access (Cook & Hussey, 1995). For individuals who can benefit from enlarged print, such as those who have low vision or who have reading disabilities, optical aids may be an appropriate technology solution. Optical aids include magnifying glasses and magnifiers on stands. These devices are simple tools and readily available. Magnifiers on stands are particularly useful if the individual is doing a task that requires the use of both hands.

Nonoptical aids consist of enlarged-print, high-intensity lamps, and contrast objects (Cook & Hussey, 1995). For instance, some forms of print come already

FIGURE 6.6   Braille 'n Speak
Photo courtesy of Blazie Engineering.

enlarged such as books and newspapers for individuals with low vision. High-intensity lamps can provide contrast on reading materials and objects, such as brightly colored objects in the environment, making them stand out against backgrounds and become more visually distinguishable.

A closed circuit television (CCTV) device (see Figure 6.7) is one of the most common examples of an electronic aid. A CCTV includes a camera, video display, and a unit that manages how the material is presented (zoom feature, scanning table). Individuals place their reading material on the scanning table, the camera captures the image, and the lens projects the image, which is shown on the video display. The scanning table can be easily moved forward and backward, and from side to side to allow maximum visibility of the material. The use of color, contrast, and type size permit users with varying acuity abilities to access and read the material.

FIGURE 6.7   Closed Circuit Television
Photo courtesy of Psycho-Educational Services.

Tactile Aids.   Access to print through the use of touch by individuals with visual impairments can be accomplished through the use of technology that produces print in a tactile format. Braille and the Optacon (Optical Tactile CONverter) II are two examples of devices that feature a tactile output mode of printed material. The Optacon consists of a camera, which the user runs along the printed material. "The Optacon uses a phototransistor array to obtain an image of the printed letter and translates this image into an equivalent (facsimile) in tactile form" (Cook & Hussey, 1995, p. 643). Thus, the user runs the camera along the print that is translated into the tactile facsimile. The user feels the tactile output and translates the messages into letters and words to "read" the print.

Braille is the most widely used tactile aid by individuals with severe visual impairments (Cook & Hussey, 1995). Braille consists of characters that have six or eight dots and can be read letter by letter, by word signs, and by contractions. Braille is produced by embossing the characters on heavy-duty paper. A brailler can be used to produce written language; naturally, the receiver of the document must be able to read Braille. Braille also can be produced via the computer and a Braille printer (see printers in this chapter) using specialized software that translates text into the embossed Braille cells.

Scanner/OCR/Speech Synthesis.   Often, individuals wish to access print from a variety of sources such as textbooks, newspapers, magazines, and so forth. Simply picking up the material and reading it may not be an option for individuals with visual impairments and in some cases for individuals with cognitive disabilities because they may not possess the visual acuity or the reading skills to access the text, respectively. A system for accessing print includes the use of a scanner, Optical Character Recognition (OCR) software/hardware, and speech synthesis. OCR systems might be thought of as "reading machines" because they provide a way of inputting print (e.g., a page in a book, a letter) into a computer, and speech synthesis/screen reading software "reads" the print (output). A scanner, using a camera, captures the print. The OCR system, which may be a piece of hardware plugged into a PC computer or software, translates the print into a format that can be "read and spoken" by the computer or translated into Braille. This system is helpful for school and work activities. For example, a middle, high school, or postsecondary student might be required to read a chapter for homework. Because of a severe reading disability, this setting demand task is challenging for the student. However, by scanning the text into the computer, the student can hear the chapter material read aloud and thus be able to access the print. In a similar way, an employee can use this technology at work to access print related to his or her work environment.

Caution must be exercised with this technology, however. First, OCR systems do not always read text with 100 percent accuracy or even read 100 percent of the text at all (tables, for example, may be lost in translation). Second, although the user can access print and hear the material read, understanding the material and knowing the vocabulary that is used within the context may require additional instruction or explanation from the teacher or employer. Access to print does not guarantee comprehension of the text.

There are two primary ways text can be scanned. First, text can be scanned using a full-page flatbed scanner where a page of text is placed face down on the device (much like a copy machine). Or text can be scanned using a hand-held scanner, where the individual moves the scanner's camera across or down a page of text. Full-page scanners provide access to entire pages, whereas the hand-held scanner may or may not accommodate a full page. If it does not, then the user must manually manipulate the scanning process. The flatbed scanner is usually heavier and more expensive than the hand-held scanner, which is portable and can plug into a laptop computer. Thus, the type of scanner should be selected depending on the needs of the user (Cook & Hussey, 1995).

There are two types of OCR systems: "stand alone" or PC-based. In the stand-alone system, all the components are built into one device, including the scanner, OCR software/hardware, and the speech synthesizer. Some stand-alone systems are portable, which can be used in the library or at work, and others are desktop units. The PC-based components consist of a full-page (desktop) or hand-held scanner, an OCR board and/or software, and a speech synthesizer. Some companies have added other features, such as highlighting words as they are spoken back by the system, and being able to alter the rate at which the text is read. This feature could help students develop reading fluency, which is a skill that contributes to comprehension. Systems aimed at developing access to print can facilitate word recognition and fluency skills but comprehension skills also must be developed to aid student understanding of class content (Bryant & Bryant, in press).

Several OCR systems are available and used in many settings. First, the Kurzweil 3000 (Lernout & Hauspie™), using a stand-alone scanner, can be used to scan and display print as it appears in the document including the color graphics and pictures. The Kurzweil then reads the document out loud while highlighting the text. With adjustable reading rates and highlighting, fluency and word recognition are addressed. The student can also use the highlighting feature to identify the main ideas or supporting details. Notes and highlighted text can be saved into a separate document for later study (see Figure 6.8).

Second, WYNN (Learning Systems Group; Arkenstone Products) was designed with assistance from students with LD in reading and from special educators. Used with a PC platform, text is represented in auditory and visual formats and includes highlighting, bookmarks, ruler guides, and annotations. WYNN includes color-coded tool bars that are labeled with pictures and words. Users can highlight text by chunks, thus focusing on groups of words rather than on word-by-word reading. Some of the features include scanning a page, customizing the document page (spacing, margins, type size), accessing a dictionary, adding voice, and decoding words.

Finally, the OPENBook software (Arkenstone Products) allows individuals with visual impairments to read and edit scanned images from books, magazines, newspapers, and other documents. Once text is scanned, OPENBook software transforms print into electronic text, which is read aloud by the speech synthesizer. OPENBook uses IBM's ViaVoice™ Outloud speech software to make the PC talk. Features include dictionary, thesaurus, spell check; page insertion and deletion;

FIGURE 6.8   Kurzweil

Reading the text aloud with highlighting words in Kurzweil 3000.

Photo courtesy of Psycho-Educational Services.

book marking; and Page Layout Navigation to move from one component to the next.

Application of a small scale OCR/speech synthesis system is available in the Quicktionary™ Reading Pen (see Figure 6.9). This portable, pocket-sized "reading pen" (smaller than a TV remote control) uses a "miniaturized" optical scanning system to enable the user to scan single words and a full line of print on a page (e.g., textbook, magazine) and have the word read aloud by means of a built-in speech synthesizer. The device offers definitions for scanned words, auditory spelling of the word, and a save feature to keep a record of scanned words. The portability of this device allows users to take the pen to various environments (school, library, work) to assist with unknown words due to word recognition or vocabulary issues.

Variable Speech Control Tape Recorders.   Books-on-tape is a popular option for individuals with visual impairments, dyslexia, and reading disabilities for listening to prerecorded text (e.g., textbooks, novels, journals, newspapers) at a rate suitable for their listening comprehension. Prerecorded text is available from a number

FIGURE 6.9   Quicktionary Pen
Photo courtesy of Psycho-Educational Services.

of sources, including the Library of Congress, Recordings for the Blind, and several private companies. Books-on-tape can be played on variable speech control (VSC) tape recorders, which allow the user to play audiotaped material slower or faster than the rate at which it was initially recorded, without the loss of intelligibility. Intelligible speech at varying rates is achieved by adjusting speed and pitch control levers. Taped texts are among the most common accommodations requested by postsecondary students for course material.

FOCUS ON 6.3

Summarize the information presented in this section into two parts: listening devices and print aids. Identify devices, their purpose, and individuals who might benefit from using the devices. Consider the setting demands in which these devices might be used.

SUMMARY

In this chapter, we have focused on AT devices that can be used to help individuals with different types of disabilities access the wealth of information found across a variety of environments. Access to the computer is one of the most critical dimensions in today's society if individuals are going to be "players" in this technology age. A variety of input and output device options were presented including ways to adapt the conventional keyboard and alternative input and output options to meet more access challenges. Certainly, telecommunications is a second major area individuals must be able to access. Simply using the telephone is a task that most of us take for granted. For individuals who are deaf or hard of hearing, access is now available and has become a legal mandate. Also, Internet access is another area that enables people to be competitive, informed, and part of the market economy. Universal design features can ensure that all individuals can enjoy the options offered by Internet service. Finally, access to information presented orally and in print are other important considerations. Numerous devices are available that can promote access for individuals with mild to severe challenges.

DISCUSSION QUESTIONS

1. Describe the features of input devices and explain considerations for selecting the devices to meet individual needs.
2. Describe the features of output devices. Explain how these devices might be used in a home, school, and work setting.

3. Describe your thoughts about how universal design features can be more widely accepted and employed. Describe potential barriers to universal design and possible solutions.

4. Describe the features of devices that promote access to listening and print.

REFERENCES

Alliance for Technology Access. (1996). *Computer resources for people with disabilities.* Alameda, CA: Hunter House Publishing.

Angelo, D. H. (1997). AAC in the family and home. In S. Glennen & D. DeCoste (Eds.), *The handbook of augmentative communication* (pp. 523–45). San Diego: Singular Publishing Group.

Bryant, B. R., & Bryant, D. P. (in press). The use of assistive technology in postsecondary education settings. In L. Brinkerhoff (Ed.), *Assistive technology.* Austin, TX: Pro-Ed.

Church, G., & Glennen, S. (1992). *The handbook of assistive technology.* San Diego: Singular Publishing Group.

Cook, A. M., & Hussey, S. M. (1995). *Assistive technologies: Principles and practices.* St. Louis: Mosby.

King, M. L., & Rental, V. M. (1981). Research update: Conveying meaning in written texts. *Language Arts, 58,* 721–28.

Lewis, R. (1993). *Special education technology.* Pacific Grove, CA: Brooks/Cole Publishing Co.

Rehabilitation Act Amendments of 1998. Section 508, U.S.C. section 2.

Smith, D. D. (2000). *Introduction to special education* (4th ed.). Boston: Allyn and Bacon.

University of Washington. (1997). *World wide access: Accessible web design.* Seattle, WA: Author.

CHAPTER SEVEN

INTEGRATING ASSISTIVE TECHNOLOGY ADAPTATIONS INTO ACADEMIC INSTRUCTION

CHAPTER AT A GLANCE

OBJECTIVES

1. Describe the components of designing, implementing, and evaluating academic instruction.
2. Explain the features of instructional software, types of software, and guidelines for evaluating software.
3. Describe the basic skills for reading, writing, and mathematics.
4. Describe assistive technology adaptations that can be used in reading.
5. Describe assistive technology adaptations that can be used in writing.
6. Describe assistive technology adaptations that can be used in mathematics.
7. Explain how to evaluate the effectiveness of instruction.

This chapter was written by Diane Pedrotty Bryant and Ae-Hwa Kim.

MAKING CONNECTIONS

Think about the reading, writing, and mathematics skills you learned in elementary, middle, and high school. These skills have served as the foundation for higher-level learning and thinking. Many students with disabilities who have difficulty acquiring these skills can benefit from assistive technology adaptations to promote learning. Identify adaptations you think might help students with learning difficulties be more successful with the basic skills. From Chapter 6, review devices that promote access to information.

INTRODUCTION TO INTEGRATING ASSISTIVE TECHNOLOGY ADAPTATIONS INTO ACADEMIC INSTRUCTION

National and state legislation and mandates have called for raising academic standards and monitoring student achievement as an effort to improve the quality of education in the United States. For example, the Goals 2000: Educate America Act, signed into law by President Clinton on March 31, 1994, focused on improved standards, professional development, use of technology in classrooms, and community involvement. President George W. Bush's "No Child Left Behind" plan to increase high standards and accountability for student performance continues the national emphasis on quality education, which applies to *all* students.

For students in the preschool, elementary, middle (or junior high), and high school years, a quality education includes access to the general curriculum and/or a functional curriculum, as appropriate, and adaptations that promote learning and access to learning. As discussed in Chapter 2, there are a variety of adaptations, such as behavioral, curricular, and instructional, that IEP teams can recommend and teachers can choose to promote academic learning and access. Assistive technology adaptations, including remedial software, stand-alone tools, and compensatory devices will be the focus of this chapter. Moreover, although instruction encompasses a broad range of subjects such as literacy, mathematics, social studies, science, and so forth, reading, writing, and mathematics will be emphasized in this chapter. Connections to other subject areas will be made as appropriate.

Reading, writing, and mathematics comprise the basic academic curriculum, which is important across all the school years. During the elementary school years, students learn knowledge and skills in reading, writing, and mathematics. In the middle and high school years, students learn more advanced mathematics and are expected to use their knowledge and skills in reading and writing to learn subject areas, such as social studies and science. Students certainly learn many more areas besides reading, writing, and mathematics, but these are the core curricular areas.

For many students with disabilities, learning the essential knowledge and skills in the core areas is challenging because of difficulties associated with learning skills to mastery (e.g., difficulty remembering basic math facts) and accessing the content (e.g., cannot read the text). Assistive technology adaptations are imperative to promote academic success for this group of students.

For general and special education teachers, integrating AT adaptations into the classroom is often quite challenging. There are numerous reasons why integration is challenging. For example, teachers may lack the essential training for using the AT adaptations and may require technical support that may be limited. Teachers may not be familiar with *how* to go about integrating the AT adaptations into instruction (Lemons, 2000), may not be familiar with how to evaluate the effectiveness of the AT adaptations, or may not view the adaptations as feasible and practical to implement. To address these challenges, preservice teacher preparation programs and inservice development are essential to help teachers become proficient and comfortable with technology integration into instruction. School districts must also ensure that technical support for teachers and maintenance of devices is readily available. The purpose of this chapter is to provide ideas of *how* AT adaptations can be integrated into the designing, implementing, and evaluating of instruction; that is, what teachers already do! (For a more thorough discussion about designing, implementing, and evaluating instruction, see Rivera & Smith, 1997).

DESIGNING INSTRUCTION

Designing instruction focuses on the students, curriculum and instruction, and adaptations. Teachers decide what they will teach, how they will teach, and what resources will be used for instruction. Teachers integrate AT adaptations into the design of instruction by thinking about their students, the curriculum and instruction, and adaptations; that is, adaptations are an integral part of focusing on and getting ready to teach.

Students

We begin this section by offering a personal perspective from a mother about her son (Personal Perspective 7.1). We learn about the parents' goals and hopes and their suggestions for educators to consider all types of adaptations to accommodate individual student's needs to promote success.

Before designing instruction, teachers must learn about the personal/social and academic needs of their students, including the experiences students bring to the educational setting and the academic levels at which they are performing. Teachers examine the IEP and other documents to gather information for instructional planning purposes. Additionally, it is critical that teachers become very familiar with each student's levels of performance according to the psycho-educational assessment in the cognitive, social, motor, sensory, and language domains to determine functional capabilities and limitations.

PERSONAL PERSPECTIVE 7.1

Ernest is 12 years old and in fifth grade at an elementary school. Within moments of his birth in 1989, we (his parents) were told he had Down syndrome. He began "school" two months later at the Infant Development Program, an early childhood and infant program. Ernest began saying words at 12 months with the help of a sign language program (called "Makaton") and an inherent love of reading books. He took his first steps at the age of 2½ with the encouragement of his friends at preschool. Ernest has grown up with two younger brothers, Eason (age 10) and Henry Lane (age 7), who are his best friends and worst enemies. He is truly the big brother, working hard to enforce the house rules, and picking up for them when their behavior lapses from the well-worn routines that make up our everyday life. Ernest watches videos constantly in his free time, cheering on the Pink Panther and Scooby Doo. Ernest rides the big school bus with his brothers and is a proud member of the school's Safety Patrol.

You both have been activists in disabilities and advocates for your son. As advocates, how have your efforts been received by professionals over the years, particularly related to any requests you might have had for technology to help your son access the curriculum?
Over the years, Ernest's disabilities have introduced us to many wonderful professionals. My husband and I have worked hard to foster a team spirit, which has resulted in a deeply committed staff and mutual trust. The vision that our family shares of Ernest's future has been well received and enlarged beyond our expectations by professionals, teachers, and students in Ernest's classes. At one time, our request for a classroom computer was seen as an abandonment of learning handwriting by Ernest's occupational therapist, but that was never our intention. Ernest has continued to work on his handwriting, although key-boarding will probably be his future means of writing. That same therapist became one of Ernest's best advocates.

What devices does Ernest use and how effective have they been in his development?
Ernest uses computers at school and at home. I'm not sure how effective they've been, as I haven't seen much direct transfer of reading or number skills from the computer games he plays. It still seems to take the one-to-one teaching with real human beings for him to make strides in his education. The computer is great at reinforcing the skills he already has. Ernest is a real whiz with computers and VCRs, and they do use computers in the Learning Lab at school.

What are your expectations for Ernest's education? And what concerns do you have as he gets closer to his high school years?
We would like to see Ernest continue learning in the regular classroom for at least part of the day, with one-to-one teaching of specific skills. Of course, this goal is getting harder as Ernest's skills are at a kindergarten level. Our ultimate expectation for his education is for Ernest to thrive in the real world as an adult. Since we will be moving on to middle school next fall, our main concern is to build bridges this year so that the teachers and administrators at his new school will understand and support our goals. Ernest will hope-fully continue to have the friendship and support of his classmates from Hill, but there will be many new children and experiences ahead in Ernest's life.

(continued)

Please explain to our readers the process that you went through in acquiring AT devices for your son.
We purchased a computer for all three of our kids five years ago. Ernest has also been fortunate because our school is technology-rich. We have not had to acquire technology specifically for Ernest, although he has had access to a very old computer in the classroom as a diversion. Ernest's special education consultant has been very good at acquiring software with discretionary funding. I had Ernest evaluated for AT a few years ago, but nothing more than pencil grips was suggested by the school district.

What types of funding sources have you been able to tap in order to help purchase AT devices?
None.

What advice about technology and school would you give other parents who have a child with Down syndrome?
I try to observe Ernest in the regular classroom (like a fly on the wall). What will it take to keep him there and reach his individual goals at the same time? Usually it's not high-tech AT. Usually it's a well-planned adapted curriculum and a talented teaching assistant. Or it's a creative regular education teacher who pairs Ernest with other children in the classroom. I try to avoid getting too focused on special equipment or specialized therapy.

Describe the challenges that you have faced as your son has transitioned from one school to another.
So far, the biggest challenge we've faced is changing the preconceived notion that Ernest belongs in a particular place due to his disabilities. Because of Ernest's unique set of skills and compliant behavior, I haven't seen a special education classroom yet that would be a good fit. When we last transitioned at age six, we realized that Ernest's success depends on the stimulation of his peers and being a fundamental part of his school. We are firm believers that the only way to learn life skills is for Ernest to experience life, even though it might be messy, more time-consuming, and less safe. Hopefully, we'll be able to carry this mind-set forward into middle school and beyond.

Here is your chance to speak to those readers who are teachers, pathologists, or other care givers. What would you want them to know about assistive technology and how it affects your son's life?
Don't let technology or therapy get in the way of working with Ernest! If there's a piece of equipment needed, please let me know and I will find a way to get it. Thus far, I haven't found AT that significantly improves Ernest's capabilities. As time has passed, we've become more accepting of Ernest's inherent abilities and disabilities. We've found that there's no technology substitute for one-to-one instruction, an adapted curriculum, and real friendships at school.

Reproduced with permission from Psycho-Educational Services.

FOCUS ON 7.1

Take a few minutes to review the case studies, Maria and Gene, in Table 7.1. Make a list of the students' functional capabilities and limitations. We will come back to Maria and Gene throughout this chapter.

The IEP, and transition plans for older students, are critical documents for teachers to examine carefully to design instruction because the curriculum and appropriate adaptations are stipulated for instruction. Additionally, the Adaptations Framework, as discussed in Chapter 2, can provide helpful information for designing instruction. Figure 7.1 provides an example of a completed Adaptations Framework for Gene, and Figure 7.2 depicts integrating AT adaptations into the design, implementation, and evaluation of instruction. As can be seen, Maria requires instruction in reading, and adaptations have been recommended for the classroom teacher. Gene needs instruction in writing along with devices to promote access to the curriculum.

Curriculum, Instructional Planning, and Assistive Technology Adaptations

Curriculum is described as a plan for the selection and organization of student experiences to change and develop behaviors. The IEP identifies the curriculum, for

TABLE 7.1 Case Studies

MARIA

Maria is a fourth-grade student. Psycho-educational assessment information and teacher observations report that Maria has normal hearing and vision and average intelligence. She speaks English at school and receives all instruction in English; she is bilingual in Spanish, which is spoken at home. She reads at a slow rate and experiences difficulty with comprehension. She has difficulty decoding and recognizes a limited number of high-frequency words. Maria tries to read words correctly although she is not always successful. She is reading at a second-grade independent reading level with approximately 45 words per minute correct.

GENE

Gene is a seventh-grade student. Psycho-educational assessment information and teacher observations report that Gene has normal hearing and low vision. He wears glasses for correction and benefits from adaptations including high-contrast color, enlarged print, and optical and nonoptical devices. He has average intelligence and speaks only English. He reads at the fourth-grade level; his comprehension is better. Gene experiences difficulties with written language. He has trouble generating and organizing ideas for writing assignments and getting his thoughts down on paper. His written production is limited for his age in terms of sentence structure, spelling, and vocabulary. The overall number of words generated is quite limited, and editing is difficult for what is written.

Setting-Specific Demands		Person-Specific Characteristics		Adaptations
Task	**Requisite Abilities**	**Functional Capabilities**	**Functional Limitations**	**Simple-to-Complex**
Write a term paper	Generate ideas; organize ideas; write the draft; revise the draft; edit the draft; turn in the paper	Hearing; cognitive ability to complete task	Low vision; ability to organize ideas; ability to generate paragraphs; ability to edit work completely	Enlarged print access; semantic mapping tool; use of high-contrast color; software support; screen reader/speech synthesis

⇧   ⇧   ⇧   ⇧   ⇧

Evaluation of Effectiveness

FIGURE 7.1   Adaptations Framework: Gene

instance, academic and life skills, to be taught. Additionally, the level of schooling (elementary or secondary), graduation requirements, state and local standards, and the textbook all influence what teachers teach (Rivera & Smith, 1997).

Instructional planning is one of the most important components of "designing instruction" because decisions are made about the "what" and "how" of teaching. Lesson plans are descriptions of specific instructional activities that occur during the school day. The process of developing lesson plans can be aided by thinking about specific decision-making questions such as:

1. What are the student's IEP annual goals and short-term objectives for the content area to be taught?
2. How will instruction be delivered?
3. What teaching techniques will be used?

Designing Instruction	**Implementing Instruction**	**Evaluating Instruction**
• Student • Curriculum • Adaptations • Classroom	• Delivery • Grouping	• Environmental factors • Use of adaptations • Monitoring student progress

FIGURE 7.2   Integrating Adaptations into Instruction

4. How will students be grouped?
5. How will materials and adaptations be integrated into instruction?
6. How will the lesson be evaluated?

Planning for the integration of devices can be assisted by thinking about the following additional questions:

1. Do I know how to use the device?
2. Is my classroom set up to accommodate the use of the device?
3. Does the student require computer access devices? (See Chapter 6 for additional information.)
4. How will I know if the device is effective?

In this chapter, we focus on AT adaptations including remedial and compensatory adaptations. Remedial adaptations involve techniques that attempt to correct a problem after other techniques have proven ineffective (Rivera & Smith, 1997). Techniques may involve additional instructional materials, a multisensory (e.g., visual, auditory, tactile) emphasis, or in the case of this chapter, instructional software and devices. Compensatory adaptations attempt to circumvent a problem and offer a solution to promote access. For example, a calculator can be viewed as an example of a compensatory adaptation for a student who cannot learn the basic facts but is receiving instruction in whole number computation.

The IEP team as well as the teacher and student identify AT adaptations as instruction progresses. Once teachers develop a good sense of their students' instructional needs and the AT adaptations that can be used to promote learning and access, additional adaptations can be identified and implemented. Integrating AT adaptations into "designing instruction" means that teachers plan how adaptations can be used to meet individual student's needs. In this section, we explain the process of evaluating instructional software, which can be used for remedial purposes; describe reading, writing, and mathematics curriculum; and present representative examples of AT adaptations for remedial or access purposes.

Instructional Software

Instructional software provides individualized experiences that many students require as well as (a) extra practice to promote mastery of skills, (b) development of writing abilities, (c) simulations and problem-solving opportunities, and (d) access to the curriculum (Lewis, 1993). Table 7.2 provides information about different types of instructional software.

Instructional software usually includes words, graphics (e.g., pictures, animation), and features of effective instruction that promote effective learning. Students who can benefit from software for remedial purposes must continue to be provided instruction, which is grounded in best practice on specific skills. For instance, instructional software should contain simple, easy-to-follow directions, models, examples, positive corrective feedback, extra practice opportunities (branching), an

TABLE 7.2   **Types of Instructional Software**

TYPE	PURPOSE	STRENGTHS
Drill and Practice	• Reinforcement of skills previously taught • Practice • Feedback	• Provides multiple practice opportunities • Can be individualized • Provides corrective feedback • May provide branching to easier skills
Simulation	• Decision-making and cause-effect situations	• Gives students opportunities to make decisions and to witness the results of those decisions • Provides opportunities to analyze situations and apply problem-solving skills
Games	• Fun, gamelike situation • Animation and sound to simulate a game format	• May be motivating • May reinforce skills

Source: Adapted from Rivera & Smith (1997).

appropriate reading level, pacing options, and documentation of students' progress (Rivera & Smith, 1997). Also, software should focus on research-based skills. For example, if software is aimed at teaching or reinforcing decoding skills, then practice with blending and segmenting should be included. Documentation (teacher's guide/directions) that accompanies the software may include content explanations of the software, lessons, and extended activities.

Software evaluation is an important component when selecting software for classroom instruction. Teachers should review software before purchasing it to determine the integrity of instructional design or consult with their technology specialist for recommendations (Rivera & Smith, 1997). Table 7.3 contains guidelines for software evaluation and selection. Table 7.4 provides examples of instructional software and AT devices by publisher or vendor.

READING

Reading is essential for success in school and life (Bondanza, Kelly, & Treewater, 1998; Snow, Burns, & Griffin, 1998). The written word is the gateway to knowledge.

TABLE 7.3   Guidelines for Software Evaluation and Selection

A. General Information

Name of software

_____

Publisher _____   Cost _____

Hardware specifications required to run software

_____

Network copy _____   Cost _____

B. Description

Grade level(s) _____

Software Instructional Area(s)

_____

Reading Level of Software Text (if applicable)

_____

Purpose

_____

____ Tutorial   ____ Drill and Practice

____ Simulation   ____ Game

Instructional Objectives ____ yes   ____ no (List objectives if stated)

_____

Information Presentation (check all that apply)

____ Speech   ____ Music   ____ Graphics

____ Text   ____ Animation

Visuals (check all that apply)

____ Color   ____ Black and White   ____ Screen Too Busy

____ Graphics Enhance Rather Than Distract

____ Print legible   ____ Print size age appropriate

(continued)

TABLE 7.3   Continued

Sound (check all that apply) ____ yes   ____ no

____ Sound is clear/audible   ____ Speech is audible

____ Sound is distracting   ____ Rate of speech is appropriate

C. Instructional Design

Directions are clear, easy to read, and short.	____ yes	____ no
Examples or models are provided.	____ yes	____ no
Pacing is appropriate.	____ yes	____ no
Practice opportunities are provided.	____ yes	____ no
Corrective feedback is provided.	____ yes	____ no
Corrective feedback is stated positively.	____ yes	____ no
Difficulty level can be individualized.	____ yes	____ no
Branching is available for extra practice.	____ yes	____ no
Reinforcement (visual and/or auditory) is present.	____ yes	____ no
A recordkeeping/evaluation option is available.	____ yes	____ no

D. Content

Appropriate to stated objectives	____ yes	____ no
Factual and accurate	____ yes	____ no
Free of gender, cultural, racial bias	____ yes	____ no
Relates to school's curriculum	____ yes	____ no
Relates to student's IEP	____ yes	____ no
Sufficient scope and sequence	____ yes	____ no

E. User demands

Academic

_____

_____

Physical/motor/sensory

_____

Computer knowledge

_____

TABLE 7.3   Continued

Technical vocabulary

Problem solving

Functions (check all that apply)

____ Save work in progress   ____ Print in progress   ____ Alter sound

____ Return to main menu at any point in program   ____ Change pace

Ability to make adjustments for (check all that apply)

____ Low vision   ____ Motor difficulties

____ Computer access

Adapted with permission from Rivera & Smith (1997), pp. 148–149. Copyright © 1997 by Allyn & Bacon

TABLE 7.4   Examples of Instructional Software and AT Devices by Publisher/Vendor

Attainment Company: Attainment Company, Inc. Verona, WI 53593-0160
   *Basic Coins CD-ROM [Computer Software]. (2000).
   *Dollars and Cents Software [Computer Software]. (2000).
   *MatchTime CD-ROM [Computer Software]. (2000).
   *Reading Lesson [Computer Software]. (2000).
   *Show Me Math Software [Computer Software]. (2000).
   *Show Me Spelling [Computer Software]. (2000).
   *TimeScales [Computer Software]. (2000).
   *Wordwise software [Computer Software]. (2000).

CAST: Center for Applied Special Technology, Peabody, MA 01960
   CASTeReader [Computer Software]. (1999). ULTimate KidBooks [Computer
      Software]. (1997).

Don Johnston Inc. : Don Johnston, Inc. Volo, IL 60073
   *Access to Math [Computer Software]. (1994).
   *Co:Writer [Computer Software]. (2000).
   *Simon Sounds It Out [Computer Software]. (1994).
   *Simon Spells [Computer Software]. (1994).
   *Start-to-Finish Books [Computer Software]. (1994).
   *Write: OutLoud [Computer Software]. (2000).

(continued)

TABLE 7.4   Continued

Edmark: Edmark Corporation, Redmond, WA 98073-9721
*Astro Algebra [Computer Software]. (1997).
*Bailey's Book House [Computer Software]. (1993).
*Carnival Countdown [Computer Software]. (1996).
*Cosmic Geometry [Computer Software]. (1996).
*Imagination Express Series [Computer Software]. (1994, 1995, 1996).
*Millie's Math House [Computer Software]. (1992).
*MindTwister Math [Computer Software]. (1999).
*Money Math [Computer Software]. (2000).
Number Heroes [Computer Software]. (1996).
Stanley's Sticker Stories [Computer Software]. (1996).
Stories & More Series [Computer Software]. (2000).
Words Around Me [Computer Software]. (1996).

InfoUse: InfoUse, Berkeley, CA 94710-2566
*MathPad [Computer Software]. (1998).
*MathPad Plus [Computer Software]. (2000).

IntelliTools: IntelliTools, Inc., Petaluma, CA 94954
*IntelliTalk II [Computer Software]. (2000).
*Number Concept 1 [Computer Software]. (1990).
*Number Concept 2 [Computer Software]. (2000).

Knowledge Adventure: Knowledge Adventure, Torrance, CA 90504
*Spell It Deluxe [Computer Software]. (2000).
*Spelling Blaster [Computer Software]. (2000).

Laureate Learning Systems: Laureate Learning Systems, Inc., Winooski, VT 05404
*Adjectives and Opposites [Computer Software]. (1996).
*Exploring Early Vocabulary Series [Computer Software]. (1996).
*First Words, First Words II, and First Verbs [Computer Software]. (1996).
*Irregular Verb Training [Computer Software]. (1996).
*Micro-LADS [Computer Software]. (1996).
*My House, My Town, and My School [Computer Software]. (1996).
*Readable Stories [Computer Software]. (1996).
*Sentence Master [Computer Software]. (1996).
*Simple Sentence Structure [Computer Software]. (1996).
*Talking Series [Computer Software]. (1996).
*Words and Concepts [Computer Software]. (1996).

Other Vendors
*Dragon NaturallySpeaking Professional [Computer Software]. (1999). Voice
Recognition Systems, Lexington, KY 40524.
*Inspiration [Computer Software]. (1999). Inspiration Software Inc., Portland, OR
97225-2167.
*KeyREP [Computer Software]. (1999). Bloorview MacMillan Centre, Toronto, ON
M4G 1R8.

TABLE 7.4 Continued

---

*Kurzweil 3000 [Computer Software]. (1999). Lernout & Hauspie Speech Products, Burlington, MA 01803.

*Mathkeys Unlocking Measurement [Computer Software]. (1996). MECC, Minneapolis, MN 55430.

*OutSPOKEN [Computer Software]. (1995). ALVA Access Group, Inc., Oakland, CA 94612.

*PixWriter [Computer Software]. (1998). Slater Software Inc., Guffey, CO 80820.

*Reading Pen [Computer Software]. (1998). Wizcom Technologies Inc., Acton, MA 01720.

*Speaking Language Master™ [Computer Software]. (2000). Franklin Electronic Publishers, Burlington, NJ 08016-4907.

*Spelling ToolKit Plus [Computer Software]. (1996). MECC, Minneapolis, MN 55430.

*Unifix® Software [Computer Software]. (1996). Didax Educational Resources, Rowley, MA 01969-3785.

*WiggleWorks [Computer Software]. (1996). Scholastic, Inc., New York, NY 10012.

*WiVox [Computer Software]. (1999). Bloorview MacMillan Centre, Toronto, ON M4G 1R8.

*WriteAway [Computer Software]. (1998). Information Services, Inc., Newbury, MA.

*Writing with Symbols 2000 [Computer Software]. (1998). Mayer-Johnson, Inc., Solana Beach, CA 92075.

A large amount of information is presented through text, so the ability to read and understand text is a necessity in today's society (Bryant, Ugel, Hamff, & Thompson, 1999). However, for many students with disabilities, the act of reading is a challenging process (Bender, 1998).

Reading refers to the product of decoding and comprehension (Gough, 1996). Decoding is translating the print into a representation similar to oral language, and comprehension is understanding the representation (Carnine, Silbert, & Kameenui, 1997). The ability to decode words rapidly and accurately is essential so readers can focus on constructing meaning from text (Moats, 1998).

As the quality of technology has been developing during the last few decades, computers have been widely acknowledged as useful instructional tools in reading instruction (Reinking, 1987). Computer-Assisted Instruction (CAI) has been applied to reading instruction, such as improving word identification and reading comprehension, for students with disabilities (Boettcher, 1983; Jones, Torgesen, & Sexton, 1987). Moreover, there is a dramatic increase in the number and the quality of commercial software reading programs for students with disabilities (Lewis, 1993). In fact, many software reading programs consider design features to help students with disabilities circumvent their disabilities in various ways (e.g., scanning option that provides access to the program for students with physical impairments). The scope of reading skills covered by reading programs varies from program to program and may include word identification, vocabulary, fluency building, and comprehension.

Word Identification.   Word identification is often referred to as the process that is used to figure out unfamiliar words (Hargis, 1999). Instruction in word identification helps students to recognize the sounds represented by letters and letter combinations and to blend these sounds to produce words (Okolo, Cavalier, Ferretti, & MacArthur, 2000). Through the use of instructional software and access adaptations, students can be provided with multiple opportunities to hear and practice word identification skills. (The software and AT devices presented in this chapter are only examples and are not meant to be endorsements. Teachers must make their own determinations about the appropriateness of software and devices based on their students' needs.)

Simon Sounds It Out (Don Johnston, Inc.) is a software program that provides practice in word identification skills. Simon Sounds It Out has a mentor approach in that a mentor guides students through individualized instruction at their own pace. A mentor instructs students on letter sounds and word families or patterns (e.g., at, en, op), and helps students to use these sounds and word patterns to construct words. Figure 7.3 provides an example of the software program. A model is provided (visually and verbally) for the skill. In this case, students are shown how to blend the onset /p/ with the rime /en/ to produce the word "pen." Students can control the difficulty level depending on their abilities. The program reports students' progress and provides printed worksheets.

Bailey's Book House (Edmark, Inc.) is a software program that provides early language activities with speech and graphics and provides feedback as reinforcement. There are two activities related to word identification skills. In Letter Machine, the students learn the alphabet by pressing a letter key to see an animation, which is related to the letter they press. For instance, if a student selects the letter "D," it triggers an animated clip of dinosaurs. Students sound out and read words in Three-Letter Carnival. In the question and answer mode, students are asked to fill the carnival cars with objects or animals that rhyme or begin with the same letter.

Let's Go Read! An Island Adventure (Edmark, Inc.) is a software program that includes over 175 lessons and 12 leveled interactive books. Students practice word identification skills, such as letter-sound correspondence, and create simple sentences through lessons. Forty common sight words are presented and students can combine letters to make words. It has a built-in speech recognition feature, so that students can record their responses during the activities. For example, students can read a sight word, which is written on a cloud, into the microphone. If it is correct, then the cloud disappears.

A *card reader machine* (Drake Educational Associates, Ltd.), which is an audiovisual learning aid and sometimes called a *language master*, provides practice in reading skills, including word identification. It utilizes audiocards—cards with a strip of audio tape on them—to record and play back a brief visual and sound exercise, through the card reader machine. Sight words can be written and recorded on the special cards by teachers or students, and students can see and hear the words by placing the card through the machine. The card reader machine provides for individualized and self-paced learning and requires little teacher supervision. Teachers can use a card reader machine to have students practice letter recogni-

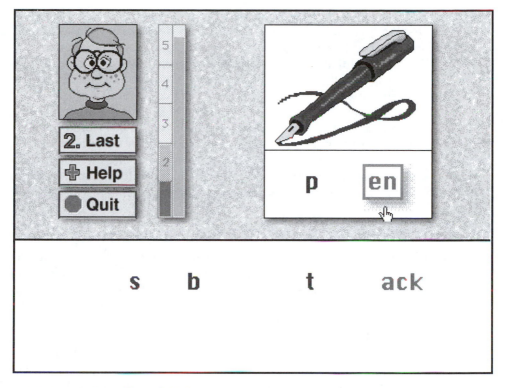

FIGURE 7.3   Simon Sounds It Out

Copyright © Don Johnston, Inc., Volo, IL. Used by permission.

tion, letter-sound correspondence, consonant sounds, vowel sounds, irregular vowel sounds, word attack, and so forth.

Vocabulary

Vocabulary knowledge is important for reading comprehension (Carnine, Silbert, & Kameenui, 1997). Typically, students with reading difficulties do not possess a rich vocabulary because they have not had multiple exposures to vocabulary development due to limited reading experiences (Simmons & Kameenui, 1990). Therefore, students need many opportunities to build their vocabulary knowledge base; technology is one avenue for this to happen.

First Words, First Words II, and *First Verbs* (Laureate Learning Systems, Inc.) are early vocabulary instructional software programs. These programs provide structured, tutorial practice in 100 early developing nouns and 40 verbs. There are six levels of training, so teachers can choose an appropriate level for each student. Words can be presented with pictures or in isolation. These programs focus on nouns and verbs by providing students with practice matching spoken verbs to their appropriate pictures.

The *Talking Series* (Laureate Learning Systems, Inc.) software complements *First Words, First Words II,* and *First Verbs* by developing the use of nouns and verbs presented in those programs. Each program includes an overlay for the Touch-Window or IntelliKeys, so students can press a word, phrase, or picture on the overlay to hear their labels. *Talking Nouns I* contains 40 words, *Talking Nouns II* contains 50 additional nouns, and *Talking Verbs* contains 40 words.

Speaking Language Master™ (Franklin Electronic Publishers) is a reference tool for students with limited vocabulary. It Includes 130,000 words, 300,000 definitions, 500,000 thesaurus entries, and a grammar guide. The headphones can be connected to it for use in the classroom. The students can create their own list of words to study. It also uses Franklin's Dynamic Phonics Guide! to hear how letters in a word sound, which relates to word identification and spelling (see Figure 7.4).

Fluency

We know that many struggling readers have problems reading accurately, quickly, and with expression. Attainment of skilled, fluent decoding allows the reader to focus on comprehension, which is the goal of any reading activity (Samuels, 1979/1999). Research has shown that fluency instruction can be an effective means of enhancing understanding of text (Meyer & Felton, 1999). Better understanding of the text allows the student to read yet more quickly and accurately.

The *tape recorder* can be used for students to practice their reading passage numerous times until automaticity is achieved. Through tape-assisted reading, students can obtain the amount of practice they require to build fluent reading behavior. First, the teacher records the reading passage. During the practice session, the student follows along as the recorded passage serves as a model of accurate and quick reading. The student then can read along with the recorded passage working on accuracy and speed. Although not intended to develop "speed reading," the tape-assisted passage can provide practice in reading accurately and quickly with expression.

FIGURE 7.4   Speaking Language Master.
Photo courtesy of Psycho-Educational Services.

Reading Comprehension

Reading comprehension is the ultimate goal of reading, which is the foundation for education (Bondanza, Kelly, & Treewater, 1998). Reading comprehension is an active process where readers construct meaning from text by incorporating text information into their prior knowledge (Bondanza, Kelly, & Treewater, 1998; Kaufman, 1992; Williams, 1998). Although the ability to comprehend is associated with decoding skills, decoding does not always lead to proficient reading comprehension (Bondanza, Kelly, & Treewater, 1998; Williams, 1998). Hence, instruction in reading comprehension is important. We present a variety of instructional software that can be used for students to practice comprehension skills.

Start-to-Finish Books (Don Johnston, Inc.) are electronic books with various functions (e.g., highlighting words, speech synthesizer). This software program focuses on reading comprehension, vocabulary, and fluency. Students who have difficulty decoding can opt to use a speech synthesizer, so that they can hear the passage read. Students can control reading rate and intonation depending on their needs or preference. Words are highlighted as they are read (see Figure 7.5). Also, the program allows students to hear any word's pronunciation in the story by

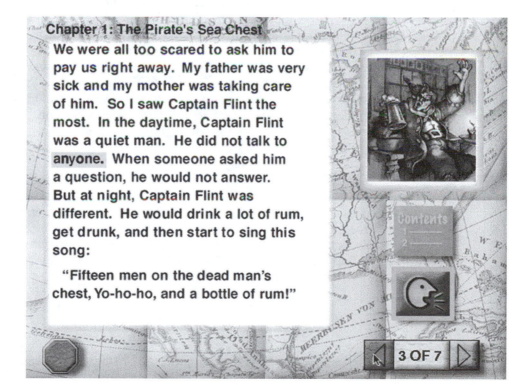

FIGURE 7.5 Highlighting Words Feature in Start-to-Finish Program
Copyright © Don Johnston, Inc., Volo, IL. Used by permission.

clicking the word. After each chapter, the students take a cloze passage quiz. A variety of teacher materials (i.e., prereading vocabulary lists, multiple-choice questions, writing activities), switch access, and an automatic record-keeping function are included. Each program contains a paperback copy of the book, audiotape of the story, and CD-ROM.

The *Stories & More Series* (Edmark Inc.) is a series of classical children's books with interactive activities. The purpose of the program is to focus on reading comprehension skills of students with disabilities. Prestory activities to activate students' prior knowledge and facilitate students' predictions about the stories are provided. To comprehend successfully, readers must make the connection between textual information and their own prior knowledge to facilitate construction of meaning (Bondanza, Kelly, & Treewater, 1998). The reader's prior knowledge plays an important role in the understanding of text (Kaufman, 1992). Activating prior knowledge is an effective strategy to improve reading comprehension. Hence, the prereading activities are important ways to promote reading comprehension.

Additionally, during-reading activities and postreading activities are important to improve reading comprehension. The program provides practice in comprehension and includes poststory activities to encourage the students to recall what they read and to demonstrate comprehension. A read-aloud function is included so that students can hear the story.

Inspiration (Inspiration Software, Inc.), which will be described in the writing section in detail, can be used to work on reading comprehension. Inspiration can be used during and after reading to organize main ideas and supporting ideas by creating semantic maps or outlines (see Figure 7.6). Students can use this software in content area classes, such as science, social studies, and English, to help them organize information they have read to facilitate comprehension. Inspiration enables students to create what is known as a graphic organizer.

FOCUS ON 7.2

Think about how the adaptations presented in the reading section can be used in the classroom. Identify some of the setting demands (tasks and requisite abilities) that might necessitate the use of any of these adaptations. Identify why each type of instructional software and AT device can help remediate difficulties or promote access to the curriculum. Share your ideas with your peers.

WRITING

Writing is a complex activity involving writing processes and mechanics (Berninger & Swanson, 1994). Writing can be divided into two levels: (a) transcription processes, such as handwriting and spelling; and (b) composing processes, such as planning, composing, and revising (Brooks, Vaughan, & Berninger, 1999). Students with disabilities may demonstrate writing difficulties due to learning or access prob-

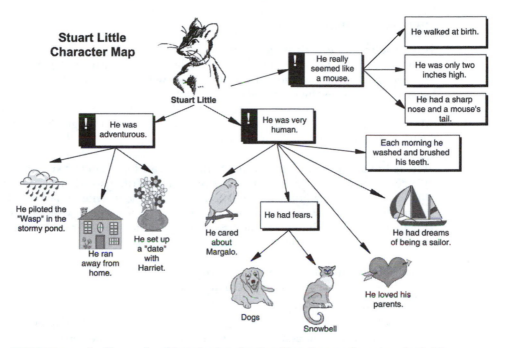

FIGURE 7.6 An Example of Inspiration for Reading Comprehension Activities

Source: Diagram created with Inspiration® by Inspiration Software, Inc.

lems. These difficulties could involve problems in the writing process as well as mechanical errors (MacArthur, Graham, & Schwartz, 1991; MacArthur, Harris, & Graham, 1994). (See Personal Perspective 7.2.)

The writing process consists of five phases: (a) prewriting, (b) drafting, (c) revising, (d) editing, and (e) publishing. Prewriting is a process that includes all the activities that a writer does to prepare for writing, including selecting a topic and planning. After selecting a topic, the writer gathers and organizes information. Drafting is the act of writing. The writer focuses on getting his or her thoughts down rather than creating a completed piece in this phase. Revising is a procedure where the writer reviews what he or she has written and makes changes in content. Editing is a process of correcting errors. In this phase, a writer focuses on mechanical errors, rather than changes in content. Publishing is a procedure in which the writer shares the writing piece. There are programs that can facilitate the writing process, especially the prewriting phase, by allowing students to brainstorm and organize ideas. Also, there are programs that provide practice in syntax, which plays an important role in the writing process.

Mechanics

Mechanics involves skills including spelling, handwriting, punctuation, and capitalization. Students should develop accurate and quick handwriting skills and

PERSONAL PERSPECTIVE 7.2

Please tell us a little bit about yourself.
I am 15 years old and I have lived in Simi Valley in the same house all my life. I live with my parents and my two dogs. I was diagnosed with learning disabilities (LD) and Sensory Integrative Dysfunction when I was 6 years old. I went to public school for kindergarten and to private school for first grade. I went back to public school for second through sixth grade. I attended a private school for seventh through ninth grade and I am starting tenth grade there in two weeks.

Please tell us a little bit about your challenges learning academic subjects.
Without a computer, I could not write a report and writing essays would be impossible. I have trouble taking notes in school because I am a slow writer. I have trouble remembering the order of words and what I want to write when writing with pencil and paper. I have trouble decoding words and sequencing sounds when I read. I have difficulties when given many directions at one time.

For what reasons do you use speech recognition?
Some of the reasons I use speech recognition are:

- Putting thoughts on paper
- School work and for writing paragraphs, reports, essays, and summaries
- Chatting with grandparents and friends on AOL instant messenger
- Writing e-mails
- Writing thank you notes and letters

Basically for everything I have to write.

How does speech recognition help you do your schoolwork?
I write better with speech recognition in school and at home because I can get my thoughts down on paper and I'm able to write more. I also write better because I can say what I want to write and I don't fall behind. I use a lot more vocabulary in what I write and I write longer sentences. I have an extensive vocabulary and now I can use it when I write.

What challenges do you find with speech recognition? How do you deal with the challenges?
Problem: I can be disruptive to other students when I use speech recognition in the classroom.
Solution: Sometimes I go to the hallway where I don't disrupt anyone or I change the settings so I can talk quieter into the microphone.
Problem: Not every computer I have has access to Dragon Dictate, the speech recognition software I use, installed on it.
Solution: I take my laptop to use when I need speech recognition.
Problem: Speech recognition has trouble understanding me when I am sick.
Solution: I don't intend on using it much when I am sick.
Problem: I get frustrated sometimes when it doesn't understand me.
Solution: I try to speak louder and clearer.

Who taught you how to use speech recognition?
A teacher who was my instructor for the first 10 hours of training and for ongoing support at school. My dad helps and teaches me at home.

How do you fix any problems you are having with speech recognition software?
I first assess the problem that I am experiencing and then I use my knowledge to try to fix any problems. If I am unable to succeed, I discuss the problem with my teacher or my dad and hopefully they can resolve the problem.

Are there other technologies that you use to help you in your academic studies?
I use a calculator, desktop computer, and a laptop computer. I use a Plantronics USB headset microphone for speech recognition on my laptop computer and my desktop computer at home. I have a watch that can hold telephone numbers that I can't remember. The calculator is for doing mathematical equations, and I have a laptop computer to use in all my classrooms with speech recognition installed on it. I also use various types of software for the computer such as:

- Text Aloud MP3: I use it to proofread papers that I have written. When I do research, I paste the text into the program and then I can have it read to me.
- Inspiration: a program for mapping ideas for writing assignments.
- Microsoft Word: for spelling and grammar.

Technology is the reason I am now succeeding in school. I'm even doing this e-mail with my speech recognition.

If you had a chance to tell teachers about speech recognition, what would you tell them?
I would first tell teachers that it is a tool, not a toy. I would also tell them that it helps me in a lot of ways. I believe that it helps me learn how to read and write and it helps me do better and to succeed in school.

Reprinted with permission from Psycho-Educational Services.

should become proficient in spelling words for successful writing (Graham, Harris, MacArthur, & Schwartz, 1998). Students with disabilities may demonstrate more spelling, capitalization, and punctuation difficulties than typically achieving students (MacArthur, Graham, & Schwartz, 1991). Students who have not mastered the mechanics of writing expend considerable energy on low-level skills (i.e., spelling, capitalization, punctuation, handwriting). Difficulties in spelling words, handwriting, or punctuation result in problems with acquiring the high-level writing processes, such as planning and revising (Graham, 1999; McCutchen, 1996).

Computers have been used to support writing for students who have difficulty writing (Okolo, Cavalier, Ferretti, & MacArthur, 2000). Technologies, such as word prediction, spell checks, and speech synthesis, can be used for the writing process by reducing the burden of the mechanics of writing. Hence students with writing difficulties can concentrate on the high-level process of writing, such as planning and content generation, rather than on the low-level process of writing mechanics (De La Paz, 1999). These technologies have the promise to help students circumvent their difficulties with writing (MacArthur, 1996, 1998). In this section, we describe various types of instructional software and AT devices that can be used to facilitate the writing process and mechanics.

Word Prediction

Word prediction software can be used to support the writing process by predicting the word. This technology was originally developed for students with physical impairments to reduce the number of keystrokes needed. However, it supports students with writing difficulties (e.g., spelling difficulty), as well as students with physical impairments, by offering a list of possible words (Okolo, Cavalier, Ferretti, & MacArthur, 2000). Word predication software predicts a word and produces a list of possible words when students start to type. The user can select the intended word from the list if it is in the list. Word prediction programs often include speech synthesis, which reads the text and the list of words, and a spell check. Speech synthesis allows postsecondary students to listen to what they have written, so they can monitor their writing (Raskind & Higgins, 1995).

Co:Writer (Don Johnston, Inc.) is a writing assistant program with intelligent word prediction. The intelligent word prediction function helps students with writing difficulties and students with physical difficulties write correct sentences by reducing the number of keystrokes needed to produce a word or sentence. When students press the initial letter of the word, Co:Writer brings up a list of predicted words (see Figure 7.7). Writing with Co:Writer helps students practice the basic writing skills (i.e., spelling, word decoding, simple sentence structure, contextual practice, and more complex sentence structure).

KeyREP (Bloorview MacMillan Centre) is a word prediction and abbreviation-expansion program that is intended to help students with writing difficulties and physical impairments write faster and more easily, although research is needed to support this purported effect. When students begin typing a word, a list of predicted words appears. Students select the word they want, and KeyREP types it into whatever application they are using. Predictions are based on the letter(s) typed,

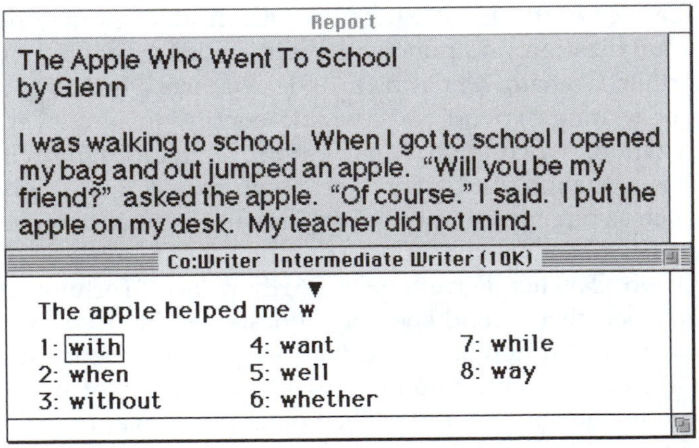

FIGURE 7.7   Word Prediction of Co:Writer

Copyright © Don Johnston, Inc., Volo, IL. Used by permission.

how frequently words are used, and personal preference. KeyREP supports abbreviation-expansion where two or three letters can expand into phrases or full sentences. *WiVox* (Bloorview MacMillan Centre) is used with KeyREP where WiVox reads each word in the KeyREP prediction list. WiVox speaks letters, words, sentences, or entire entries. WiVox reads the words, letters, or sentences in a word processor, e-mail, or web page document.

Word Processors

Many researchers have found that word processors help students compensate for writing difficulties (Collins, 1990; MacArthur, Graham, & Schwartz, 1991; Primus, 1990). There are several ways for word processors to facilitate the writing process. First, writing with a word processor means that corrections can be made easily. This feature allows students to focus on the content at first rather than on the mechanical process. Students can then revise what they wrote during the editing process. Second, word processors with desktop-publishing features allow papers to be produced with minimal errors. Third, word processors can be used in groups of students. Student can work together on the same computer during the writing process (Okolo, Cavalier, Ferretti, & MacArthur, 2000).

Write:OutLoud (Don Johnston, Inc.) is a talking word processor with a talking spell checker, so students can hear what they type. Equipped with a text-to-speech function, Write:Outloud can speak words and sentences, or read whole passages. The program also highlights word by word as students write. Because Write: OutLoud speaks while students write, the students can hear what they have written and hopefully they will be able to detect inaccuracies.

IntelliTalk II (IntelliTools, Inc.) is a talking word processor combining speech, graphics, and text. IntelliTalk includes functions, such as a speech synthesizer, talking spell checker, and built-in scanning. Text-to-speech features allow students to listen to letters, words, sentences, and entire entries as they write. Picture menus provide prompts for students who have difficulty reading the typical text-based menu in a word processor.

Semantic Mapping Software

Semantic mapping software can be used for generating and organizing information or ideas in the writing process.

Inspiration is a visual learning tool that enables students to organize the ideas they brainstorm. A wide range of functions, such as transforming a diagram into an outline, diagramming, creating concept maps, providing templates and worksheets, providing symbols or photographic quality images, and connecting to the Internet are examples of some of the instructional features. Inspiration connects with activities associated with the writing process, including brainstorming, planning, organizing, outlining, and webbing. Students can create diagrams, concept maps, semantic webs, graphic organizers, and outlines. For example, the compare-contrast graphic can be used to organize thoughts before writing begins. Ideas can always be rearranged as the paper unfolds and new ideas or a better organization emerges (see Figure 7.8).

Writing Programs

There are programs that are intended to teach and reinforce the writing process, although research is needed to support this intention. These programs often target primary-grade students who are in the beginning stages of learning the writing process, but they may also be used with older students who require remediation.

Writing with Symbols 2000 (Mayer-Johnson, Inc.) is a symbol-supported reading and writing program that contains over 8,000 pictures. Students can write with picture stories, read and follow picture directions, and communicate with pictures and speech. Features include a built-in talking word processor that highlights the words as students write and a spell checker that uses pictures.

ULTimate KidBooks (CAST) is a multimedia publishing program that enables teachers to create electronic books that use images and text. It is a template into which content can be entered. It focuses on accessibility by providing a variety of functions, including highlighting, text enlargement, speech synthesis, and built-in switch access.

Stanley's Sticker Stories (Edmark, Inc.) is a writing program that includes a word processing function with animated characters. The program provides students with a way to create stories and make their own animated storybooks. Students can create stories by choosing sticker characters, dialogue for characters, backgrounds, and music. A Sticker Spelling Book is provided for spelling, and stories can be read for students with limited reading skills.

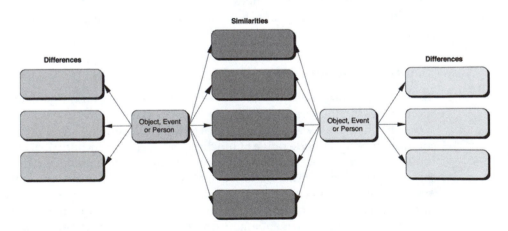

FIGURE 7.8   Brainstorming Format for a Compare-Contrast Paper Using Inspiration

Source: Diagram from Inspiration(R) by Inspiration Software, Inc.

Spelling Programs

The goal of spelling instruction is to help students become fluent spellers of words they are likely to use in their writing and develop strategies for determining the spelling of unknown words (Graham, 1983). There are programs that focus on spelling. In addition, there are spelling devices, such as portable electronic spelling dictionaries, for supporting the selection of correct spellings of words.

Simon Spells (Don Johnston, Inc.) is a spelling program with a mentor approach. The mentor guides students through individualized instruction at their own pace by providing verbal and written feedback. Simon Spells provides a function that presents words phonemically and in context. It includes 1,000 high frequency and beginning words. Reports of students' progress and printed worksheets for practice are features that are included in this program.

Show Me Spelling (Attainment Company, Inc.) teaches functional spelling. It allows students to spell up to 500 words. Two modes are included: instructional mode and question mode. In the instructional mode, students can choose adjectives, adverbs, prepositions, or all words. They type in the spelling for the picture on the screen and click the "Show Me" button to see the correct spelling. It includes options to give hints, to highlight vowels, or to provide other cues. In the quiz mode, students are asked for the correct spelling of a list of words; the program then reports students' scores.

Spelling Blaster (Knowledge Adventure) uses phonics and context clues to build spelling skills. The program provides spelling patterns and word families; uses phonics and rhyming words; edits misspelled words; and identifies correct spellings. It includes over 140 spelling lists and crossword puzzles.

Syntax Programs

Instruction in syntax is important for students who are developing their writing skills. Knowledge of syntax plays an important role in the writing process during the drafting, revising, and editing stages. There are several programs that focus on syntax.

Micro-LADS (Laureate Learning Systems, Inc.) is a seven-module series with 45 syntactic rules. It focuses on grammatical constructions and vocabulary. Pictures are used to help develop grammatical structures. It presents two or three pictures, depending on the grammatical construction, with optional speech and/or text. It then asks the students to select the picture that represents the correct construction. Micro-LADS provides a speech synthesizer, switch or touch screen access, automatic record-keeping function, and control of difficulty level.

The *Sentence Master* program (Laureate Learning Systems, Inc.) is a program that focuses on spelling and writing. It provides four-level exercises, each containing eight stories that provide repetition on 150 common words and use the words in a short story. First students practice words sequentially. Then the Sentence Master introduces an animated story that contains only those words that have been practiced. The most frequently used words, such as "the," "is," "but," "and," are

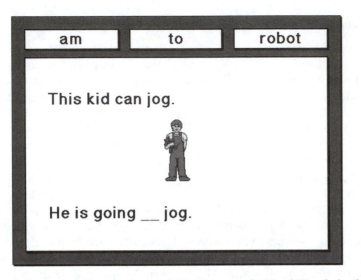

FIGURE 7.9   Instruction on Most Frequently Used Words in the Sentence Master

Source: Created by Laureate Learning Systems, Inc.; copyright © Laureate Learning Systems, Inc.

emphasized (see Figure 7.9). It includes a speech synthesizer and automatic record-keeping.

FOCUS ON 7.3

Think about how the AT adaptations presented in the writing section can be used by students at the elementary, middle, high school, and postsecondary level. Identify some of the setting demands (tasks and requisite abilities) that might necessitate the use of any of these devices. Identify student challenges in meeting the setting demands. Discuss students' functional limitations that might be circumvented by using some of these AT adaptations. Share your ideas with your peers.

MATHEMATICS

Mathematics is an important topic of instruction for all students. We know that mathematical difficulties emerge at the elementary level and persist across the grade levels into adulthood (Garnett, 1987). Research shows that students with mathematical problems experience developmental lags, which may hinder their ability to perform mathematical skills as successfully as their same-age peers (Cawley, Baker-Kroczynski, & Urban, 1992). Students with mathematical problems tend to plateau in mathematical knowledge, thus impeding retention of the curriculum presented at different grade levels (Cawley & Miller, 1989). For instance, if mastery of basic facts is lacking, then students will probably exhibit difficulties solving more advanced mathematical algorithms. Instructional software for computation; time, money, and measurement; algebra; and word problem solving is widely available; these are the most common types of instructional software (Lewis, 1993). Thus, students with mathematical difficulties should be evaluated for appropriate AT adaptations to promote learning and access to the curriculum (Rivera & Smith, 1997).

Number Concepts

Number concepts consist of numeration, place value, numeral recognition, counting, and an understanding of quantity. Number concepts include skills that are the basic foundation of higher-order mathematical thinking (National Council of Teachers of Mathematics [NCTM], 1989). Too often, not enough emphasis and time is spent on number concepts particularly for students who struggle with mathematics (Rivera, 1997). AT adaptations may be helpful in providing students with multiple opportunities to engage in a variety of activities to develop a deeper understanding of number concepts.

Number Concepts 1 (IntelliTools, Inc.) emphasizes counting 1 to 10; the concepts of greater than, less than, and equal; and beginning addition and subtraction. Number Concepts 1 focuses on basic mathematical thinking and the ability to count. In the "Questions & Answer Mode," randomly generated problems appear for students to solve. In the "Explore Mode," the students create their own problems. Number Concepts 1 offers switch access, overlay access, automatic record-keeping, and Oshi's additional support. Number Concepts 2 emphasizes skip counting, place value, factoring, and the hundreds chart.

Unifix Software (Didax Educational Resources) is a math program that offers a pictorial representation of abstract math concepts. Unifix Software is based on the manipulative mathematics materials, called Unifix, which is a combination of interlocking cubes and other materials (see Figure 7.10). Students can manipulate the cubes to study patterning, counting, addition, and subtraction. Unifix Software provides multiple representations of number concepts. The number concepts are represented visually through sets of objects, symbolically through numbers, and auditorily through sounds associated with the cubes. Unifix Software supports switch access.

Millie's Math House (Edmark, Inc.) is a math program that emphasizes counting to 30, addition, and subtraction. Millie's Math House consists of seven activities in which students practice numbers, shapes, sizes, patterns, addition, and subtraction as they build mouse houses, create wacky bugs, count animated critters, make jelly-bean cookies, and answer math challenges posed by Dorothy the duck.

Computation

Students with mathematical disabilities demonstrate difficulties with computing basic mathematics facts accurately and fluently (Geary, 1990) and whole-number problems. The development of fluency or automaticity in math fact responding is an important instructional skill for acquiring more advanced mathematical concepts.

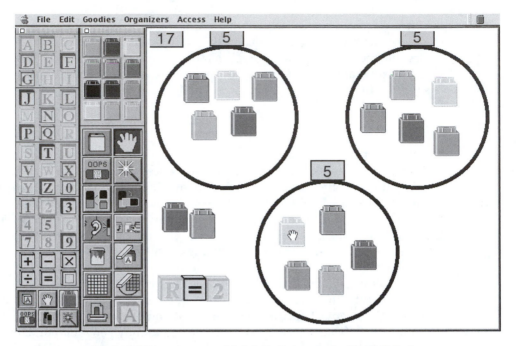

FIGURE 7.10   Pictorial Experiences with Math Concepts in Unifix® Software

Unifix® software is a registered trademark of Philograph Publications, Ltd.

Computer-assisted instruction can provide the practice opportunities students with mathematical disabilities may require to master basic mathematics skills (Okolo, Bahr, & Rieth, 1993) and for offering the capability of individualizing instruction.

MindTwister Math (Edmark, Inc.) provides practice in essential math facts (addition, subtraction, multiplication, and division) and works on problem-solving skills (i.e., visualization, deduction, sequencing, estimating, and pattern recognition). MindTwister Math is a multiplayer game format. For example, one game asks students to share the controls of a submarine as they steer around a grid in search of numbers that match a specific rule. As students play, they practice a wide range of skills, including rounding, math facts (such as addition through division), decimals, estimating, and reading graphs.

Show Me Math Software (Attainment Company, Inc.) emphasizes addition/ subtraction, multiplication, and division. It includes Show Me Addition/ Subtraction, Show Me Multiplication, and Show Me Division. Each program features assessment and an instructional mode. Teachers can determine students' weaknesses and evaluate their progress. In the instructional mode, students practice solving problems.

MathPad (IntelliTools, Inc.) is an electronic numbers processor that allows students to solve basic addition, subtraction, multiplication, and division problems on the computer. MathPad consists of toolbar, worksheet, and problem list features. MathPad allows the teacher or student to enter problems directly into the program or to import problem lists and sets up problems using the correct vertical format automatically. MathPad can be used by students who have difficulty doing math with pencil and paper or who need help organizing math problems. This program supports switch or overlay access.

MathPad Plus (IntelliTools, Inc.) contains the same functionality as MathPad with some additional features. Students can do addition, subtraction, multiplication, and division using fractions and decimals. MathPad Plus provides the students with a function to view problems as pie charts, fraction bars, or decimal grids, which can be manipulated on the screen. The screen is used as a worksheet on which the students enter numeric or word problems.

Access to Math (Don Johnston, Inc.) is a talking math worksheet program. Access to Math provides teachers with math worksheets for addition, subtraction, multiplication, and division. Students complete math worksheets on or off the computer. Speech feedback, color coding of number columns, and grid support are features that are provided by this program (see Figure 7.11).

Big: Calc (Don Johnston, Inc.) is a talking calculator, which can be used alone or with other programs. By allowing students to hear numbers, students can access math. There are six different calculator styles: phone pad, number line, giant calc, keyboard, business calc, and pyramid. Students can solve math problems ranging from simple addition and subtraction to currency and numbers involving decimals and negative integers. Switch and touch screen access are also available with this program (see Figure 7.11).

Geometry

Geometry is a skill that is taught throughout the grade levels (NCTM, 1989). Through various materials and adaptations, the abstract nature of geometry can become more concrete for those students who struggle with mathematics.

Cosmic Geometry (Edmark, Inc.) focuses on a variety of math principles related to geometry, including attributes of shapes and solids; geometric terminology; 2D and 3D coordinates; length, perimeter, area, and angle; surface area and volume; and symmetry. Carnival Countdown mentioned earlier has a component to teach geometry. In "Block Roundup," students learn the concepts of size, area, perimeter, symmetry, and fractions. Students build colorful patterns with strings of clowns,

FIGURE 7.11   Access to Math and Big:Calc
Photo courtesy of Psycho-Educational Services.

or divide them up into sets. Also, they paint, glue, hammer, and measure shapes, and they can break larger shapes into smaller parts, or calculate the area or perimeter of a design.

Algebra

Algebra is an area sorely neglected in math instruction for youngsters with learning and behavior problems (Rivera & Smith, 1997). Secondary-level students are often faced with abstract mathematical concepts, such as algebra, that require a solid foundation in mathematical skills (e.g., computation, math properties) and language.

Astro Algebra (Edmark, Inc.) emphasizes algebra, graphing, ratios, coordinates, and operations. In Astro Algebra, students travel through the galaxy solving problems that cover a wide range of pre-algebra and other algebra-related topics (e.g., graphing, ratios, coordinates, and operations). Students travel with four crew members, who help them strategize, calculate, and check their work. The ship's powerful tools are available to graph functions; work with exponents; and translate between fractions, decimals, and percents. The students have opportunities to practice algebraic and problem-solving problems. Students are exposed to math principles, including functions; graphing on a number line and coordinate grid; ratios and proportions; slope and intercept; fractions, decimals, and percents; exponents; problem solving and reasoning; and algebraic terminology. A step-by-step calculator, a talking reference database, and progress record function are included.

Time, Money, Measurement

Time, money, and measurement are skills that are emphasized by the NCTM (1989) as important life skills for all students to possess. Students with mathematical disabilities exhibit difficulties with these areas because they usually do not receive sufficient instruction and the concepts can be abstract. Activities that provide lots of practice and concrete representations of the concepts are helpful (Rivera & Smith, 1997).

MatchTime CD-ROM (Attainment Company, Inc.) is a basic program for students who are learning to tell time. MatchTime applies a programmed learning approach for students who struggle with time concepts. It has four difficulty levels, and each level provides a pre-set sequence of multiple-choice matching exercises. Students need to demonstrate mastery before moving onto the upper level. In Levels 1 through 3, students are required to find the clock that matches the large sample clock. Level 1 teaches matching the hour hand for 3, 6, 9, and 12 o'clock. Level 2 teaches minutes, but only in 15-minute intervals. Level 3 teaches all the minutes. In Level 4, the students are introduced to the concepts of "earlier" and "later." Level 4 has students selecting clocks that are up to four hours earlier or later than the sample. Spoken cues are provided in all exercises.

TimeScales (Attainment Company, Inc.) consists of three modules of increasing difficulty: (a) hours of the day, (b) minutes of the hour, and (c) from time to time.

The hours-of-the-day module is limited to hourly increments. The minutes-of-the-hour module introduces minutes within hours. The time-to-time module provides students with practice calculating the passage of time. Each module has a multiple choice and set-the-clock option.

Basic Coins CD-ROM (Attainment Company, Inc.) is a program that focuses on functional money skills using computer coins. Basic Coins CD-ROM involves the penny, nickel, dime, quarter, half-dollar, and the new golden dollar coins. It consists of three parts: (a) name, (b) match, and (c) purchase. In the first part, the computer names coins and gives their values. Next, students identify the correct value of coins by matching. Then students practice buying from a computerized vending machine. Basic Coins CD-ROM is touch screen and IntelliKeys compatible.

Dollars and Cents Software (Attainment Company, Inc.) is a program that emphasizes life skills and math. It includes First Money, Spending Money, and Making Change. First Money is the first step in independent money management. It provides students with voice prompts and graphic cues to help them move through the program. First Money focuses on money names and equal value. For example, students learn that a quarter equals two dimes and a nickel. Spending Money is the second step. Students practice buying products; they learn to select bills and coins; and receive change through the activity. Spending Money features an exercise or shopping option. In exercises, teachers determine instructional components. For example, the teacher determines if students pay with coins, with bills, or both. In shopping, the teacher decides how much the student should spend, and the program generates a shopping list. Making Change is the most advanced money program where students play the role of store clerk. The program generates purchasing situations, and the students calculate the price and give change. All programs feature animated graphics and human-quality speech. It is TouchWindow and IntelliKeys compatible.

Word Problems

Word problem solving is an area that warrants instructional emphasis across elementary, middle, and high school grades (NCTM, 1989; Rivera, 1997). Good problem solvers engage in a variety of activities (e.g., drawing pictures or diagrams, identifying important parts, disregarding extraneous information, rereading) to represent and solve word problems (Montague, 1988). Students with mathematical disabilities exhibit quantitatively similar strategies as their peers but qualitative differences for problem-solving abilities (Montague & Applegate, 1993). For instance, students have been observed rereading problems, yet they appear to have difficulties translating information into mathematical equations (Montague & Applegate, 1993). Thus, research has demonstrated for students with learning disabilities that word problem solving is difficult across elementary (Parmar, Cawley, & Frazita, 1996), secondary, (Montague & Applegate, 1993), and postsecondary levels (Zentall & Ferkis, 1993).

The majority of CAI studies (e.g., Bahr & Rieth, 1989) have focused on the effects of software (e.g., drill-and-practice, game formats) on the acquisition and fluency of computational skills. Other studies (e.g., Howell, Sidorenko, & Jurica, 1987; Shiah, Mastropieri, Scruggs, & Fulk, 1995–1996) have compared the effects of CAI to teacher-directed instruction. Thus, we have come to understand that curricular and instructional software design features are critical features that contribute to success (Babbitt & Miller, 1996).

Number Heroes (Edmark, Inc.) focuses on basic math concepts and problem-solving skills. With the help of Fraction Man, Star Brilliant, and other math superheroes, students practice math concepts, multiplication and division, fractions, 2D geometry, and probability by solving problems. Students identify, subtract, and multiply fractions to make fireworks with Fraction Man. The students read graphs and charts and determine probability. Students practice the concept of perimeter, area, congruence, similarity, symmetry, rotation, and tessellation by building geometric shapes. Students apply math logic by playing games with contestants, and they have to solve addition, subtraction, multiplication, and division problems. Number Heroes includes two calculators that display the steps for solving a problem and convert between fractions and decimals.

FOCUS ON 7.4

Conduct research on mathematics disabilities. Describe the types of problems encountered by people who struggle with dyscalculia. Identify mathematical skills and concepts that are frequently taught across grade levels. Identify devices that might be helpful for students to learn, and practice those skills and concepts.

IMPLEMENTING INSTRUCTION

Implementing instruction focuses on grouping students for teaching the lesson, delivering instruction, using materials, and integrating AT adaptations to promote learning and access to the curriculum. In this section, we describe groupings into which AT adaptations can be integrated and provide examples of how lessons can be delivered with AT adaptations as a part of effective instruction for Maria and Gene.

Grouping

Grouping for instruction refers to the ways in which the instructional process is structured to promote student learning (Rivera & Smith, 1997). Whole-group instruction involves the teacher presenting a lesson to the entire class, which is a common arrangement found at the elementary and secondary level. Typically, whole-group instruction is chosen to teach content area subjects, such as science, social studies, and health; this is particularly true at the secondary level. Although there are advantages for this grouping arrangement (Gersten, Carnine, & Woodward, 1987), limited opportunities exist for individualized instruction. Also, with this grouping arrangement, teachers must ensure that students who are using AT adaptations for access are using the devices effectively; this could be challenging to manage in whole-group instruction.

Small group instruction usually involves a group of two to six students who are grouped homogeneously to facilitate instruction or heterogeneously by ability if working independently as a group (Rivera & Smith, 1997). For example, small groups may be formed to provide instruction in academic areas, such as reading or mathematics; students in this grouping arrangement usually are reading at about the same reading level or requiring instruction on the same math objective. Research supports this grouping arrangement for struggling students (Vaughn, Thompson, Kouzekani, Bryant, & Dickson, 2002). Cooperative learning is a good example of small group instruction where students work collaboratively to achieve common academic and social goals (Johnson, Johnson, & Holubec, 1994). When integrating AT adaptations into small group instruction, teachers can monitor implementation more carefully. Groups will have to be situated strategically in the classroom to access furniture and electrical outlets if the AT adaptations, such as a computer or tape recorder, necessitate these considerations. (See Rivera & Smith for a more thorough discussion of grouping for instruction.)

Instructional Delivery

We provide a lesson for Maria and Gene to show how instruction can be delivered to teach an objective and to integrate AT adaptations. First, review Figure 7.1 for Maria and Figure 7.2 for Gene to determine the AT adaptations recommended by the IEP team for them to master reading fluency (Maria) and writing (Gene). Now, review the lesson plans in Table 7.5 for Maria and Table 7.6 for Gene to see an example of the delivery of instruction and the integration of AT adaptations into teaching.

FOCUS ON 7.5

Using the lesson plan in Table 7.5 or 7.6, write another lesson plan integrating AT adaptations for Maria, Gene, Jon (see Chapter 3), or another student of your choice. Share your plan with your peers.

EVALUATING INSTRUCTION

The final part of this chapter focuses on the effectiveness of the AT adaptation. Lesson plans should contain specific evaluation plans related to the instructional objective (see Tables 7.5 and 7.6 for examples of progress monitoring related to objectives). Additionally, teachers can evaluate the effectiveness of AT adaptations

TABLE 7.5   Maria's Lesson Plan with AT Adaptation Integration

Objective: The student will read passages with improved rate and accuracy.

INSTRUCTIONAL ACTIVITY

Passage Reading: Students build reading fluency through tape-assisted reading, repeated reading, and paired reading.

MATERIAL	GROUPING
Short section of decodable text	Individual partners
Tape recorder	
Recorded passage	
Timer and graph paper	

DELIVERY OF INSTRUCTION

1. Record a passage of text from a decodable book at the student's independent reading level.
2. Tell the student to go to a designated area for tape-assisted reading.
3. Have the student listen to the recorded passage one time while following along in the book.
4. Have the student practice the passage outloud with the recorded text 3–4 times.
5. Have the student read the same reading passage to another, stronger reader.

PROGRESS MONITORING

6. Have the student read the same passage for one minute doing "best reading."
7. Have the student chart on graph paper the number of words read in one minute.

by examining environmental factors, use of adaptations, and monitoring user progress as discussed in Chapter 2. Examples of evaluation checklists are provided in Tables 7.7, 7.8, and 7.9. Teachers can develop their own checklist or add to the ones provided in this chapter. Combining lesson plan progress monitoring and evaluation of the effectiveness of AT adaptations should provide a comprehensive picture of student progress.

FOCUS ON 7.6

Return to Maria's and Gene's lesson plans and review how their progress was monitored. Examine the information in Tables 7.7–7.9. Develop your plan for evaluating the effectiveness of AT adaptations and share with the class.

TABLE 7.6 Gene's Lesson Plan with AT Adaptation Integration

Objective: The student will write a four-paragraph paper using compare-contrast text structure.

INSTRUCTIONAL ACTIVITY

Map and Write: Students write a paper by using text structures.

MATERIAL	GROUPING
Inspiration compare-contrast template and mapping	Whole group
WriteOutloud/Word processing	Small group
Enlarged font	Individual

DELIVERY OF INSTRUCTION

1. Select a topic from the textbook (social studies or science) to be studied that includes two concepts that can be compared and contrasted.
2. Brainstorm with students as a whole group what they know about the two concepts.
3. Have students create a semantic map using Inspiration in small groups to organize their brainstormed ideas about the two concepts.
4. Have students work in small groups to identify the similarities and differences between the two concepts and use Inspiration's compare-contrast template to organize their thoughts.
5. Have students write a four-paragraph paper: two paragraphs to discuss the concepts and two paragraphs to compare and contrast the concepts. Have Gene use the information from the two Inspiration activities to organize his thoughts and WriteOutloud/word processing to generate the paper and edit his work.

PROGRESS MONITORING

6. Correct the papers in terms of accuracy in describing the concepts and comparing and contrasting them.
7. Correct the papers in terms of word production, complete sentences, and spelling.

SUMMARY

In this chapter, we focused on integrating AT adaptations into the design, implementation, and evaluation of instruction with an emphasis on academic instruction at the elementary, middle, and high school levels. The student is at the heart of the discussion in this chapter. Both remedial and compensatory adaptations fall under the realm of AT adaptations and serve an important purpose in remediating and providing access to instruction, respectively. Instructional software requires careful consideration and selection to ensure that it meets the needs of students and

TABLE 7.7   Environmental Factors

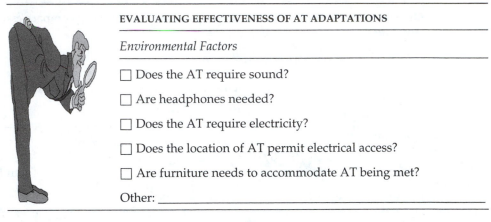

EVALUATING EFFECTIVENESS OF AT ADAPTATIONS

Environmental Factors

☐ Does the AT require sound?

☐ Are headphones needed?

☐ Does the AT require electricity?

☐ Does the location of AT permit electrical access?

☐ Are furniture needs to accommodate AT being met?

Other: _____

TABLE 7.8   Use of Assistive Technology Adaptations

EVALUATING EFFECTIVENESS OF AT ADAPTATIONS

Use of AT Adaptations

☐ Is more training required?

☐ Is the adaptation reliable?

☐ Is technical support available?

☐ Can the student keep pace with peers?

☐ Is there a fatigue factor?

Other: _____

TABLE 7.9   Monitoring User Progress

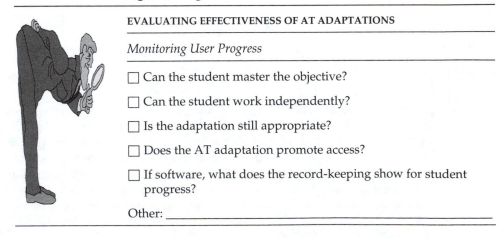

EVALUATING EFFECTIVENESS OF AT ADAPTATIONS

Monitoring User Progress

☐ Can the student master the objective?

☐ Can the student work independently?

☐ Is the adaptation still appropriate?

☐ Does the AT adaptation promote access?

☐ If software, what does the record-keeping show for student progress?

Other: _____

incorporates best practice in instructional design and curriculum. We provided a wealth of information about AT adaptations in reading, writing, and mathematics that teachers can consider as they make decisions about the tools that may help their students acquire, practice, and master the very important skills inherent in the core subject areas. Implementing instruction involves grouping arrangements and the delivery of instruction with a focus on AT integration. Finally, we provided information about evaluating the effectiveness of instruction. Careful monitoring of AT use and student progress informs instructional decision making and knowledge about the effectiveness of AT adaptations to remediate and promote access and independence.

DISCUSSION QUESTIONS

1. Explain the challenges teachers might encounter when integrating AT adaptations into instruction.
2. Compare and contrast remedial and compensatory AT adaptations.
3. Identify questions to consider when designing lessons and possible answers for the questions.
4. Describe the components of designing, implementing, and evaluating academic instruction.
5. Explain the features of instructional software, types of software, and guidelines for evaluating software.
6. Describe the basic skills for reading, writing, and mathematics and difficulties students might exhibit in these areas.
7. Compare and contrast the AT adaptations that were described in reading. Describe how the adaptations might help students with different functional limitations in reading.
8. Compare and contrast the AT adaptations that were described in writing. Describe how the adaptations might help students with different functional limitations in writing.
9. Compare and contrast the AT adaptations that were described in mathematics. Describe how the adaptations might help students with different functional limitations in mathematics.
10. Describe how a classroom might be set up to support technology adaptations.
11. Describe how you would obtain training to learn how to use the devices (see Chapter 2 for a refresher on training.)
12. Develop your own case study and lesson plan.
13. Describe how you would evaluate the effectiveness of AT adaptations in a classroom or other environmental setting.

REFERENCES

Babbitt, B. C., & Miller, S. P. (1996). Using Hypermedia to improve the mathematics problem-solving skills of students with learning disabilities. *Journal of Learning Disabilities, 29*(4), 391–401, 412.

Bahr, C. M., & Rieth, H. J. (1989). The effects of instructional computer games and drill and practice software on learning disabled students' mathematics achievement. *Computers in the Schools, 6*, 87–101.

Bender, W. (1998). *Learning disabilities*. Boston: Allyn and Bacon.

Berninger, V. W., & Swanson, H. L. (1994). Modifying Hayes and Flower's model of skilled writing to explain beginning and developing writing. In E. C. Butterfield (Ed.), *Children's writing: Toward a process theory of the development of skilled writing* (pp. 57–82). Greenwich, CT: JAI.

Boettcher, J. V. (1983). Computer-based education: Classroom application and benefits for the learning-disabled student. *Annals of Dyslexia, 33*, 203–19.

Bondanza, A., Kelly, K., & Treewater, A. (1998). *Means of improving reading comprehension*. (ERIC Document Reproduction Service No. ED 424 567).

Brooks, A., Vaughan, K., & Berninger, V. (1999). Tutorial interventions for writing disabilities: Comparison of transcription and text generation process. *Learning Disability Quarterly, 22*, 183–290.

Bryant, D. P., Ugel, N., Thompson, S., & Hamff, A. (1999). Instructional strategies for content-area reading instruction. *Intervention in School and Clinic, 34*(5), 293–302.

Carnine, D. W., Silbert, J., & Kameenui, E. J. (1997). *Direct instruction reading* (3rd ed.). Upper Saddle River, NJ: Prentice-Hall.

Cawley, J. F., Baker-Kroczynski, S., & Urban, A. (1992). Seeking excellence in mathematics education for students with mild disabilities. *Teaching Exceptional Children, 24*, 40–43.

Cawley, J. F., & Miller, J. H. (1989). Cross-sectional comparisons of the mathematical performance of children with learning disabilities: Are we on the right track toward comprehensive programming? *Journal of Learning Disabilities, 23*, 250–54, 259.

Collins, T. (1990). The impact of microcomputer word processing on the performance of learning disabled students in a required first year writing course. *Computers and Composition, 8*, 49–68.

De La Paz, S. (1999). Composing via dictation and speech recognition systems: Compensatory technology for students with learning disabilities. *Learning Disability Quarterly, 22*, 173–82.

Garnett, K. (1987). Math learning disabilities: Teaching and learners. *Reading, Writing, and Learning Disabilities, 3*, 1–8.

Geary, D. C. (1990). A componential analysis of an early learning deficit in mathematics. *Journal of Experimental Child Psychology, 49*, 363–83.

Gersten, R., Carnine, D., & Woodward, J. (1987). Direct instruction research: The third decade. *Remedial and Special Education, 8*(6), 48–56.

Gough, P. B. (1996). How children learn to read and why they fail. *Annals of Dyslexia, 46*, 3–20.

Graham, S. (1983). Effective spelling instruction. *Elementary School Journal, 83*, 560–68.

Graham, S. (1999) Handwriting and spelling instruction for students with learning disabilities: A review. *Learning Disability Quarterly, 22*(2), 78–98.

Graham, S., Harris, K. R., MacArthur, C., & Schwartz, S. (1998). Writing instruction. In B. Wong, *Learning about learning disabilities* (2nd ed.). San Diego: Academic Press.

Hargis, C. H. (1999). *Teaching and testing in reading: A practical guide for teachers and parents*. Springfield, IL: Charles C. Thomas Publisher.

Howell, R., Sidorenko, E., & Jurica, J. (1987). The effects of computer use on the acquisition of multiplication facts by a student with learning disabilities. *Journal of Learning Disabilities, 20*, 336–40.

Johnson, D. W., Johnson, R. T., & Holubec, E. (1994). *The new circles of learning: Cooperation in the classroom and school*. Alexandria, VA: Association for Supervision and Curriculum Development.

Jones, K. M., Torgesen, J. K., & Sexton, M. A. (1987). Using computer guided practice to increase decoding fluency in learning disabled children: A study using the hint and hunt I program. *Journal of Learning Disabilities, 20*(2), 122–28.

Kaufman, M. (1992). *Enhancing reading comprehension and critical thinking skills of first grade ESOL students through the use of semantic webbing*. (ERIC Document Reproduction Service No. ED 345 579).

Lemons, C. J. (2000). *Comparison of parent and teacher knowledge and opinions related to augmentative and alternative communication*. Unpublished master's thesis, The University of Texas, Austin.

Lewis, R. B. (1993). *Special education technology.* Belmont, CA: Wadsworth.

MacArthur, C., Graham, S., & Schwartz, S. (1991). Knowledge of revision and revising behavior among learning disabled students. *Learning Disability Quarterly, 14,* 61–73.

MacArthur, C. A., Harris, K. R., & Graham, S. (1994). Improving students' planning processes through cognitive strategy instruction. In E. C. Butterfield (Ed.), *Children's writing: Toward a process theory of the development of skilled writing* (pp. 173–98). Greenwich, CT: JAI.

McCutchen, D. (1996). A capacity theory of writing: Working memory in composition. *Educational Psychology Review, 8,* 299–325.

Meyer, M., & Felton, R. H. (1999). Repeated reading to enhance fluency: Old approaches and new directions. *Annals of Dyslexia, 49,* 283–306.

Moats, L. C. (1998). Reading, spelling, and writing disabilities in the middle grades. In B. Wong, *Learning about learning disabilities* (2nd ed.). San Diego: Academic Press.

Montague, M. (1988). Strategy instruction and mathematical problem solving. *Reading, Writing, and Learning Disabilities, 4,* 275–90.

Montague, M., & Applegate, B. (1993). Middle school students' mathematical problem solving: An analysis of think-aloud protocols. *Learning Disability Quarterly, 16,* 19–32.

National Council of Teachers of Mathematics. (1989). *Curriculum and evaluation standards for school mathematics.* Reston, VA: Author.

Okolo, C. M., Bahr, C. M., & Rieth, H. R. (1993). A retrospective view of computer-based instruction. *Journal of Special Education Technology, 12*(1), 1–27.

Okolo, C. M., Cavalier, A. R., Ferretti, R. P., & MacArthur, C. A. (2000). Technology, literacy, and disabilities: A review of the research. In R. Gersten, E. P. Schiller, and S. Vaughn, *Contemporary special education research* (pp. 179–250). Mahwah, NJ: Lawrence Erlbaum Associates.

Parmar, R. S., Cawley, J. F., & Frazita, R. R. (1996). Word problem-solving by students with and without mild disabilities. *Exceptional Children, 62*(5), 415–29.

Primus, C. (1990). *Computer assistance model for learning disabled.* Washington, DC: Office of Special Education and Rehabilitation Services, U.S. Department of Education.

Raskind, M. H., & Higgins, E. (1995). Effects of speech synthesis on the proofreading efficiency of postsecondary students with learning disabilities. *Learning Disability Quarterly, 18,* 141–58.

Reinking, D. (1987). *Reading and computers: Issues for theory and practice.* (ERIC Document Reproduction Service No. ED286 162).

Rivera, D. P. (1997). Mathematics education and students with learning disabilities: Introduction to the special series. *Journal of Learning Disabilities, 30*(1), 2–19, 68.

Rivera, D., & Smith, D. D. (1997). *Teaching students with learning and behavior problems* (3rd ed.). Boston: Allyn and Bacon.

Samuels, S. J. (1979/1999). The method of repeated readings. *The Reading Teacher, 50* (5), 376–81.

Shiah, R-L., Mastropieri, M. A., Scruggs, T. E., & Fulk, B. J. M. (1994–1995). The effects of computer-assisted instruction on the mathematical problem solving of students with learning disabilities. *Exceptionality, 5*(3), 131–61.

Simmons, D. C., & Kameenui, E. J. (1990). The effect of task alternatives on vocabulary knowledge: A comparison of students with learning disabilities and students of normal achievement. *Journal of Learning Disabilities, 23,* 291–97.

Snow, C. E., Burns, S., & Griffin, P. (1998). *Preventing reading difficulties in young children.* Washington, DC: National Academy Press.

Vaughn, S., Thompson, S., Kouzekani, K., Bryant, D. P., & Dickson, S. (2002). *The effects of grouping arrangements on reading instruction.* Submitted for publication.

Williams, J. P. (1998). Improving the comprehension of disabled readers. *Annals of Dyslexia, 48.*

Zentall, S. S., & Ferkis, M A. (1993). Mathematical problem solving for youth with ADHD, with and without learning disabilities. *Learning Disability Quarterly, 16,* 6–18.

CHAPTER EIGHT

ANCHORING INSTRUCTION FOR STUDENTS WITH DISABILITIES

CHAPTER AT A GLANCE

OBJECTIVES

1. Explain the theoretical basis for anchoring instruction.
2. Define anchoring instruction.
3. Explain how to develop an anchor.
4. Describe the steps in implementing anchoring instruction.
5. Explain the benefits associated with anchoring instruction.
6. Explain the challenges associated with anchoring instruction.

MAKING CONNECTIONS

In this chapter, we offer an insightful way to integrate instructional technology into classroom instruction. Think about types of instruction that teachers used when you attended school (school years and postsecondary). Describe technology practices that were used and the effect of these practices on your learning.

This chapter was written by Herbert Rieth and Linda Colburn.

INTRODUCTION TO ANCHORING INSTRUCTION

It is becoming evident that schools have an obligation to prepare children for a more technologically literate world. Expanding global competition has brought attention to the necessity of preparing future generations of Americans "to add value within an increasingly integrated world economy" (President's Committee of Advisors on Science and Technology [PCAST], 1997, p. 11).

The skills required to be both effective workers and effective citizens are increasing in complexity (Berryman, 1993; National Education Goals Panel, 1998). The skill requirements of business and industry are changing, and changes in the workplace have created a need for broader skills, and in some organizations higher levels of skill (Berryman, 1993; Scott, Cole, & Engel, 1992). The presence of computers in the workplace has educational implications, since "they force a replacement of observational learning with learning acquired primarily through symbols, whether verbal or mathematical" (Berryman, p. 367). Competition abroad has helped us to identify that increased productivity depends upon "higher worker skills and the creation of a high-performance work environment" (National Education Goals Panel, 1998, p. 92).

Technology Literacy and Instructional Goals

In this century there are many new and different types of literacy that citizens will require to work effectively. A Nation at Risk was the first formal national document to include computer literacy as a critical element of the national indicators of educational progress (Scott, Cole, & Engel, 1992). Developing technology literacy requires that we do more than just teach students how to use word processing, databases, and spreadsheets (Goldberg & Richards, 1995). Students will need to know how to listen, identify reliable information (from a vast resource available to them via the Internet), represent information in multiple formats, create products, and share understandings with wider audiences than in past generations.

Recent reports indicate that meeting the educational goals of the twenty-first century will require more higher-order thinking and problem-solving skills, with less emphasis on the memorization of isolated facts (PCAST, 1997). In order to facilitate the development of higher-order thinking and problem-solving skills to meet the national goals, teachers will have to provide students with opportunities to solve problems embedded in authentic real-life tasks. In addition, students will have to be educated to "handle new situations and meet new intellectual challenges" (Salomon, 1993, p. 128). The potential for using technology to achieve these goals, as well as to provide students with access to information as they need it to solve associated tasks, is currently receiving considerable attention (Cognition and Technology Group at Vanderbilt [CTGV], 1994; Lunenburg & Irby, 1998; Means & Olson, 1995).

Research in Cognitive Science

Research in the area of cognitive science has prompted educators to rethink what is taught, and how it is taught (Bransford, Brown, & Cocking, 1999). This research has influenced a shift to a more constructivist model of instruction that focuses on the construction of new knowledge as learners continually analyze and reorganize the connections between existing knowledge and new information and experiences. In addition, as students encounter information that is inconsistent with their current beliefs, they are taught to ask questions and seek information to resolve conflicts. The resultant information is used to build on, or strengthen, their knowledge.

These research findings have been incorporated into the National Education Goals Report (1994) that concludes that students must be able to reason, solve problems, apply understanding, and write and speak well. If we reexamine these and other national goals (Office of Technology Assessment [OTA], 1995; PCAST, 1997), and consider the current literature on instruction (Airasian & Walsh, 1997; Berryman, 1993; Feng, 1995; Jonassen, 1995; Kinzer, Singer Gabella, & Rieth, 1994; Means, 1994; Means & Olson, 1995; Roblyer, Edwards, & Havriluk, 1997; Scott, Cole, & Engel, 1992), we can conclude that generative learning and constructivist approaches are effective, and are therefore recommended for use in the schools.

Research in cognitive science has helped influence a shift in the focus of education from the teacher to the student. Increasingly, students are recognized as the focal point in the teaching and learning process (Barnes, 1989; Campione & Brown, 1990; Wang & Palinscar, 1989). This recognition has precipitated a change in the role of student from that of passive observer to that of active participant. As active participants, students offer ideas, raise questions, and build on others' ideas to construct new knowledge (Barnes, Britton, & Torbe, 1990; Hayworth & Conrad, 1990; King, 1994). Students are taught and encouraged to challenge long-held beliefs about what it means to know and to learn. They learn from each other and begin to understand that education is the process of learning, as well as the process of knowing.

Cognitive research also has shown that learning improves as students are provided opportunities to actively engage in their education by interacting and collaborating with fellow students as they endeavor to solve real-life problems (Bransford, Sherwood, Hasselbring, Kinzer, & Williams, 1990; Bransford, Vye, Kinzer, & Risko, 1990). Additionally, as students work in small groups to resolve real-life questions that have no single correct answer, they are forced to evaluate data, analyze information, identify issues, discuss different viewpoints, and use their background knowledge to develop problem-solution strategies (Boeher & Linsky, 1990; Hudspeth & Knirk, 1989; Ornstein, 1995).

Research results have prompted a shift in the focus of instruction to teaching students to find and use knowledge rather than simply to memorize information (PCAST, 1997). This view of teaching is in direct contrast to traditional didactic teaching models, where teachers do much of the thinking for their students and routinely provide them with "rules" and "facts" that must be memorized and recorded on paper as evidence of subject content mastery (Willoughby, 1990). Research suggests that more often than not students are unable to use these rules or facts outside of the content area in which they were learned or as a tool to solve daily living problems (Bransford et al., 1990b; Cognition and Technology Group at Vanderbilt [CGTV], 1991a, b; 1992a, b, 1993; Whitehead, 1929).

In summary, recent research in cognitive sciences has provided new information about the ways that individuals learn and think. This research has influenced a shift in instruction to a more constructivistic model in which students actively participate with their peers in the construction of new knowledge that is used to solve real-life problems. In the following paragraphs we will provide a description of one instructional technique (anchoring instruction) that has incorporated many of these research findings into an instructional framework.

FOCUS ON 8.1

Discuss with a partner valuable learning experiences that you have had as a student and compare/contrast those with the instruction that traditionally occurs in the classroom.

DEFINING ANCHORING INSTRUCTION

Anchoring instruction is an instructional technique that is based on research in the field of cognitive sciences. It begins with an event or problem situation that is presented using a video segment or movie. The video segment or movie (subsequently referred to in this text simply as video) is used to provide background information about the target event or problem situation to create a rich context that facilitates the development of a mental model/portrait or an "anchor" to facilitate learning.

The development of instructional anchors has been influenced by efforts to reduce the amount of "inert knowledge." Inert knowledge includes memorized information that is stored as factual knowledge, but is rarely accessed to solve problems (Bransford, Brown & Cocking, 1999; CTGV 1991a, b, 1993a, b; Whitehead, 1929). The resulting effect of inert knowledge is that students are unable to recognize the relationships between their knowledge of facts and its use in solving authentic real-world problems. This inability to access pertinent information to solve problems results in a failure to transfer information from one context to another (Bransford et al., 1990a).

The use of video-based anchors enables teachers to use dynamic moving images and sounds to go beyond lecture or text-based instruction. Vye and colleagues (1991) suggest that the visual format may aid in the formation of more precise mental models and, as a result, increase the likelihood that learners can use their newly acquired information to solve practical problems. Additionally, video-based anchors enable teachers to provide more inclusive instruction. The use of video bypasses the text, thereby enabling both disabled and nondisabled learners to have increased access to content. Thus students who are not successful readers can be active participants in the learning process. Because of this inclusion there is greater shared understanding across students, which in turn increases opportunities for discussion and participation.

In anchoring instruction, teachers strive to develop student problem-solving skills, rather than simply asking them to memorize information that might be used at a later time, usually on a written test. Additionally, teachers expect students to use their knowledge to solve realistic problems. For example, the *Jasper Woodbury* video series (CGTV, 1992b), a series of mathematics problem-solving videos developed by CTGV, employs the anchored instruction. In one adventure of this series, students have to apply mathematical concepts and understandings to plan a lengthy boat trip between two communities while adhering to a budget. Accordingly, they must select a route between the two communities, calculate the duration of the trip, plan navigational strategies, identify refueling facilities, identify facilities to replenish supplies including food, and calculate gas consumption in order to complete the journey. In this scenario students must immediately demonstrate not only that they learned the information but that their level of understanding is such that they can use the new information to solve authentic problems.

Anchoring instruction is enhanced by the random access capabilities of videodiscs and CD-ROM technologies that allow the user to return almost instantaneously to any segment of the event or information under discussion in the classroom setting. This rapid access to information can have powerful effects on learning and cognitive development by increasing the students' opportunities for finding relevant information embedded within the context of the video presented in the laserdisc or CD-ROM format (McLarty, Goodman, Risko, Kinzer, Vye, Rowe, & Carson, 1990). The random-access feature of the technologies allows students to explore repeatedly from multiple perspectives the content presented within the video. This revisiting feature has been found to promote a higher level of analysis than a single viewing of the information (Williams Glaser et al., 1999).

The video content is selected thoughtfully to: (a) provide learners with a rich context; (b) provide a context that is shared, as all students in a classroom view the same content; and (c) generate student interest in the curriculum, while enabling them to identify and explore the learning context from many different perspectives (McLarty et al., 1990). For example, on several occasions the authors have used the film *To Kill a Mockingbird* as a video anchor to facilitate learning in social studies and literacy by students with and without disabilities (Kinzer, Singer Gabella, & Rieth, 1994; Williams Glaser et al., 1999). The film, which is set in the rural south during the Great Depression of the 1930s, provides students with a rich context and setting for the time period as they explore themes of money, power, and human relationships. One goal of the lessons is to support the development of knowledge about these themes. Initially, students explore the video using their existing knowledge as a springboard for discussions about the identified themes. The video provides a context for learning and enables students to develop a much deeper understanding of the subject matter under investigation as they engage in extensive research about the issues of civil rights and prejudice presented in the video (Williams Glaser et al., 1999).

Anchoring the instruction in the video provides students with opportunities to encounter certain contextual experiences or events that they would not encounter within more traditional instructional environments. For example, the *To Kill a Mockingbird* video anchor is especially helpful in providing opportunities for students to explore environments (e.g., a segregated courtroom, small rural towns, depressed economic times) and information that would not be easily accessible in traditional classroom settings. The video also includes a series of courtroom scenes, which serve as a context from which teachers base classroom discussions supporting students as they link new information about the rural South, the Great Depression, judicial process, and segregation to previously acquired knowledge.

The anchor also provides a focal point for class discussions and increases interactions between students and teachers. For example, during earlier classroom research, using *To Kill a Mockingbird* as an anchor the authors identified a higher number and cognitive level of interactions between teachers and students (Williams Glaser et al., 1999). Further, the authors reported that as students became expert with the anchor they began to compare events depicted in the anchor to their own experiences. The resulting discussion became much more dynamic and complex. Students used the anchor as a point of departure to ask and answer questions and discuss complex issues. They made choices regarding what information they were looking for and how they should go about finding the answers. They began seeking knowledge, asking for more information, discussing their ideas, extending the ideas of others, and going beyond the textbook. They became collaborators, and they became teachers. They did not wait for teachers to provide them with a list of facts or other related information. They made decisions on the issues they found to be most compelling, and determined the best ways to use the available resources to find the answers to the questions they posed. Almost immediately, the students began to make links between some of the issues they identified during the fall semester and the curriculum presented during the spring semester. Interestingly, in several instances, the students felt these links were important to their understanding of new information.

Anchoring instruction involves modifying the classroom environment to support more student centered learning. In this type of environment, students typically have increased opportunities to recognize, evaluate, and use a variety of resources to effectively answer questions they think are important. By allowing students to have a voice in the classroom and by providing them with opportunities to work together to solve difficult problems, they are being better prepared for life beyond the classroom.

Instruction anchored in video is designed to maximize students' attention as they engage in learning. Ideally, the video anchor is intrinsically interesting, thereby facilitating student task engagement and inquiry (Bransford et al., 1990b). Students assume responsibility for their learning as their knowledge of the anchor increases. In the *To Kill a Mockingbird* example, as students become experts with *To Kill a Mockingbird,* they begin to work in small groups on research topics of interest to them, using information they identified through research, and presenting it in the format they choose. Additionally, the anchor provides opportunities for students to acquire new knowledge about the conditions in which various concepts and facts are used (CTGV, 1992a). As students explore a task embedded in a familiar anchor, they begin to understand why their implicit knowledge is necessary, and they begin to make connections to its availability in other situations. For example, students who learned about the Great Depression in the United States through viewing and discussing content presented in *To Kill a Mockingbird* were able to identify related events that contributed to the depression in Germany following World War I.

By allowing students to generate their own paths to a solution, they become conscious, creative problem solvers (Bransford et al., 1990; CTGV, 1991, 1992a, 1992b; Vye, Row, Kinzer, & Risko, 1990). The theories that provide the underpinnings for anchoring instruction suggest that this method of instruction may be a valuable tool to mitigate the problems associated with text frequently encountered by students with disabilities. By providing novice or struggling readers with a visual representation of real world problems in context, they may be more likely to recognize characteristics and concepts that relate to teaching and learning in ways that were difficult to obtain from text alone.

In another example of anchoring instruction, Xin, Williams Glaser, and Rieth (1996) used the commercial videodisc *The Great Quake of 89* as an anchor to enhance vocabulary acquisition by a group of 10 fourth-grade students who were also enrolled part-time in a resource program for students with learning disabilities. The students received the video-based lessons for 20 minutes a day, 3 days a week, for 6 weeks. The results indicated that students increased their performance on review tests by an average of 27 percent as compared to their scores attained when non-video-based instruction was used. In addition, students reported that they preferred the video-based instruction and student task engagement rates exceeded 85 percent when anchoring instruction was used. Basically, students learned more and were most satisfied when video-based instruction was provided.

Despite the growing body of research regarding the effectiveness of anchoring instruction, some educators and researchers have raised concerns that students might "lose ground" in the basic skills if they spend more time learning how to use computer technologies and acquiring new problem-solving skills (Herman, 1988). Research investigating the use of anchors indicates, however, that students involved in multimedia intervention have performed equally well on tests of content knowledge as students in comparison traditional instructional environments (Pellegrino, Hickey, Heath, Rewey, Vye, & Cognition and Technology Group at Vanderbilt, 1992).

FOCUS ON 8.2

Identify ways that anchoring instruction would be a positive intervention for students with disabilities.

IMPLEMENTING ANCHORING INSTRUCTION

Rieth and Kinzer (2000) have described a four-phase process for implementing instructional anchors. As mentioned previously, anchoring instruction begins with a focal event or problem situation presented via a video segment or movie that provides the opportunity for students to create a mental model to facilitate learning and the development of problem-solving skills.

Phase 1: Watching the Video Anchor

The whole class watches the video together in order for all students to view the same information and to develop a shared context. Subsequently, the shared context is used as a basis for classroom discussions that provide opportunities for students to: (a) identify and define real-world problems or issues related to the video (students are asked to relate the information presented in the video to other experiences and knowledge that they have accumulated); (b) generate strategies for solving problems or addressing issues presented in the video; and (c) identify the concepts and ideas presented in the anchor. Students are not allowed to watch the video passively. They are prompted to identify and record related real-world problems and problem-solving strategies, and note concepts and ideas presented in the anchor. Students are encouraged to review segments of the video to clarify information, to ask questions, and to have discussions. Teachers report that they are teaching more effectively and that students are more deeply engaged in learning (Kinzer, Colburn, & Rieth, 2000).

Phase 2: Retelling and Segmenting

In retelling, students list events or scenes from the video that they identify as critical to their understanding of the story. These events are written on sentence strips so that when questions arise regarding the order of events, students can revisit the video as necessary and then properly reorder events. Subsequent class-wide discussions enable students to confirm conclusions, identify contradictions, and correct misconceptions about the content.

The segmenting activity is designed to develop a shared expertise in the anchor. Students construct several strategies for breaking larger chunks of video into three or four smaller segments. Prevalent segmenting strategies include: (a) identifying breaks in the video based on scene changes; (b) identifying breaks in the video based on characters' appearance within a scene; and (c) identifying breaks in the video based on shifts in the plot sequences. All segments identified as important to the students' understanding of the story are given an identifying name and listed with start and end times, and a master list of segment names and time codes is created. For example, one *To Kill a Mockingbird* video segment is labeled "The Hickory Nuts" and start and end times are listed. The entire class has an understanding of just what scene is referred to by this title and students know exactly where to locate it on the laser disc for later revisiting.

Phase 3: Characterization

For character analysis, the class is broken into small groups of approximately five students. Each group examines, in detail, one character from the story. They identify their character's basic personality traits, and the societal influences that shaped the characters' personality and behavior. Subsequently, they identify a short video clip to substantiate their analysis of the individual's character traits. Each group presents their character analysis to the class and shows a supporting clip. Afterward, students ask questions, critically reflect on their classmates' analysis, and discuss related events and actions contained in the video. Alternatively, this can be accomplished through a guided whole-class discussion with the teacher assisting the students as they consider the issues and their own interests in following a particular theme or strand.

Phase 4: Student Research

Students are divided into small groups of four or five to develop a research question around issues arising from their discussion of the anchor. The video anchor functions as a focal point as students use textbooks, reference books, photographs, electronic encyclopedias, and the Internet to acquire the information needed to answer their selected research question. Group members work to divide the workload so each member of the group contributes to the research and participates in the creation of a final multimedia presentation, where groups showcase their work and share their understanding with their classmates. The audience of peers has opportunities to applaud and consider the group's efforts in post presentation discussions.

During this phase the teachers serve as facilitators who coach students about research strategies, mediate discussion, help students link new information to previously acquired knowledge, demonstrate presentation techniques, and prompt students to build on each other's work.

Because anchoring instruction relies heavily on video and students work extensively in cooperative learning groups that place a premium on listing and participating, students with visual and auditory impairments will require scaffolding if they are to participate. For example, students with visual impairments can be paired with a peer who could provide an ongoing narration of events that are occurring on the screen to supplement information that the student acquires while listening to the movie content. This should provide sufficient scaffolding to enable students with visual disabilities to effectively participate in the subsequent discussions and benefit from anchoring instruction. Relatedly, students who are deaf or hearing impaired can watch the film with their classmates and with the assistance of an interpreter and/or through their lip-reading skills, participate actively in the subsequent discussions and research activities.

FOCUS ON 8.3

Choose a movie and character that you are familiar with and create a character map.

DEVELOPING ANCHORS

The 4D Model (Thiagarajan, Semmel, & Semmel, 1974) for instructional development is one approach to developing anchors. The model includes four stages of instructional development: (a) define, (b) design, (c) develop, and (d) disseminate.

The first stage is to *define* the instructional content to be taught. In the *To Kill a Mockingbird* example the researchers centered instruction around the concepts of fairness and justice. Thus, the initial steps involved defining the aspects of fairness and justice that we wanted to teach. Defining also involves specifying the desired instructional outcomes. In the previously cited *To Kill a Mockingbird* example, some of the desired instructional outcomes included higher-level student questions and responses; that is, interpretive questions and responses rather than factual questions and factual responses (Williams Glaser et al., 1999).

The second stage in developing an anchor is to *design* the anchor and the related learning activities. The first step is to select the video anchor based on the instructional goals, objectives, and intended learner outcomes. There are two primary strategies for identifying video for developing anchors. The first is to use commercially available video (e.g., *To Kill a Mockingbird*), that can be implemented intact, without any modifications, or repurposed by selecting vignettes that more closely meet the instruction goals and objectives. The second strategy is to custom design and develop video that might be either staged or captured spontaneously on site. Typically, the identification and selection of the video anchor is one of the more time-consuming tasks since the anchor must be a rich source of content and concepts. Once the anchor has been selected, the next task is to develop related learning activities including activities, projects, work sheets, and curricular materials.

During the third stage, *develop*, prototypical materials and lessons are developed and formatively and summatively evaluated. Once sample lessons are scripted, they are shared with content experts (e.g., fellow teachers, curriculum coordinators) for evaluation. The evaluation helps ensure content validity, clarity of directions, and the richness and high interest of the instructional activities. Subsequently, lessons are implemented and evaluated with the target population. Attainment or nonattainment of prescribed student outcomes is used to guide any modifications of the anchoring instructional unit.

Once the anchors and related materials have been evaluated extensively and found to be effective, they are ready for dissemination to other professionals. Therefore, in the final stage, *disseminate,* the anchors and related materials are shared with other educators. Dissemination occurs in multiple formats, including distribution by publishers, descriptions provided in professional journals, professional presentations at conferences and/or staff development activities, and sharing with state and/or local education agencies. The goal is to share the information as broadly as possible with professional audiences.

FOCUS ON 8.4

As a group, select two themes (e.g., fairness and justice) and identify a movie that you could use to focus on those themes. Design an activity to help students develop their understanding of the two themes.

BENEFITS OF ANCHORING INSTRUCTION

Overall, there is research that provides testimonial to improved educational outcomes associated with the use of anchoring instruction (Bransford et al., 1999). While most of the evidence relates to general education student outcomes, Kinzer and colleagues (1994), Xin and colleagues (1996) and Williams Glaser and colleagues (1999) have provided evidence of improved outcomes in classrooms that include students with disabilities. The primary benefits of anchoring instruction include the (a) contextualization learning; (b) promotion of learning; (c) active involvement in learning activities; (d) social construction of knowledge; (e) development of problem-solving skills; (f) enhancement of knowledge transfer; and (g) promotion of student ownership of knowledge (Bransford et al., 1990a; CGTV, 1990, 1992a, b, 1993a, b; Kinzer & Rieth, 1999).

Anchoring instruction features contextualized learning. For example, *To Kill a Mockingbird* includes a visual portrayal of the rural South during the Great Depression. The video provides a rich portrait that enables students to develop mental models about the effects of an economic depression on people and their daily lives. The scenes in the video provide a unifying context for all the students, from which teachers can base classroom discussion as they help students link new information to their existing knowledge.

Generally, research findings have indicated that student learning has improved with the anchoring of instruction (Bransford et al., 1990a, b; Kinzer et al. 1994; Williams Glaser et al., 1999). For example, Williams Glaser and colleagues (1999) reported that the number of daily interactions recorded between students and teachers during anchoring instruction in an eighth-grade classroom substantially exceeded the number recorded during a baseline period when students received more traditional didactic instruction. The authors indicated that the anchoring instruction intervention produced broad effects since, regardless of the specific anchored instructional activity, the overall effect was to increase opportunities for students to participate actively in instructional activities. In addition, the authors reported that the intervention also resulted in an increase in the quality of questions that were being asked by the classroom teachers during large group discussions.

As stated previously, anchoring instruction focuses on the student as the focal point of the teaching and learning process (Barnes, 1989; Campione & Brown, 1990; Wang & Palinscar, 1989). Students are responsible for investigating problem situations. They are expected to offer ideas, raise questions, conduct research, synthesize information, and develop presentations to be shared with their peers rather than having the teacher perform these activities for them. Concurrently, the role of the teacher changes from being the central purveyor of knowledge to that of a facilitator who asks questions, provides direction, and generally encourages students in their learning.

Anchoring instruction focuses on the social construction of knowledge where learners construct knowledge as they continually reorganize connections between existing information to make sense of new information and new experiences. As students encounter information that is inconsistent with existing information, they must ask questions and seek answers to resolve conflicts. They use this information to build or strengthen their knowledge.

In solving problems that are multifaceted, students have opportunities to transfer knowledge across subject matter areas and across problem-solving situations. They learn that knowledge is not static nor subject matter areas compartmentalized. They learn that knowledge is to be applied to solve problems in daily living rather than simply memorized for retrieval at some later point in time.

Finally, anchoring instruction empowers the learner. Students have choices in selecting and conducting research projects, they have input regarding interpretation of events and activities. These opportunities to choose support students' development of a sense of ownership and motivation. For example, the authors have repeatedly observed high rates of engagement on the part of students participating in anchored lessons. This is illustrated by a recent experience where a class of ninth-grade students worked diligently on their group research projects throughout every class period for a two-week period. They came in at lunch and stayed after school to work. In fact, they finished on the last day of school, voluntarily choosing to continue to work long after fellow ninth graders had stopped working on school work and were waiting out the final few days watching movies or packing up classrooms. Additionally, we have repeatedly interviewed students who were having difficulty in school and who were often truant, but who attended classes featuring anchoring instruction despite their absence in their other classes. These examples provide concrete references to the power of anchoring instruction to promote student engagement and sense of ownership of knowledge.

FOCUS ON 8.5

What are some ways that a classroom teacher could be a better facilitator using these principles?

CHALLENGES OF ANCHORING INSTRUCTION

While there are many benefits associated with anchoring instruction it is not without challenges to teachers and students. The challenges that must be negotiated include: (a) role changes for the teacher and the students; (b) the time required to develop anchoring instructional units; (c) the content and video support necessary to assist teachers who opt to use anchoring instruction and identification of products/techniques that enable those with certain disabilities so they are not left with others operating equipment for them; (d) access to materials necessary to develop anchoring instruction units, and (e) strategies to assess group and individual student performance.

As stated previously, the role of teachers and students changes during anchoring instruction. Teachers are asked to relinquish the role of central purveyor of knowledge, while students are given greater responsibility for their learning. The challenges for teachers are associated with relinquishing their pivotal and controlling role as they learn to facilitate and coach students who will have more responsibility for actively participating in the learning process. For teachers who feel that they are successful in their role in providing didactic instruction, this is a very difficult task. They find it more difficult to ask students to consider the possibilities rather than simply telling them the answer (Williams Glaser et al., 1999). For their part, some students find it difficult to become more responsible for assuming a more active role in their learning. They have difficulty adjusting to their greater responsibility and increased participation in their learning. To date, the authors have found that staff development training for teachers and modeling and support have been beneficial strategies to counteract this challenge.

A second challenge is the considerable time required to develop anchoring instructional units. The time requirement falls into two categories. The first is related to the development of the curricular materials required to implement anchoring instruction. This is a process that requires planning to identify the goals and objectives of the instructional unit and to identify the outcomes expected of the students. Once the planning is completed, lessons must be developed, implemented, evaluated, and modified. Materials and worksheets must be developed to compliment and supplement the material presented in the video. For example, materials are required to facilitate characterization. In some cases this involves copying or scanning images and designing work activities for participating student groups. All of these activities add to an already full school day.

In addition, the selection and location of appropriate video content can be a time-consuming activity. For example, a decision must be made to select available video that may or may not need to be repurposed. The video must fit the instructional goals and objectives and facilitate the attainment of prescribed student outcomes. In the event that new video must be developed, the task becomes increasingly time consuming. To date, the most effective strategy for counteracting the time required to develop new anchors has been collaboration among a group of teachers interested in implementing instructional anchors. The participation of multiple teachers tends to distribute the time across the group and reduce the response cost for individual teachers.

Relatedly, teachers also have encountered difficulty gaining access to the Internet and materials including video, video equipment, and computer equipment. Teachers must have access to video anchors. Access is made more manageable with the use of commercially available video (e.g., *To Kill a Mockingbird*). In addition, teachers must have access to equipment to show the video. Access to the technology necessary to implement anchoring instruction can vary across schools and classrooms and can become an obstacle that delays or prevents implementation of anchoring instruction. In some school sites access is highly competitive and therefore teachers must wait their turn, which can produce a slowdown in the delivery of the target instructional units. Access to the Internet is another issue that must be resolved if computers are to become integral to teaching and learning. In some cases teachers don't have access to telephones in their classrooms (OTA, 1995), making Internet access through modems impossible. To solve these challenges, some schools have raised funds to increase the pace of wiring the school for Internet access. Some schools have sought funds for computer equipment through corporate sponsors or federal and/or state government agencies, while others have identified the development of technology infrastructure to be a superordinate priority and appropriated funds to purchase needed hardware and software.

To sustain teachers through the process of integrating technology, it is essential that they receive support from colleagues, administrators, and students (Colburn, 2000). The implementation of instructional innovations frequently creates resistance (Fullan & Stiegelbauer, 1991). One strategy for reducing resistance is to provide support through staff development activities that involve demonstrations, opportunities for discussion, and the identification of resources to help implementation. Access to a content and/or technology support person is essential. It has been our experience that teachers will abandon technology as they encounter problems with the operation of the equipment or with software (Rieth, Bahr, Polsgrove, Okolo, & Eckert 1987). Access to equipment in good working order is critical to successful implementation (Colburn, 2000).

Because anchoring instruction relies heavily on video and small group discussions, teachers may be required to scaffold instruction to ensure the participation of students with visual and/or auditory impairments. Scaffolding may require that the teacher arrange for an interpreter for a student with an auditory impairment or arrange for a peer to assist a student with a visual impairment as they watch the movie that is serving as the anchor. While these activities appear reasonably simple for the teacher to accomplish, they add to the overall response cost associated with anchoring instruction and therefore cannot be casually dismissed as considerations.

The final challenge to anchoring instruction is related to evaluating student performance. In anchoring instruction, students frequently work in small groups. Therefore, in order to assign grades the teacher must not only evaluate the group product but also determine the contribution of individual group members. Relatedly, since many projects result in multimedia products that involve text, graphics, sound, and video, there are added assessment considerations. To date, a series of strategies have been initiated to address this challenge. One strategy involves teachers frequently observing and engaging in discussions with groups to obtain a sense of the contributions of individual members. Another strategy involves teachers and students generating rubrics that are used in the evaluation process (Prestidge & Williams Glaser, 2000). A third strategy—the use of portfolio assessment, where students compile dossiers that include a series of products that they develop—has also experienced increasingly widespread use in schools to address this challenge.

In closing we will share observations provided by a teacher who implemented anchoring instruction. The comments vividly convey the teachers' perceptions about the realities of implementing this instructional innovation and provide insight into its potential sustainability. While discussing the use of *To Kill a Mockingbird* to anchor instruction the teacher indicated that the video promoted extensive active student participation as they asked lots of questions about the content and its meaning. The teacher also reported "students demonstrated that they could work together, support and rely on each other," and "they genuinely enjoyed helping each other." In addition, to the high rates of student engagement and interactions, the teacher also reported that the video enabled students to attain a higher level of content understanding, to better synthesize information, and to critically evaluate content. The video reportedly enabled students to better understand the plot and the storyline and instilled confidence that they had a "chunk of information they could rely on, feel good about, refer back to." The video reportedly enabled students to gain a much richer understanding of the poverty and racial discrimination that occurred during the Depression of the 1930s. "The research piece made them think beyond the text as they explored various real-life applications." Finally, the teacher was amazed with the students' dogged efforts to complete their projects at the end of the school year. "I have never seen kids still so focused this late in the year. By this time they usually have shut down; they are finished for the year. Having them work this hard is really, really impressive" (See Personal Perspective 8.1.).

FOCUS ON 8.6

Select two challenges to the use of anchoring instruction and describe how you could address them.

SUMMARY

This chapter described anchoring instruction as an approach for providing more student-centered learning in the classroom. Anchoring instruction was introduced

---

PERSONAL PERSPECTIVE 8.1

Interviews were conducted with a ninth-grade language arts instructor who spent two years implementing anchoring instruction in four ninth-grade language arts classes that included five or more students with disabilities per class.

What did the movie do for the students that they couldn't get from the book?
I know they understood plot, theme, and setting, but they missed out on irony and fore-shadowing. Overall they got a lot out of it. They provided a lot of thoughtful comments. In particular, the research piece made them think beyond the text. A lot of extension there—they had to go beyond the book to explore various real-life concrete things. When they watched the video there was a lot of "I didn't know that," and "This has never occurred to me before."

Did students participate in group discussion?
They all participated and they were all invested in it. The students didn't come in to class working well together. They surprised me by working so well together. The small group work was a change for me—it was really cool—I was very impressed with the outcomes, which seemed to be due to the strength of the assignments. Students weren't isolated; they integrated and worked together. They had to share, get consensus, then would go off on their research assignments and bring information back to the group. With the small group activities they all had a chunk of information that they could rely on, feel good about, refer back to, even when faced with something new—they felt they could fall back on the video. For all of them to have that confidence was amazing to me.

How did you feel about your participation in anchoring instruction?
There were reactions I did not expect. Certainly I did expect the excitement and the will-ingness to try. However, I didn't have to cajole them to participate. They understood the big picture—they were willing to take risks. Based on their prior work, I thought of the students in particular ways. I thought I knew their limitations. The anchoring instruction threw out a lot of preconceived notions that I had about what the students were capable of.

---

with a description that linked this instructional approach to technology literacy and cognitive science with an emphasis on student-centered learning involving active participation in the construction of new knowledge in a real-life problem context. Anchoring instruction was defined as an instructional technique that involves a problem situation situated in a video context that includes opportunities for students to reflect on the problem and pose solutions. Implementing anchoring instruction was described as a four-phase process including watching the video anchor, retelling and segmenting events, characterization, and student research. These phases span a period of time as students engage in a variety of whole and small group activities with an emphasis on developing critical thinking and research skills. The process of developing anchors was described via the 4D Model, which includes four stages: define, design, develop, and disseminate. Finally, the benefits and chal-lenges of anchoring instruction were presented. The benefits include contextual-ized learning, promotion of learning, active involvement, social construction of knowledge, development of problem-solving skills, enhancement of transfer knowledge, and promotion of student ownership of knowledge. The challenges of changes in teacher roles, time required to implement, access to necessary materials, content and video support, and assessment strategies were duly noted, yet the information presented in this chapter suggests that teachers find the benefits of anchoring instruction outweigh the challenges and will make the effort to integrate the approach into their teaching.

DISCUSSION QUESTIONS

1. Explain the theoretical basis for anchoring instruction.
2. Define anchoring instruction.
3. Explain how to develop an anchor.
4. Describe the steps in implementing anchoring instruction.
5. Explain the benefits associated with anchoring instruction.
6. Explain the challenges associated with anchoring instruction.

REFERENCES

Airasian, P., & Walsh, M. (1997). Constructivist cautions. *Phi Delta Kappan* 78 (6) 444–49.

Barnes, D., Britton, J., & Torbe, M. (1990). *Language, the learner and the school* (4th ed.). Portsmouth, NH: Boynton/Cook, Heinemann.

Barnes, H. (1989). Structuring knowledge for beginning teachers. In M. C. Reynolds (Ed.), *Knowledge base for the beginning teacher* (pp. 13–21). Oxford: Pergamon Press.

Berryman, S. E. (1993). Learning for the workplace. In L. Darling-Hammond (Ed.), *Review of Research in Education Vol. 19* (pp. 343–401). Washington, DC: American Educational Research Association.

Boehrer, J., and Linsky, M. (1990). Teaching with cases: Learning to question. In M. D. Svinicki (Ed.), *The changing face of college teaching* (pp. 41–57). San Francisco: Jossey-Bass

Bransford, J. D., Brown, A. L., & Cocking, R. R. (1999). *How people learn.* Washington, DC: National Academy Press.

Bransford, J., Kinzer, C., Risko, V., Rowe, D., & Vye, N. (1989). Designing invitation to thinking: Some initial thoughts. In S. McCormick & J. Zutell (Eds.), *Cognitive and social perspectives for literacy research and instruction* (pp. 35–54). Chicago: The National Reading Conference.

Bransford, J., Sherwood, R., & Hasselbring, T. (1988). The video revolution and its effects on development; some initial thoughts. In G. Forman & P. B. Pufall (Eds.), *Constructivism in the Computer Age* (pp. 173–201). Hillsdale, NJ: Lawrence Erlbaum Associates.

Bransford, J. D., Sherwood, R. D., Hasselbring, T. S., Kinzer, C. K., & Williams, S. M. (1990a). Anchored instruction: Why we need it and how technology can help. In D. Nix & R. Spiro (Eds.), *Cognition, education and multimedia: Exploring ideas in high technology* (pp. 115–141). Hillsdale, NJ: Lawrence Erlbaum Associates.

Bransford, J., D., Vye, N., Kinzer, C., & Risko, V. (1990b). Teaching thinking and content knowledge: Toward an integrated approach. In B. F. Jones & L. Idol (Eds.), *Dimensions of thinking and cognitive instruction* (pp. 381–415). Hillsdale, NJ: Lawrence Erlbaum Associates.

Campione, J. C., & Brown, A., L., (1990). Guided learning and transfer: Implications for approaches to assessment. In N. Fredrickson, R. Glaser, A. Lesgold, & M. Shafto (Eds.), *Diagnostic monitoring of skill and knowledge acquisition.* Hillsdale, NJ: Lawrence Erlbaum Associates.

Cognition and Technology Group at Vanderbilt. (1990). Anchored instruction and its relationship to situated cognition. *Educational Researcher, 19* (6), 2–10.

Cognition and Technology Group at Vanderbilt. (1991a). Educational Technology. Technology and the design of generative learning environments. 31, 34–40.

Cognition and Technology Group at Vanderbilt. (1991b). Video environments for connecting mathematics, science, and other disciplines. Paper presented at Wingspan Conference on Integrated Science and Mathematics Teaching and Learning, Racine, WI.

Cognition and Technology Group at Vanderbilt. (1992a). Anchored instruction in science and mathematics: Theoretical basis, developmental projects, and initial research findings. In R. Duschl & R. Hamilton (Eds.), *Philosophy of science, cognition psychology, and educational theory and practice* (pp. 244–273). Albany, NY: SUNY Press.

Cognition and Technology Group at Vanderbilt. (1992b). The Jasper experiment: An exploration of issues in learning and instructional design. *Educational Technology Research and Development, 40,* (1), 65–80.

Cognition and Technology Group at Vanderbilt. (1993a). Anchored instruction and situated cognition revisited. *Educational Technology, 33,* 52–70.

Cognition and Technology Group at Vanderbilt. (1993b). Toward integrated curricula: Possibilities form anchored instruction. In M. Rabinowitz (Ed.) *Cognitive science: Foundations of instruction* (pp. 33–55). Hillsdale, NJ: Lawrence Erlbaum Associates.

Cognition and Technology Group at Vanderbilt. (1994). From visual word problems to learning communities: Changing conceptions of cognitive research. In K. McGilly (Ed.), *Classroom lessons: Integrating cognitive theory and classroom practice* (pp. 157–200). Cambridge, MA: MIT Press.

Colburn, L. K. (2000). *An analysis of teacher change and required supports as technology is integrated into classroom instruction.* Unpublished dissertation, Vanderbilt University, Nashville, TN.

Educational Testing Service Policy Information Center Report. (1996). *Computers and classrooms: The status of technology in U.S. schools.* On-line: http://www.ets.org/ research/pic/cc sum.html.

Feng, Y. (1995). *Some thoughts about applying constructivist theories of learning to guide instruction.* Proceedings of the International Conference of the Society for Information Technology and Teacher Education (SITE). San Antonio, Texas, March 22–25, 1995. (ERIC Document Reproduction Service No. ED 381 148).

Fullan, M. G., & Stiegelbauer, S. (1991). *The new meaning of educational change* (2nd ed.). New York: Teachers College Press.

Goldberg, B., & Richards, J. (1995). Leveraging technology for reform: Changing schools and communities into learning organizations. *Educational Technology, 35* (5) 5–16.

Hayworth, J. G. and Conrad, C. F. (1990) Curricular transformation: Traditional and emerging voices. *Curriculum in transition: Perspectives on the undergraduate experience.* Needham, MA: Ginn Press.

Hudspeth, D., & Knirk, F. G. (1989). Case study materials: Strategies for design and use. *Performance Improvement Quarterly* 2, 30–41.

Jonassen, D. (1995). Supporting communities of learners with technology: A vision for integrating technology with learning in schools. *Educational Technology* July, 60–64.

King, A. (1994). Guiding knowledge construction in classroom: Effects of teaching children how to question and how to explain. *American Educational Research Journal, 31* (2), 338–368.

Kinzer, C. K., Colburn, L. K., & Rieth, H. J. (2000). *Evaluating the use and implementation of anchored instruction to enhance the literacy and social studies skills of mildly disabled learners: Year 1 Progress Report.* Washington, DC: Office of Special Education Programs.

Kinzer, C. K., & Rieth, H. J. (1999). *Evaluating the use and implementation of anchored instruction to enhance the literacy and social studies skills of mildly disabled learners.* Washington, DC: Grant funded by Office of Special Education Programs.

Kinzer, C. K., Singer Gabella, M., and Rieth, H. (1994). An argument for using multimedia and anchored instruction to facilitate mildly disabled students' learning of literacy and social studies. *Technology and Disability, 3* (2), 117–128.

Loveless, T. (1996). *Why aren't computers used more in schools?* Faculty research working paper series R96-03. (ERIC Document Reproduction Service No. ED 415 831).

Lunenburg, F., & Irby, B. (1998). *Goals 2000 and integrated technology: A national status report.* Paper presented at the Annual Meeting of the American Education Research Association, San Diego April 12–17, 1998.

McLarty, K., Goodman, J. R., Risko, V. J., Kinzer, C. K., Vye, N. J., Rowe, D. W., & Carson, J. L. (1990). Implementing anchored instruction guiding principles for curriculum development. In J. Zutell & S. McCormick (eds.), *Literacy theory and research: Analysis from multiple perspectives* (39th NRC Yearbook, pp. 109–120). Chicago: National Reading Conference.

Means, B. (1994). Using technology to advance education reform. In B. Means, (Ed.), *Technology and education reform: The reality behind the promise* (pp. 1–21). San Francisco: Jossey Bass.

Means, B., & Olson, K. (1995). *Technology's role within constructivist classrooms.* Paper presented at the annual meeting of the American Educational Research Association. San Francisco. (ERIC Document Reproduction Service No. ED 383 283).

Meister, G. R. (1984). *Successful integration of microcomputers in an elementary school.* (ERIC Document Reproduction Service No. ED 256 059).

Moursand, D. (1997). The growth of instructional technology. *Learning and Leading with Technology, 25*(2), 4–5.

National Education Goals Panel. (1998). *Data for the National Education Goals Report Volume One: National Data.* Washington, DC: U.S. Government Printing Office.

Office of Technology Assessment. (1995). *Teachers and technology: Making the connection.* (OTA-CHR-616). Washington, DC: U.S. Government Printing Office.

Ornstein, A. C. (1995). Beyond effective teaching. *Peabody Journal of Education, 70*(2), 2–23.

Panyan, M., Hummel, J., Steeves, J., McPherson, S., Givner, C., & Nunn, J. (1989). *Technology Integration Project: The evaluation of the integration of technology for instructing handicapped students (elementary level).* Center for Technology and Human Disabilities: A joint project of the Maryland State Department of Education and Johns Hopkins University. U.S. Department of Education Contract #300-86-0125.

Pellegrino, J. W., Hickey, D., Heath, A., Rewey, K., Vye, N. J., & Cognition and Technology Group at Vanderbilt. (1992). *Assessing the outcomes of an innovative instructional program: The 1990–1991 implementation of the "Adventures of Jasper Woodbury."* Technical report. Nashville, TN: Learning Technology Center, Vanderbilt University.

President's Committee of Advisors on Science and Technology. (1997). *Report to the President on the use of technology to strengthen K-12 education in the United States.* Washington, DC: Executive Office of the President of the United States.

Prestidge, L., & Williams Glaser, C. (2000). Authentic assessment: Employing appropriate tools for evaluating students' work in 21st century classrooms. *Intervention in School and Clinic 35*(3), 178–82.

Resnick, L. B. (1987). *Education and learning to think.* Washington, DC: National Academy Press.

Rieth, H. J., Bahr, C., Polsgrove, L., Okolo, C., & Eckert, R. (1987). The effects of microcomputers on the secondary special education classroom ecology. *Journal of Special Education Technology, 8* (4), 36–47.

Rieth, H. J., & Kinzer, C. K. (2000). Multimedia-based anchored instruction. In D. D. Smith (Ed.) *Introduction to special education: Teaching in an age of challenge.* (4th ed.). Boston: Allyn and Bacon.

Roblyer, M., Edwards, J., & Havriluk, A. (1997). *Integrating educational technology into teaching.* Upper Saddle River, NJ: Merrill.

Salomon, G. (1993). No distribution without individuals' cognition. In G. Salomon (Ed.), *Distributed cognitions: Psychological and educational considerations* (pp. 111–138), New York: Cambridge University Press.

Scott, T., Cole, M., and Engel, M. (1992). Computers and education: A cultural constructivist perspective. In G. Grant (Ed.), *Review of Research in Education, Vol 18* (pp. 191–251). Washington, DC: American Educational Research Association.

Thiagarajan, S., Semmel, D. S., & Semmel, M. I. (1974). *Instructional development for training teachers of exceptional children: A sourcebook.* Reston, VA: Council for Exceptional Children.

Vye, N. J., Rowe, D. W., Kinzer, C. K., & Risko, V. J. (1990). *Effects of anchored instruction for teaching social studies: Enhancing comprehension of setting information.* Paper presented at the meeting of the American Educational Research Association, Boston.

Vye, N. J., Sharp, D. M., McCabe, K., & Bransford, J. D. (1991). Commentary. In B. Means, C. Chelmer, & M. Knapp (Eds.), *Teaching advanced skills to at-risk students* (pp. 54–67). San Francisco: Jossey Bass.

Walberg, H. J. (1991) Productive teaching and instruction. In H. C. Waxman & H. J. Walberg (Eds.), *Effective teaching: Current research* (pp. 33–62). Berkeley, CA: McCutchan Publishing.

Wang, M. C., & Palincsar, A. S. (1989). Teaching students to assume an active role in their learning. In M. C. Reynolds (Ed.), *Knowledge base for the beginning teacher* (pp. 71–84). Oxford: Pergamon Press.

Wang, M. C., & Walberg, H. J. (1991). Teaching and educational effectiveness: Research synthesis and consensus from the field. In H. C. Waxman & H. J. Walberg (Eds.), *Effective teaching: Current research* (pp. 81–104). Berkeley, CA: McCutchan Publishing.

Whitehead, A. N. (1929). *The aims of education and other essays.* New York: Macmillan.

Williams Glaser, C., Rieth, H. J., Kinzer, C. K., Colburn, L. K., & Peter, J. (1999). A description of the impact of multimedia anchored instruction on classroom interactions. *Journal of Special Education Technology, 14*(2), 27–43.

Willoughby, S. S. (1990). *Mathematics in a changing world.* Alexandria, VA: Association for Supervision and Curriculum Development.

Xin, F., Williams Glaser, C., & Rieth, H. J. (1996). Multimedia reading: Using anchored instruction and video technology in vocabulary lessons. *Teaching Exceptional Children, 29*(2), 45–49.

CHAPTER NINE

ASSISTIVE TECHNOLOGY DEVICES TO ENHANCE INDEPENDENT LIVING

CHAPTER AT A GLANCE

INTRODUCTION TO INDEPENDENT LIVING
- Personal Perspective 9.1

DEVICES FOR DAILY LIFE
- Focus on 9.1

SWITCHES AND SCANNING
- Focus on 9.2

ENVIRONMENTAL CONTROL UNITS
- Focus on 9.3

ACCESS TO MANAGEMENT DEVICES
- Focus on 9.4

MOBILITY
- Focus on 9.5
- Personal Perspective 9.2

OBJECTIVES

1. Explain what "independent living" means.
2. Describe ways in which assistive technology adaptations can be used to promote independence in daily living activities.
3. Describe switches and scanning and provide examples of when they can be used.
4. Describe environmental control unit systems and provide examples of how they are used in homes, work, and school.
5. Explain how assistive technology adaptations can be used for management purposes.
6. Describe the role of federal legislation in promoting independence and identify environmental accessibility issues that must be addressed.

■　■　■　■　■　■

MAKING CONNECTIONS

Think back to Chapter 2 and the purpose of assistive technology, that is, to promote independence. Consider ways from the content you have read so far that assistive technology enables people to be independent. Identify in your own life how you live independent of others and the impact of losing your independence.

INTRODUCTION TO INDEPENDENT LIVING

Individuals with disabilities have a right to live independently and experience full integration into society. Being able to live independently is fundamental to life. For example, independent living skills are identified in the adaptive areas (e.g., communication, self-care, home-living, social, community use, self-direction, health and safety, leisure, work) of the most recent definition of mental retardation (Luckasson et al., 1992). Skills such as caring for one's personal needs, engaging in recreational activities, and being able to go to work are activities that empower people and make them independent of others.

Assistive technology is intended to promote independence and enable users to access their environments and the associated tasks. Maintaining control over and having choices is a critical feature of independent living. Individuals with disabilities now have more ability to engage in independent living with the increased availability of AT devices and services.

Independent living means "control over one's life based on the choice of acceptable options that minimize reliance on others in making decisions and in performing everyday activities" (Frieden, Richards, Cole, & Bailey as cited in Nosek, 1992, p. 103). Individuals who possess independent living skills are more empowered than those who lack these abilities. Independent living skills involve mobility (in the home and within the community, including the use of public transportation), activities of daily living (grooming, eating, dressing), use of personal assistants (i.e., attendants), communication, work, and use of leisure time (Nosek, 1992).

In many cases, people with disabilities lack opportunities to exercise choice and control over many parts of their lives. When people do not have these opportunities they may remain or become helpless and dependent on others. Making choices and having some control in one's life is very important for achieving quality of life for persons with disabilities (Gardner, 1990; Schalock & Kiernan, 1990). For example, some adults with disabilities live in group homes, which provide treatment and supervision (O'Brien, 1991). Typically, their daily schedules, activities, meals, and bedtimes are managed by professionally approved caretakers. Unfortunately, choice and environmental control may be limited (O'Brien, 1991). If independence is the ultimate goal for individuals with disabilities, then procedures and support systems must be in place to promote independent living skills and the ability to make choices (Mithaug & Hanawalt, 1978). In this chapter, we discuss independent living needs and considerations for promoting independent living. We talk about environmental controls, switches, and organizational devices. We include in this chapter in a Personal Perspective by Dr. Peg Nosek (Personal Perspective 9.1). We believe that Dr. Nosek's reflections convey the spirit of this chapter.

DEVICES FOR DAILY LIFE

Independent living involves performing the activities and tasks associated with daily life. Very often individuals with physical disabilities, sensory impairments, and cognitive challenges find some of these activities challenging; assistive technology devices help promote independence and provide choices for decision making across environments and setting demands. Most AT devices for individuals with physical disabilities focus on adapting the reach necessary to do a task, adapting devices for grasping and manipulation, making two-handed activities into one-handed activities, and increasing the pressure exerted by one's hands (Cook & Hussey, 1995). To be independent to the maximum extent possible, people must be able to care for their own needs at home and school in the areas of eating and food preparation, dressing, grooming, and safety. Examples of devices are explained for different activities related to daily life for home, school, work, and leisure.

Eating and Food Preparation

There are many types of simple AT adaptations that can be used to promote independence. For example, to enable people to manage eating, handles on utensils can be built up or handles can be angled to facilitate grasping and manipulation. Suction devices can be added to the bottom of plates to prevent them from moving and to provide stability and sides of dishes can be built up for easier scooping. Drinking devices include cups with covers to prevent spilling and handles to help with grasping. Preschool and schoolage students are taught how to use these devices as part of their total curriculum in self-help to foster independence in eating across the lifespan.

Food preparation can be accomplished through a one-handed can opener, mechanical "reachers" to get items off shelves, jar openers, and bowls with suction devices to prevent spilling. Other devices are available that help with daily household tasks. For instance, North Coast Medical provides a variety of functional adaptations for tasks. Their adaptations or devices include an adjustable gripping tool to grasp plugs and tops on jars, door knob turns, which can be adapted with easy-to-open handles that are pushed down to turn the door knob, a key turner with a large handle for improving leverage, and long-handled brooms and dustpans to minimize bending.

Other helpful kitchen devices for individuals who have low vision or who are blind include color-coded measuring devices and speaking liquid level indicators, respectively (Independent Living Aids). Also, high-contrast cutting boards, spatulas

PERSONAL PERSPECTIVE 9.1

Dr. Margaret (Peg) A. Nosek received a Ph.D. in Rehabilitation Research and a Master of Arts in Rehabilitation Counseling from the University of Texas, Austin, and a Master of Arts in Music from Case Western Reserve University. She is currently a professor and executive director of the Center for Research on Women with Disabilities in the Department of Physical Medicine and Rehabilitation at Baylor College of Medicine. She is an internationally recognized authority on women with disabilities and independent living for persons with disabilities. She has done considerable research and writing on developments in public policy that affect the ability of people with disabilities to live independently in the community. She is recognized as one of the first to apply scientific methodologies to the study of the health of women with disabilities and the independence of people with disabilities. More than $6 million has been awarded by the National Institutes of Health, Centers for Disease Control and Prevention, National Institute on Disability and Rehabilitation Research, and various private foundations to support her research, with another almost $5 million funding for projects she has done in collaboration with other researchers. Dr. Nosek's accomplishments are reflected in her 54 articles published in refereed academic journals, 18 chapters in academic textbooks, over 100 presentations at national conferences of scholarly organizations, and many presentations at international conferences outside of the United States. Dr. Nosek is the recipient of numerous awards for her research and advocacy by local, state, and national organizations. As a person with a severe physical disability, she has been both a pioneer and an activist in the disability rights movement, including vigorously supporting passage of the Americans with Disabilities Act. The President's Committee on Employment of People with Disabilities has honored her as a "Disability Patriot."

Tell our readers about your memories of your childhood years and how assistive devices played a role in your development.
I was diagnosed at the age of two with spinal muscular atrophy, which is a progressive neuromuscular disorder that results in slow loss of muscle function. As a child, I began walking with a waddling gate. Walking became more difficult for me as I grew older; I started using a wheelchair for mobility in the 4th grade, at which time I was also diagnosed with scoliosis. Because of a lack of arm strength, I was never able to propel the chair independently. This limited my ability to move around my environment and explore. I think it is absolutely critical for kids to be able to explore so they can learn about boundaries. A lot of kids aren't mobile right from the start. I was lucky because I could get around during my early years, but I was not mobile at a critical time in my life, adolescence. I even had to be carried in and out of my own house. I started acting out a little in order to draw people toward me because I couldn't get around. I used humor so that people would like to be around me. I didn't get my first electric wheelchair until I was 25. That's why I love seeing little kids in power wheelchairs. It's an equalizer, a liberator. For the first time I could go somewhere without people knowing where I was going. I could take off and explore my city. If I was at a party and someone was boring me, I could actually leave. I didn't have to wait for someone interesting to come up to me and talk. I could go find them. Having mobility impacted my personal life, my social life, and my self-esteem. I could actually take risks—it was exhilarating!

(continued)

As an adult, you have traveled considerably in your role as professional and advocate. Discuss some of the issues that have arisen with regard to assistive technology use as you have traveled about.

When I am at home, I have access to everything I need. Everything in my house is set at my comfort level, both physically and emotionally. When I travel, the need for a personal assistant goes way up. I need two assistants, one for my daily needs, and one to make up for the technology I can't take with me. I can't use airport wheelchairs because of my unique seating and positioning needs. When I first started traveling with my power chair, it was almost always damaged when I arrived at my destination. The airlines just weren't equipped to deal with heavy power chairs. One time my chair fell off the transport truck on the way to the plane and was crushed like a coke can. There was over $5,000 worth of damage! When I got to my destination, they brought the chair to me and said, "Here it is." But the airlines have made some strides in recent years. Now they have people who listen to me and believe me when I say something. Also, most airlines have aisle chairs for bathroom needs.

How have your daily living needs changed as you've gotten older, and how have your assistive technology needs also changed over time?

When I was young, my parents used a travel chair with four little wheels to get me around. As I got older, I had a much better chair that gave me the support my body needs. As I got weaker, I needed more assistive technology, like reaching devices. I depend on my computer for my productivity. I just can't imagine living without a computer. The benefits of computer development are phenomenal. Now that I use a ventilator, I depend on technology even more. The precautions, backup systems, that's all new. So it's an interesting progression of technology in my life.

You have been a strong advocate for many years for disability rights. How do you see assistive technology fitting into the advocacy discussion?

In my opinion, assistive technology equals liberation. Imagine life without it—I would be dead or severely limited or bed-bound. But many people are unserved or underserved. People who are poor, people who don't have insurance, older people, people who don't speak English and don't have access to this kind of information all have problems getting AT devices and services. To me, it's very important for people to accept their disability and to get connected to the service delivery systems. I count my blessings that I'm connected and have good doctors. I see so many people who refuse to use a wheelchair or hearing aids. I remember my grandmother who had developed serious mobility impairments from arthritis and could have benefited from using a wheelchair. But she said, "I'm no cripple." And she said that as I was sitting right next to her in my chair. This attitude has to change. It's okay to use a wheelchair. It's okay to use hearing aids. They're not a stigma.

You have done considerable research on women with disabilities. Describe briefly any relationship, if there is one, between women's issues and the use of assistive technology devices.

There's a huge connection. Technology developed in response to the needs of veterans injured in war so they could get back to work. A lot of technology is developed for men's needs and industrial applications. There are no effective bladder management systems for women—catheterization or diapers, that's it. Women's bladder and menstrual needs are not considered. You can't even get a seat cushion to keep your legs together. There are no gender differences in seat cushions—never been considered. There are also technology issues related to pregnancy and child raising. In a wheelchair, you can't lean over very easily, not to mention when you're pregnant. That makes it hard to lift a baby out of a crib. You have to ask someone else in the family to do it. Applications of AT for child raising are simply not there. "Through the Looking Glass," a research and training center for parents with disabilities in California, has worked to address the needs of women with disabilities and child raising. There are a lot of low-tech tricks that woman have made up to help them care for children, and TLG has helped disseminate this information. They have a web site at www.lookingglass.org that's worth checking into. Megan Kirschbaum, the director, has done some really good work in this area.

You live in one of the largest cities in the United States, Houston. Describe some of the most complicated issues surrounding transportation needs for people with disabilities in urban settings. How do these issues differ with regard to rural issues, and how does assistive technology play a role in each setting?
In Houston, there are a lot of miles between Point A and Point B, so the transportation system faces many problems in serving everyone, especially people with disabilities. It was such a feeling of conquest when I first rode in one of their accessible buses, because we had to fight hard to get it to happen. When we first approached the transportation system, the city was adamant that they would not spend the money to create accessibility to the mainline buses. But at the very first meeting after we filed a lawsuit the city backed down, and the next thing you know they bought 400 buses with lifts. They also have a door-to-door system for those who can't use buses. Like I said, the first time I rode the bus I felt like a conquering hero. I also felt like a neighbor for the first time. I just had an unbelievably warm feeling of inclusion. That said, sometimes the lifts break down and buses just go by if a driver doesn't want to take the time to pick you up.

As for rural areas, when I graduated from UT I moved to the Davis Mountains of west Texas to live with Justin Dart and his family for four months. I was completely dependent on him and his truck for getting anywhere. In rural areas, like large urban areas, life depends on being able to get around. If there is any public transportation at all, it probably includes only a door-to-door service for people with disabilities. Such systems have an even greater problem dealing with large distances, and breakdowns can be devastating. In Fort Davis there were no accessible services when I lived there. It was an interesting, and a bit of a frightening, experience.

Assistive technology encompasses highly technological devices but also includes very simple devices. Describe for our readers how your home is set up to foster independence in daily living and the role assistive devices play in contributing to your independence on a daily basis.
We always lived in inaccessible houses while I was growing up in Ohio. I had to be carried in and out of my parents' house. This really affected my feelings of self-worth and personal development. My father did not want a ramp because he feared it would lower the resale value of the house. I felt restricted and dependent. Later, when I attended the University of Texas at the age of 25, I lived in the dorm and later in cooperative housing, and both were completely accessible to me with no more than an automatic door button and a widened door to the bathroom. When I graduated I lived in an apartment, then bought my own house. I looked for a house with a minimum of steps near an accessible bus line

(continued)

that would be reasonably modifiable, with wider doors and ramps, for instance. I've outfitted the house with lowered light switches, a toilet seat extension, handheld shower, rope on the door for opening and closing, and lots of other gadgets. I have sticks with rubber tips in every room that I use to turn pages, move pencils around, and pull things close. I also have lamps that I just have to touch to turn on and off. When I was younger, one of the hardest challenges I faced was to do something so that I could turn over by myself at night. My dad and an occupational therapist helped me rig up some pulleys and rope suspended from the ceiling over my bed that could be used with my wheelchair's joystick and power supply to lift up my knees so I could wiggle around and get comfortable. That was a great help for many years.

As a leader in the disability movement, you undoubtedly have strong opinions with regard to the timely acquisition of assistive devices for people who need them. What have you seen as barriers to device acquisition and are you optimistic concerning the future in this area?
There are several barriers, the first of which deals with the importance of connecting with an agency that can purchase or provide devices. It's also important to get an accurate evaluation. We really don't have a good system to determine how people can be assessed. There is a lack of laboratories to try things out—no place you can go to try out keyboards to use with your computer. We need a place where people with disabilities can go to get matched with the technology that exists in the marketplace. Also, policies are ridiculous—it's often an all or nothing package. With my van, for example, I wanted a simple lift, but I had to get a whole package that cost $16,000 and included a kneeling system and other features that I knew I didn't want or need. Many of the components that have broken down are not under warranty any more and I can't afford to get them repaired. Now I don't use them, and I didn't need them to begin with. All I needed was a lift but I had to buy the whole package because of the liability policies of the state rehab agency that paid for it.

Another major issue involves funding. Medicare and some insurance plans are limited and won't pay for some devices, for example. And organizations are restrictive also. For instance, the Muscular Dystrophy Association will pay for a manual chair but not a power chair. So we need to work hard to get funding issues taken care of. After lack of information, I think funding is the single biggest barrier.

Finally, we need to make professionals more aware of AT issues. I count my blessings that I had a doctor who knew about the latest AT and could help me get set up with a nice compact, quiet ventilator for my wheelchair. Not all professionals are that well connected. We need to work on information dissemination for professionals.

Finally, as a person who has numerous degrees and has spent a number of years in our educational system, what would you want to share with prospective or current teachers about assistive technology use by their students in and out of the classroom?
AT is a way of thinking. It has to do with acceptance of disability as a given and something that can be accommodated. It has to do with creativity and inventiveness. AT is a great equalizer that provides people with the opportunity to participate.

The role of the teacher is to help students learn how to think, how to be creative, how to solve problems. "Low functional fixity" means you are creative and look at objects and think about a multiplicity of applications. "High functional fixity" means you only see one or two uses for the object; you're more rigid in how you look at an object and how it can be used. For example, take a brick. Some people only see a brick as something you use to build a house. But others see a brick as something that can be used to hold a door open or that can serve as a counterweight or something that can be used to raise a table a few inches so a wheelchair can fit underneath it. Teachers need to be flexible and have low functional fixity so that, for example, they can figure out ways their students with disabilities can do science experiments on their own and participate in field trips.

Also, remember that it's not good enough to assign one student to another student with a disability to do things for them while they just sit and watch. Every student needs to participate and be as independent as possible. And when the limits of independence have been reached, they need to learn how to work together with others to get their needs met.

Reproduced with permission from Psycho-Educational Services.

with a pinch-design (enabling more effective food flipping during cooking), Braille and talking scales and measures, and the use of Braille Dymo™ tape to label microwave ovens, stoves, and canned goods are additional devices, to mention a few. Additionally, new devices are becoming available that will help individuals who are blind or visually impaired to identify canned and labeled goods via bar code, thus possibly reducing the need to label everything purchased. Figure 9.1 provides examples of AT devices for eating.

Dressing and Grooming

There are many adaptations for clothing that can be made to promote independence in dressing. For example, hook-and-loop tape instead of ties on shoes helps fasten shoes; other devices help individuals who have limited range of motion for bending, limited fine-motor control, or only the use of one hand to put on socks and pantyhose. Adapted button hooks (hooking device that helps pull the button through the button hole) and zipper pulls assist with dressing.

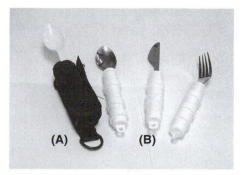

FIGURE 9.1   (A) Utensil Grips; (B) Large-Handled Utensils
Photo courtesy of Psycho-Educational Services.

To promote independence in the grooming area, modified handles (length and built-up) can be used for toothbrushes, combs, and brushes. For bathing, hand-held shower heads, shower chairs, wall grab bars, and scrub sponges with handles can be used by individuals with motor challenges. For individuals who have low vision, the bathroom should include high-contrast colors rather than the typical white found in many showers and bathtubs. Colored towels and mats and contrast on shower chairs help individuals discern items needed for grooming. Figure 9.2 provides examples of AT devices for dressing and grooming.

Safety

Home safety is always a concern for any individual. For example, *alerting devices* can be used for individuals with hearing impairments. A flashing light or vibration can signal the doorbell or fire alarm. Some companies (e.g., Whirlpool, GE) provide instructions in Braille or on audiocassettes for ovens, refrigerators, and laundry appliances (Smith, 2000). People who are blind often find that door intercoms enable a greater sense of security by eliminating the need to open the door to find out who has knocked or rung.

Mounting Devices and Page Turners

In order to promote independence, individuals must be able to use their adaptations across environments and tasks. Very often adaptations or devices must be mounted to furniture or wheelchairs. Mountability refers to the ability to attach devices to surfaces. For example, a computer, communication device, or tray might need to be mounted on a wheelchair or switches may need to be mounted on hardware close to the user's face or hand or on a surface with a sticking device to prevent slipping. Devices such as switches to turn appliances on and off might need to be mounted to a bed or table. Mounting systems, such as those sold by Tash, Inc. and Able Net, Inc., for instance, ensure that the adaptations are accessible for individuals to use as needed.

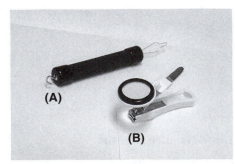

FIGURE 9.2   (A) Zipper Pull;
(B) Grooming Clippers
Photo courtesy of Psycho-Educational Services.

Page turners can be used at home, school, and work for individuals who can read various types of text but have motor challenges that impede the ability to turn the pages. Page turners promote independence because individuals can read the material at their own rate and activate the turning device when they are ready for more text; individuals do not have to rely on others to do this task. For instance, the GEWA Page Turner BLV-6 (Zygo Industries, Inc.) provides the user with control of the page-turning process whether in the sitting or lying position. The Page Turner can also be operated with multiple or single switches and by environmental control units (see below for a discussion on environmental control units). An example of a page turner is shown in Figure 9.3.

Leisure

Leisure activities, such as reading, sewing, and card playing, are another area in which individuals with disabilities should have access and independence to choose what they wish to engage in for recreation. For instance, books-on-tape (e.g., novels) from the Recording for the Blind and Dyslexic (RFB&D) can provide access to reading material for those who need AT adaptations to access print. A variety of categories, such as textbooks and novels, are available to rent. A special tape player can be purchased from RFB&D to accommodate the tapes. The National Library Service (NLS) for the Blind is another resource that provides popular reading; NLS loans playback equipment.

Built-up handles on scissors can help with sewing and cutting for those with fine motor difficulties, and holders for cards and pool cues can aid in playing card games and shooting pool (Cook & Hussey, 1995). For instance, North Coast Medical offers Lo Vision® (playing cards for individuals with as little as 5 percent normal vision. The cards contain numbers, letters, and suit symbols that are enlarged and each suit is color-coded. Braille dominoes, a volley beep ball, Braille bingo boards, and large-print bingo cards (Independent Living Aids) enable individuals who are blind and who have low vision to participate fully in games played by children and adults alike.

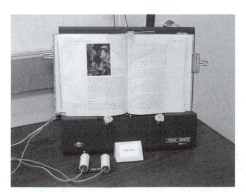

FIGURE 9.3 Page Turner
Photo courtesy of Psycho-Educational Services.

In the area of entertainment, there are several adaptations that can be used to enable individuals with sensory impairments to access the entertainment world. For example, for individuals who are hard of hearing or deaf, closed-captioned television programs are now available. As a part of the Americans with Disabilities Act, televisions must now include built-in decoding capability. More and more broadcasts include closed-captioned programming, including, for instance, news stations such as CNN, sporting events, prime-time shows, and public-service programs. For individuals with visual impairments, access to some forms of television and other forms of entertainment, such as movies, is becoming increasingly available through audiodescription (Smith, 2000). Audiodescription involves the verbal description of the onscreen story and is made available during the silent portions of the show through earphones and a small FM receiver (Smith, 2000). Thus, the entertainment world is becoming increasingly accessible for individuals with sensory impairments. Technology devices enhance and expand opportunities for leisure activities. Examples of leisure devices are shown in Figure 9.4.

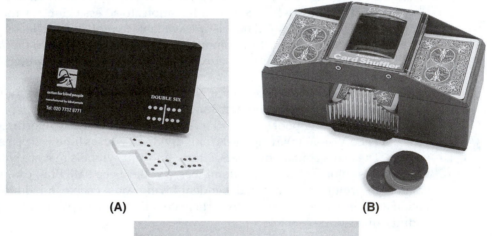

(A)   (B)

(C)

FIGURE 9.4   (A) Dominoes; (B) Card Shuffler; (C) Bingo Cards

(A, C) Photos courtesy of Psycho-Educational Services; (B) Photo courtesy of North Coast Medical, Inc., Morgan Hill, CA.

FOCUS ON 9.1

Keep a list for one day of your activities of daily living. Think about a specific type of disability and the types of AT devices you would need in order to continue your level of engagement successfully. Share the list in class with a small group. Identify the commonalties and differences among the lists.

SWITCHES AND SCANNING

Switches are considered to be input devices and are used to input a signal into a computer (see Chapter 6), a battery-operated toy, a communication board, an environmental control unit (see next section), and so forth. Switches can generate simple responses when an individual pushes the switch to get an action or more complex responses when multiple switches are used. Some devices, such an electronic communication board or software, offer many choices from which the users can select their response. For example, a communication board may have several food options for the user to select from when indicating that he or she is hungry. Scanning is a procedure that draws attention to each item that the user can choose to select (Lewis, 1993). A switch can be pushed to activate the scanning procedure and pushed again when the food item of choice is highlighted. Switches and scanning are considered to be *indirect selection methods,* meaning that there are several steps involved in inputting a signal and that the individual has to do more than just push a key on a computer (*direct selection method*), for example, to input a signal. Switches and scanning offer individuals with disabilities the ability to manipulate their environment independently and to make choices.

Switches

Questions for decision makers to consider when assessing and choosing switches are included in Table 9.1. Once a switch is selected, users may need time learning how to use the device. Switch instruction should include identifying the switch, activating the switch, and deactivating the switch (Lewis, 1993). For instance, SwitchIt!® Suite (Intellitools, Inc.) provides four developmental programs to teach the use of switches and to match the user's cognitive and developmental level. Students learn cause-effect, turn taking, concept building, and scanning. Characteristics and types of switches are two important topics to think about when selecting switches.

Characteristics of Switch Devices.   Many characteristics must be considered when selecting switches, such as the design of the switch, how a person uses the switch, and how a person receives feedback about the switch's activity. The design of the switch includes its size, the number of activation sites, and the size of the sites. For example, a large switch, such as the Jelly Bean® (switch (Able Net, Inc., Figure 9.5), has a 2½-inch activation site to be pushed. This design is particularly effective for users who have limited range of motion and who need a device with a large surface

TABLE 9.1   Questions for Decision Makers to Consider for Independent Living Adaptations

SWITCHES

- What devices does the user need to access with a single switch or switch array?
- What are the cognitive, motoric, and sensory abilities of the user?
- What are the best design features for the user?
- What is the best way for the user to activate and deactivate the switch?
- What effort and fatigue factors are involved in using the switches?
- What is an appropriate type of feedback (visual, auditory) for the user?
- Can the user operate a switch and scanning set up?

SCANNING

- Does the user possess the cognitive, sensory, and motor abilities to access scanning formats and techniques?
- What tasks will require scanning?
- What format is best suited for the user?
- What technique is best suited for the user?
- What type of switch will be used with the scanning procedure?

ENVIRONMENTAL CONTROL UNITS

- What does the user want to be able to do with the ECU?
- What type of input device most appropriately matches the needs of the user?
- What type of feedback (visual, auditory) is most appropriate for the user and the environment?
- What locations will the ECU be used?
- What are the user's cognitive and positioning abilities?
- What services are available (funding, maintenance, training)?

for interaction purposes. A joystick, on the other hand, has a switch array (activation choices include up, down, left, right) with multiple activation sites. This design requires that the user grasp and manipulate the joystick to activate different sites that have distinctive movements. The user needs to have enough range of motion to activate the different choices (Cook & Hussey, 1995).

Switches can be designed for operation in several ways including momentary, latched, and timed activation. *Momentary* operation means that the switch is activated for as long as the user presses the switch. *Latched* operation means that the user presses the switch to turn it on and presses it again to turn it off. Finally, *timed* operation means that the switch can be programmed (using a timer) to stay on for a set period of time and will turn itself off when the time runs out.

There are several ways switches can be used including activation, deactivation, and effort. Switches can be activated using movement, respiration, and phonation (Cook & Hussey, 1995). *Movement* activation can occur with the head, arms,

FIGURE 9.5   Jelly Bean Switch
Photo courtesy of Psycho-Educational Services.

legs, and eyes and can occur mechanically or electrically. Mechanical activation of switches, which uses force, is the most common type of switch activation; these are sometimes called "push switches." Electric activation of switches is based on electrical signals in the body, such as electrodes near the eyes that measure eye movements (Cook & Hussey, 1995). Electromagnetic (light or radio waves) and proximity (heat-sensitive) activation of switches does not require direct body contact. A head-mounted light pointer and remote control are examples of electromagnetic switches. *Respiration* involves breathing where individuals use the breathing actions of inhaling and exhaling to activate the switch. Individuals who do not have fine- and gross-motor control, such as those with quadriplegia, may find this option appropriate for their needs and abilities. *Phonation* activation involves the use of the voice or sound. Voice recognition is a good example of phonation activation (see Access to Information in Chapter 6).

Just as switches need to be activated, users must also be able to release or deactivate them. Like mechanical activation, deactivation also involves the use of force. Therefore, an individual's ability to use force to activate and deactivate switches must be examined. Finally, the amount of effort needed to activate and deactivate switches is a critical component of switch use. Whether it is the use of the head, arm, leg, or hand; the use of inhalation and exhalation; or the use of articulation and loudness, the amount of effort must be considered. Also, the link between effort and fatigue must be considered. If a switch requires a great deal of effort and tires the user quickly, then the usefulness of the switch across time, environments, and tasks is questionable.

In order to know that the activation and deactivation of the switch was successful, the user must receive some type of feedback. For example, an auditory click or response (voice output) tells the user that the switch was depressed successfully. Visually, an action, as with cause-effect software or turning a lamp on or off, provides feedback that the signal was received.

Types of Switches.   There are many types of switches available to match the needs of users. Cook and Hussey (1995) identified six types of single-switch options: the paddle switch, which can be activated by body movement; the wobble (provides auditory feedback) and leaf switches, which can be activated by body movement in two directions; level switches, which are much like wobble switches but move in only one direction; pneumatic switches, which involve sips and puffs; and pillow switches, which respond when pushed. Switches can be used singly or several can be plugged into a switch interface. For example, Macintosh Switch Interface (Don Johnston) and DJ PC Switch Interface (Don Johnston) offer multiple switch access for computer use. Switches and the devices to which they will be attached should be examined to determine the type of adapter that will be necessary to link the switch to the device. Cordless switches eliminate the need for adapters but usually have to be directed toward the control panel.

Scanning.   Questions for decision makers to consider when assessing and choosing scanning options are included in Table 9.1 (Church & Glennen, 1992). Individuals should receive training in the scanning procedure selected. Don Johnston offers a variety of software to teach the use of switches and scanning across age levels. For instance, the Press-to-Play Series™ contains single-switch stories that teach switch skills. Single-Switch Software for Teens includes age-appropriate activities that focus on cause-effect and linear scanning. Scanning formats and scanning techniques must be considered when selecting a scanning procedure.

Scanning Formats.   Scanning formats generally involve a visual display presented in some sequential manner. The user activates a switch when the scanning procedure highlights his or her choice; thus, multiple choices for a task can be provided from which the user chooses. For instance, a child views four types of toys each in its own box on a computer screen. The scanning procedure moves from left to right sequentially highlighting each box as it goes along. The child pushes the switch when the box containing the preferred toy is highlighted. In another example, a student might be working on sound/symbol identification. Several pictures of objects with the same sound and one object with a different sound are displayed in a linear format. The student's task is to activate the switch when the object with the different beginning sound is highlighted.

There are several types of scanning formats; selection of the type should match the user's needs and abilities and the amount of items and information that needs to be addressed. *Linear scanning* involves the vertical or horizontal arrangement of arrays with items to be scanned. The scanning procedure moves left to right or top to bottom scanning each item one at a time and the user activates the item of choice when it is highlighted. *Rotary scanning* involves the presentation of the items in a circle where again items are scanned one at a time.

To increase the number of items that can be scanned, thus the information that the user can access, *group-item scanning* can be used. Several items are presented in a group; the groups are scanned sequentially. The user selects the group with the item. The scanning continues of the items in the group until the user selects the specific item. For example, there are three groups: food, school, and recreation. The user selects food. Under food, specific food choices are available, such as french fries, milk, and so forth. The user selects the specific desired food. In *row-column scanning* each row is illuminated. The row with the item is selected; each column in the row is illuminated until the user selects the desired item (Cook & Hussey, 1995). For instance, three rows are presented containing letters of the alphabet. The row in which the desired letter is located is selected, then the column in which the letter is located is selected.

Scanning Techniques. There are three types of scanning techniques: automatic scanning, step scanning, and inverse scanning. Each type's features must be considered carefully to match the needs of the user. *Automatic scanning* involves scanning items continuously at an established rate, which can be increased or decreased, until the user activates the switch on the desired item. This technique requires the ability to track and attend and requires a certain level of cognitive ability (Cook & Hussey, 1995). *Step scanning* requires the user to activate the switch through each item. The user controls the rate of scanning, and switch activation to select the item or a timing device is triggered to accept the choice. The user must be able to exert sufficient effort to use this technique and not be highly susceptible to a fatigue factor. *Inverse scanning* requires the user to hold down the switch and release it when the item of choice is illuminated. The user must be able to activate the switch for a period of time and have the motor control to release it at the time the item needs to be selected.

FOCUS ON 9.2

Review catalogues or conduct an online search of switches and scanning software. Identify characteristics and types of switches and scanning formats and techniques. Make a list of the devices and software and for whom they are intended. Share this information with the class.

ENVIRONMENTAL CONTROL UNITS

Environmental control units (ECU) help people with disabilities operate electrically powered devices, such as appliances, and foster independent living in home, school, and work. These enabling devices give individuals control over their environment and promote independence. ECU systems can range from simple applications, such as turning on and off a light, to more complex systems that manage appliances, heating and cooling, and security alarms found in "smart homes" (Church & Glennen, 1992). Typically, ECUs are used by individuals with physical challenges, such as gross- and fine-motor difficulties, who need an alternate way to manage common devices and appliances.

Generally speaking, ECUs operate in this manner:

- An *input device* controls the ECU; a keypad, keyboard, joystick, switches, and voice control are examples of input devices.
- A *control unit* receives the message from the input device and translates the message into an output signal that goes to the device. Transmission options for sending messages include ultrasound, infrared, radio control, and AC power signals.
- The *device,* such as a lamp, receives and responds to the output signal.

It is helpful to understand the capabilities of the different types of input devices and transmission options so decisions can be made about the needs of the user, the environmental demands, and the most appropriate ECU match. Questions for decision makers to consider when thinking about ECUs are included in Table 9.1.

Input Devices

Input devices consist of direct selection, switches and scanning, and voice control (Angelo, 1997). *Direct selection* means that the user chooses any device to control; pressing a keypad is a way that the user can choose the device to activate. For example, four devices (e.g., 1. lamp, 2. television, 3. VCR, 4. fan) might be connected to the ECU system. The user wishes to turn on the fan so number 4 is pressed on the keypad; this is direct selection where the device is selected and the action happens. Depending on the user's abilities, the keypad can be pressed simply by using a finger or may involve technology such as a headstick, mouthstick, joystick, or ocular eye gaze monitor (Church & Glennen, 1992). The same idea can be applied to a computer-controlled ECU where the user moves through the menus until the ECU system is highlighted; then the user gives commands to the devices by pressing individual keys. This is a good input choice for someone who spends a lot of time at the computer (Angelo, 1997).

Switches and scanning are other types of input devices. A switch may be a good choice when the user needs an alternate type of input device (see discussion about switches beginning on page 205); scanning works well for users who have the cognitive abilities to respond to multiple choices. For example, a switch can be used to activate an appliance. Several switches can be used to activate different appliances. Switches can also be paired with a scanning array, such as a linear presentation of the appliances. By activating a switch, the scanning of each appliance in a linear fashion (horizontally or vertically) can occur; the user activates the switch when the appliance of choice (e.g., fan) is highlighted. There are also scanning arrays that offer branching options so that if the fan is highlighted the branching feature offers more choices: on, off, slow, medium, high speed. Items for selection, such as appliances, are usually arranged in the scanning array in order of preference and frequency of use; thus, allowing the user independence, choice, and decision-making opportunities.

Voice control involves the user's speaking commands into a microphone for the ECU. The ECU interprets the message and activate the appliance. Voice control is a voice recognition system, which involves training the machine to recognize the user's voice (Angelo, 1997). This input device is a good choice for users, who may not be able to use upper body extremities, to activate the ECU by using other types of input devices such as keypads, joysticks, switches, and so forth. Actual words are not essential to activate the system; rather, the machine is trained to recognize the user's voice, pitch, loudness, and articulation (Cook & Hussey, 1995). Therefore, in order for the input device to be effective, the user must be consistent in oral expression and operate in an environment where background noise will not interfere with the system.

Transmission Options

There are four transmission options for output signals: ultrasound, infrared, radio control, and AC power signals. *Ultrasound* involves high-frequency sound waves that are not discernible to the human hearing range. A frequency is emitted through the input device and the control box activates the appliance. Ultrasound can only be used with appliances that are in same room as the input device (ultrasound transmitter). *Infrared* transmission involves infrared pulses being sent from a remote control to the control box. Because the remote control is portable, it can be used from various locations in the room as long as the device is pointed directly at the control box and there is nothing in the way to interfere with the transmission. Devices that have built-in infrared controls, such as televisions and VCRs, can only be operated with infrared signals (Lewis, 1993). *Radio control* (electromagnetic) uses the same radio waves that are used in toys, garage door openers, and radios. The advantage to this transmission device is that the user does not have to be in the same room as the control box when activating the radio control signal. Finally, *AC power signals* take advantage of existing house wiring to transmit signals to activate appliances. The input device can be a remote unit or part of the control box (Angelo, 1997).

Use of ECUs at Home, School, and Work

ECUs can be used in the home to activate appliances and telephones. For example, Zygo Industries, Inc. offers the GEWA Prog, which is based on infrared transmission and operated using a hand-held transmitter. Input device options include either a keypad or switches and scanning techniques. The GEWA Prog can work up to 100 feet in distance and does not have to be aimed directly at the control box (receiver). The GEWA Prog with its INFRA-LINK system for lighting switches, wall sockets, opening windows, intercoms, alarm systems, and elevator controls can be used in the "smart home" concept. Lights, TV, VCRs, and computers can all be connected to the GEWA Prog.

Sicare Pilot (Tash, Inc.) is a voice-activated device for environmental control at home and work. It can also be operated using a switch or single switch and scanning. Sicare Pilot converts spoken commands into signals that control numerous devices and appliances, such as computers, televisions, and lights, within multiple environments. Sicare Pilot uses both infrared and radio transmission and provides both visual and auditory feedback to the user. For individuals with visual impairments, at least one thermostat is needed that has large print and tactile markings. There is also a need for more innovation in the thermostat area for those wanting electronic thermostats; presently access by individuals who are blind is difficult at best. For telephone control, GEWA Infra-Link Speaker-Telephone offers user access to the phone with the use of a single switch to answer the phone or dial a number. Thus, this environmental control device provides complete access to users who might otherwise not be able to use telephones, both at home and work.

A school application is the final example of environmental control. The PowerLink® 3 Control Unit coupled with the AirLink Cordless Switch (Able Net,

Inc.) enables students to access and participate in school activities that involve electrical devices. For instance, using the cordless switch, the student can activate a device independently, such as a tape recorder, through the PowerLink® 3 Control Unit (see Figure 9.6). This process allows the student access to school tasks and participation with peers.

FOCUS ON 9.3

Using the case study you developed in Chapter 2, design a "Smart Home" for your individual. Explain the input device and transmission option. Your design should include examples of adaptations for different rooms in the house. Present your design in class to the other students.

ACCESS TO MANAGEMENT DEVICES

For individuals to be independent, they must demonstrate management skills for daily life activities at home, school, and work, and they must possess some degree of organization. The first step in being able to manage oneself in daily life and organization is access to information. This section focuses on AT adaptations, which involve visual and auditory feedback, that help individuals with disabilities access information to enhance their abilities to manage their daily activities.

Time and Money

There are many adaptations that can assist people in managing daily life tasks related to time and money. Time and money management are two major areas that require people to have tools that promote access to information, and thus, promote independence. In the area of time management, access to time is the first step. For individuals who have low vision or who are blind, a variety of calendars, clocks,

FIGURE 9.6   Power Link
Photo courtesy of Psycho-Educational Services.

and watches with enlarged numbers, and tactile and auditory cues such as Braille numbers on watches and talking clocks are available (Independent Living Aids). For individuals who are hard of hearing, access to alarm clocks as a wake-up device can be accomplished through clocks that produce large sounds. For instance, the Big Number Very Loud Desktop Alarm Clock (Independent Living Aids) produces a sound up to 90 decibels. To help with remembering time-sensitive "things to do," such as being somewhere by a certain time, the TimePAD (Attainment Company, Inc.) can provide up to five recorded messages, which can be activated by a timer.

Money management involves being able to access information related to money and numbers. Calculators are a useful tool to help with money management. Calculators with big keys such as the Big Display Calculator and the Talking Calculator, which speaks each entry and calculation (Attainment Company, Inc.), and large-keyed calculators can help individuals who can benefit from vision aids, calculation assistance, and access to the keypad. The Large Print Check and Deposit Register (Independent Living Aids) enables individuals with low vision to manage their checkbook and to write checks. Also, the Note Teller™ Talking Money Identifier (Independent Living Aids) is a portable talking money identifier that will verbally announce the denomination of all bills from one dollar to one hundred dollars. It automatically turns itself on when a bill is inserted and off when a bill is removed. It is available in English and Spanish.

Organization

Promoting organizational skills enables people to tackle the daily tasks of home, school, and work. There are many assistive technology adaptations that can help people manage their daily routines and access information. The uses of personal data managers can promote remembering and organizing personal information. Personal data managers are available as hand-held units and allow the user to store and access personal information. Information input and access occur via a keyboard or keypad and are displayed on an LCD display. Pocket-size data managers (e.g., StepPAD, Memo Talker, Voice Organizer™, Voice It™) enable the user to enter and access information by speaking into the device. Stored data are spoken back in the user's own voice. Some of the features of data managers include calendars, daily schedules, timing devices, memo files, address books, and telephone directories. Figure 9.7 provides an example of a management device.

FOCUS ON 9.4

Identify ways you manage your time and money and keep yourself organized. Go online and locate the devices presented in the Access to Management Devices. Determine the tasks for which the devices would be well suited and the requisite abilities that are needed to use the devices. Identify the features of the devices.

FIGURE 9.7   Management Tool
Photo courtesy of Psycho-Educational Services.

Describe problems people with disabilities might exhibit for which these devices could be used to held manage their lives independently.

MOBILITY

Legislative mandates have been passed over the years that have facilitated the use of AT devices and services (Bryant & Seay, 1998; Raskind & Higgins, 1998). For instance, Title II of Section 504 of the Rehabilitation Act stated that public entities have to provide appropriate auxiliary aids and services to a student with a disability in order for the student to participate in any publicly funded program (Day & Edwards, 1996). Section 504 requires that all aspects of the learning environment, including the classroom, school, and transportation, be accessible. Chapter 4 provides information about mobility for people with physical impairments. Here we provide general information about mobility issues for people with variety of disabilities, including those with cognitive and sensory impairments.

In 1990, Congress passed the Americans with Disabilities Act (ADA), which extended the benefits and protections of the Rehab Act to individuals with disabilities in the private sector. Although the law does not specifically discuss AT devices and services (Day & Edwards, 1996), AT is clearly an important tool in providing people with disabilities an opportunity to be successful in all areas covered by the ADA including employment, transportation (e.g., buses, trains), public accommodations (e.g., hotels, restaurants, banks, theaters), and telecommunications. Therefore, barriers to mobility for all people with disabilities, particularly individuals with physical disabilities or who have low vision or are blind, must be addressed.

Architectural barriers must be removed. Thus we see wider doorways, elevators with timing mechanisms for wheelchair accessibility, accessible restrooms (doors, towel racks, sinks), cutaway curbs, and so forth. In classrooms, lower chalkboards and water fountains, adapted playground equipment, and wheelchair ramps are all examples of ways that promote access, address barriers, and create independence. Ramps (8.3% slope) in buildings and lifts in transportation vehicles help people who use wheelchairs to access buildings, public buses, and vans. These are but a few of the issues surrounding access to mobility for people with various disabilities.

In describing the nature of mobility needs for people who are blind or have visual impairments, the Committee on Vision for the National Research Council (1986) noted:

> There are two major elements of the mobility problem that result from blindness. First, the blind traveler with no pattern vision must avoid obstacles and detect drop-offs. The second problem, which is less obvious and equally serious, is navigation. Sighted travelers have many landmarks, most of which are known through vision, to guide their way. These landmarks not only identify the location but are used in the memorial representation or cognitive map of the area. Deprived of vision, the blind person must use other types of landmarks and information to orient and navigate (p. 20).

For individuals who have low vision or who are blind, orientation and mobility training is beneficial to promote freedom, movement, and independence. For instance, adults might use the long cane to help them move about their environments. Tactile maps help individuals identify key areas (e.g., elevators) and services (e.g., restrooms). Something as simple as uniform riser heights on stairs and tread widths can promote mobility (Smith, 1998). Orientation and mobility have been used for decades to help people who are blind move about effectively in their environments.

Over time, a number of mobility aids have been developed to help people with visual impairments travel about. Such aids include long canes, guide dogs, and electronic travel aids (ETA). To date, most ETAs have failed to provide needed improvements over traditional long canes and guide dogs, so their use has been minimal. It is hoped that a dialogue between consumers and engineers/developers will result in the creation of sophisticated yet practical devices to enhance the mobility needs of people who are blind or who have low vision. Clearly, the mobility issues of people with these conditions goes far beyond technology. Many have to do with planning and preparation (see Figure 9.8 for travel tips).

In their excellent text *Finding Wheels,* Corn and Rosenblum (2000) recount several anecdotes of how people with visual impairments have developed mobility competencies. For the most part, the people they describe in their anecdotal studies utilize traditional devices to enhance their mobility. A particularly poignant example of the social ramifications associated with mobility challenges was provided by Pablo, a 19-year-old living in the Midwest. He shared:

> When I turned 16 I was really upset that I couldn't go get my driver's license like all the other kids in my class. One night I got really mad at Gabriel [Pablo's brother] over something stupid and started yelling my head off about how everyone hated me and treated me like a little kid. I hung out in my room, listening to my music real loud, something my mom forbids me to do. . . . For about an hour, she let me sit in my room blasting my music and then she came in and we ended up talking for a long time about what was really bugging me. I told her all the kids in school were

talking about nothing other than getting their licenses, driving, insurance, and earning enough money to buy their own cars. I told her how lonely I felt, being the only junior who wasn't driving in the whole school and how this made me feel like a little kid (p. 12).

Corn describes a number of mobility issues in our interview with her (see Personal Perspectives 9.2). In commenting on different mobility concerns for people with low vision or blindness, Corn (personal communication, August 17, 2001) observed:

The person with low vision uses his or her vision as a primary or secondary mode for travel. Those with sufficient vision will travel just as those with typical sight will use their vision to find curbs, steps, landmarks, streets, and so forth. These individuals may use a monocular telescope or other optical device to see detail such as to read street signs or to find an office location on a building directory. They may use a hand magnifier or a closed-circuit television to read bus time tables or maps. Those with higher levels of low vision may ride a bicycle and or seek a low vision driver's license. In most states with regulations allowing low vision driving, a bioptic telescopic system is required. People with low vision may also use lenses for controlling light. For example, some eye conditions have an accompanying photophobia—extreme sensitivity to light. These individuals may use darkly tinted lenses, sometimes called light-absorptive lenses. Others will use therapeutic contact lenses that have painted irises to control how much light enters the eyes. People with low vision who have lower levels of vision may use a white cane in conjunction with their vision. For example, the white cane may alert the user to steps or drop-offs, especially if the person has very low visual acuity and/or a restricted visual field.

There are also some visual impairments that result in different levels of functioning with different environmental conditions, those that fluctuate at different times of day, and those that are degenerative. For example, a person with retinitis pigmentosa may have good visual functioning during the day but have difficulties in the evening under lower levels of light. Those with diabetic retinopathy may have fluctuations throughout the day. Others with degenerative conditions may need to adapt to changes in their visual abilities over time.

Perhaps one of the largest differences in mobility for people who have low vision and those who are blind relates to constancy. The person who is blind experiences a constant need to function with other senses. Many people with low vision need to adapt to different environments or other changes throughout the day. Even when a visual condition is stable, they may move about without restrictions in one environment and encounter some difficulties in another. However, people with low vision, who can use their vision for getting about, will want to use their vision as a primary method of learning about their environment. Vision is immediate and provides information in the near, intermediate, and far distance.

People who are functionally or totally blind will use nonvisual methods for learning orientation—where they are in their environment, mobility—the methods of traveling indoors and outdoors, and wayfinding—how to plan and execute routes. Self-protective techniques, traveling with a sighted guide, using a cane, and using a dog guide are among the methods used during travel by those who are blind. Though used less frequently, electronic travel devices are available to provide information about environments that are not within reach of one's cane or foot.

When orientation and mobility instruction is provided, most individuals are able to learn to travel in familiar and unfamiliar environments as independent travelers. In recent years, research has looked at using global positioning systems with blind travelers. Children who have never had vision must learn in a careful and systematic way how the physical world is structured. What is a roof of a house, what is an intersection, how does traffic flow? These are only a few of the concepts and mental mapping that a congenitally blind person needs to learn.

When someone loses some or all vision after the early years, they retain visual images and concepts that are helpful during the rehabilitation process. However, losing one's vision and losing one's ability to move about and go spontaneously and without thought for movements and location can profoundly impact one's adjusting processes.

Thousands of people who are blind travel to work, appointments, stores, and other places every day. They can even travel to foreign countries. A few simple tips and tricks makes traveling easier for them.

Plan Your Trip in Detail
Learn about the city layout, rules of traffic, and the location of city landmarks with respect to your hotel, bus schedules, and the airport layout. Discover exactly where you will go to get a taxi or other transportation, and decide beforehand where you will go to eat. Carry a piece of paper with the addresses of all the places you want to visit written in the native language to make traveling easier. With precision planning, very little is left up to chance, and you can relax on your trip.

Make Reservations for Everything
You know to make reservations for your hotel and airplane, bus or train travel, but you can also make reservations at museums, restaurants, and taxi services. When making reservations, tell everyone you have a visual impairment, and tell them exactly what type of help you may need. Ask if the museums allow touch tours to take place. That way, they know you are coming and can prepare for your arrival, and you know what to expect.

Buy Before You Go
Purchase your museum, airplane, train, and bus tickets, and anything else you can buy and have delivered before you go. This will eliminate the hassle of standing in endless lines only to be told you have been waiting in the wrong line. You will also become aware of the individual feel of each ticket so it won't get confused with other tickets and receipts acquired in a day.

Bring a Cane
Though guide dogs are acceptable in most parts of North America and Europe, some countries do not have a general policy regarding the dogs, so you may not be allowed into individual businesses. A cane is allowed everywhere and is a readily acceptable

FIGURE 9.8   Travel Tips for People Who Are Blind: How to Make the Trip a Little Easier

(continued)

FIGURE 9.8   Continued

symbol that you have a visual impairment, which helps in many instances. Other devices, like electronic travel aids, are also allowed everywhere.

Let People Help
Many people have a difficult time adjusting to the thought of a capable person who is blind. Therefore many people all over the world want to help. Be gracious in accepting their assistance; after all, the sighted feel better about themselves when they are helpful.

Ask Questions
Depending on the culture, some people may ignore you completely. One way to overcome these difficulties is to learn a few words of the foreign language before you travel. Don't be shy about asking questions or asking for assistance.

Know about Flying
If you choose to fly on your travels, you may be asked to preboard, postboard, or demonstrate your ability to fasten or unfasten a seat belt. You may also be asked to move if you are seated in the emergency exit row. It is unlawful for airlines to require you to do any of these things, but still it occurs. Also, bring carry-on luggage to avoid having to navigate through crowds and obstacles.

Book Your Travel with an Experienced Agent
If you choose to use an agent, book with someone who knows what services are available for people who are blind. Braille labels on elevators and hotel doors, easily accessible stairways, tour guides who tell interesting verbal tales—all of these make traveling easier. By using the services of a good agent you will save a lot of grief and have a better time. Campanian is a tour company specializing in travelers who are blind, and AggieWorld does the same.

People with visual impairments can have just as much fun on trips as their sighted counterparts. All it takes is a little preplanning and a few accommodations. Blindness should not stop anyone from seeing the world!

Adapted with permission from *Travel Tips for the Blind: How to Make the Trip a Little Easier.* http://blindness.about.com/library/weekly/aa080101a.htm.

FOCUS ON 9.5

Conduct a tour of your college or school building, public facilities, or governmental buildings. Identify ways in which mobility has been made accessible for individuals with disabilities. Share your information with other students in the class. Interview an individual who is blind or who has a physical disability that necessitates the use of a wheelchair. Talk with this person about accessibility issues. Share this information in class.

PERSONAL PERSPECTIVE 9.2

Anne Corn is a professor of special education at Vanderbilt University in Nashville, Tennessee. She has been a teacher of students with visual impairments and since 1976 she has prepared teachers and researchers in this field. Her experiences as an advocate for those with mobility impairments have taken several foci. She has conducted research and written curricula for people with visual impairments to become efficient nondrivers; she has given lectures on driving for those with low vision using bioptic telescopic lenses, and she has developed and coordinated a program that prepares orientation and mobility instructors for blind and visually impaired children and adults. In addition, she has served or committees related to mobility impairments and public transportation, and in the mid-1980s she was a member of the Urban Transportation Commission of Austin, Texas.

In your book, titled *Finding Wheels*, you briefly discuss your mobility experiences as a child with low vision. Can you summarize those experiences for us?
I had what may be considered pretty typical travel experiences for a child growing up in New York City. I walked, or took a city bus to elementary school (in poor weather) using landmarks. I took my first bus to visit my aunt around fifth grade. I went with friends into Manhattan by junior high. I knew all of the subway stops by the colors of the lighting and tiles at each station and I had memorized the order of the stops. I used these methods because I couldn't read the numbers (e.g., 42nd) as the train was coming into a stop. When I began to take a bus into unfamiliar areas, I needed to ask drivers to let me know when we arrived at a certain stop. At times drivers were helpful; other drivers were annoyed because I could obviously see and they thought I was giving them a hard time. Then again, there were New York City bus drivers who just didn't care. In those situations, I just asked for assistance from other passengers. I also learned to read maps well for both the bus and subway routes.

When friends started to take driving lessons, I felt left out. One friend thought it would be a good idea for me to go with her when her father taught her to drive. I believe my friend (who is now a pediatrician) wanted me to feel included. I went but felt that I'd rather not be there.

Your book does a nice job of chronicling four individuals' experiences with transportation issues. Tell us how orientation and mobility training affects all aspects of mobility for people who are blind or who have low vision.
By the time you were 3 or 4 years old you could probably use your finger to point in which ways your parents should turn a car to go from the grocery store to your house. At some level you understood streets, roads, intersections, that some buildings had one story and some had more. You may have watched people cross streets, understood that there are stop signs and lights and that pedestrians and drivers do certain things to navigate or find their way. Consider if you've never seen how the physical world was put together. Consider if you were placed in the back seat of a car and never saw the car itself. The car may seem like a moving couch and the physical world outside would not truly exist. A congenitally blind child must learn about all of the ways in which people move, indoors and outdoors. They must develop concepts and learn of how their bodies can move in relation to objects. Remember that with vision, you can glance about your surroundings and know

(continued)

what is there. Those who are blind must learn to "put the pieces together." They must also be courageous enough to learn the skills that enable them to be independent travelers. Lessons in orientation can begin while a child is still in his or her crib and should progress until the child is an independent traveler. For adults who lose some or all of their vision, orientation and mobility instruction helps to reinstill a sense of independence.

What has been your biggest mobility challenge and how did you deal with it?
My biggest challenge was not being able to drive. Choosing my location of housing, relying on others' schedules, and trying not to impose on others were true challenges. Now that I can drive, I live where I want to live rather than first starting with a map of grocery stores and bus routes. I live in a semi-rural area where there are no buses. I guess I was never destined to live in New York City.

You obviously travel a great deal as part of your professional duties. What AT devices for mobility have you found to be particularly helpful?
I use an 8X monocular telescope as a pedestrian. I will use it for seeing street signs, time schedules in airports, menus at fast food restaurants, finding a store at a distance, and so forth. For driving I use a 4X behind-the-lens bioptic telescopic system for driving. Also, for reading maps, I use a 20 diopter hand-held magnifier.

As a leader in the field of vision, how have your personal experiences with mobility shaped your message to your university students and your colleagues?
I believe a teacher of any student who experiences a mobility disability must consider how that person views his or her freedom and independence. For a person with a visual impairment, getting from place to place is so tied to one's life options, social life, and employability that their instructors are compelled to address mobility issues in a sensitive and proactive way. They must provide options whenever possible. For example, many children and youths with low vision, and some who are blind, do not receive orientation and mobility instruction, which is today a related service under IDEA.

If you could snap your fingers and invent a device that could serve as a mobility aid, what would it be?
I believe the driverless car is in the future. I don't need to invent it because in Spain they're already working on a prototype. This would help people with low vision and blindness—and probably many fully sighted persons as well.

Here's your chance to tell our readers one thing above all else that you want them to know about mobility issues for people who are blind or who have low vision. Have at it.
Every day of our lives we move about. We learn that moving about can be within one's home or within one's community. We can move to obtain a drink from the refrigerator or we can move from one city to another. Our choice of where we live, our choice of vocation or recreation, our relationships with others, and our sense of self are all tied to how freely we are able to move about. As a person with low vision, I keenly felt the restrictions of not being able to come and go, to be restricted by what my visual impairment imposed in the society in which I lived. While some people may be happy to be "couch potatoes" or to sit at home and collect supplemental security disability income, others want to maintain an active lifestyle. It is through the educators', parents', and clinicians' efforts that a person with low vision or blindness can take an active part in life. Many years ago I heard a speaker who was blind talk to a group of professionals. He said that every day of his life he

used social skills and mobility skills. Still, he saw that these two areas of unique learning needs for persons with visual impairments took a very low priority in the field of education. From my many years of experience as a person with low vision and as a teacher and teacher-educator, I wholeheartedly agree with this speaker's appraisal.

The Expanded Core Curriculum for Students with Visual Impairments is designed to meet the unique learning needs of students with visual impairments. It contains eight areas of instruction. Perhaps when this curriculum is readily accepted and valued by educators and parents, we will see more students receive instruction in the areas of orientation and mobility, visual efficiency, social skills, and independent living skills. Each of these are addressed within the curriculum and all contribute to a student's mobility and freedom.

Reproduced with permission from Psycho-Educational Services.

SUMMARY

Individuals with disabilities have a right to independence and full integration into society. Living independently involves access to the activities and tasks associated with daily life. Because some of these activities and tasks might be challenging, AT adaptations can be used to help people circumvent disabilities whenever possible. People must be able to care for their own needs at home and school in the areas of eating and food preparation, dressing, grooming, and safety. Environmental control units can help people with disabilities operate devices and foster independent living at home, school, and work. These enabling devices give individuals control over their environment and promote independence. Switches and scanning devices also can contribute to independence for individuals who may need alternate input device options. Finally, as a result of legislation, individuals with disabilities are entitled to access transportation, buildings, public facilities, and so forth to promote mobility in and integration into the community.

DISCUSSION QUESTIONS

1. Discuss your perceptions of how individuals with disabilities have been integrated into the community more fully and provide examples to support your views.
2. Think about an individual you know who has a developmental or acquired disability. Discuss the impact of the disability on that individual's independence and the measures that have been taken to foster independence.
3. Conduct an inventory of a classroom, workplace, or community facility to determine how assistive technology adaptations might be used in different environments.
4. Describe the characteristics of switches including design, use, and feedback.
5. Describe the six types of switches.
6. Explain the four types of scanning formats.
7. Describe the three types of scanning techniques.

8. Explain how an ECU system works including input devices and transmission options.
9. Identify examples of ECU systems in catalogues and share how they work in school, the workplace, and the community.
10. Explain assistive technology adaptations that can be used to help individuals with management skills.
11. Compare and contrast mobility issues for individuals with different disabilities. Think about accessibility in terms of architectural barriers, transportation (public and private), recreational facilities, and so forth.

REFERENCES

Angelo, D. H. (1997). AAC in the family and home. In S. Glennen & D. DeCoste (Eds.), *The handbook of augmentative communication* (pp. 523–45). San Diego: Singular Publishing Group.

Aveno, A. (1989). Community involvement of persons with severe retardation living in community residences. *Exceptional Children, 55*(4), 309–14.

Church, G., & Glennen, S. (1992). *The handbook of assistive technology.* San Diego: Singular Publishing Group.

Cook, A. M., & Hussey, S. M. (1995). *Assistive technologies: Principles and practices.* St. Louis: Mosby.

Corn, A. L., & Rosenblum, L. P. (2000). *Finding wheels.* Austin, TX: Pro-Ed.

Gardner, J. F. (1990). Introduction: A decade of change. In J. F. Gardner & M. S. Chapman (Eds.), *Program issues in developmental disabilities* (2nd ed., pp. 3–17). Baltimore: Paul H. Brookes.

Lewis, R. (1993). *Special education technology.* Pacific Grove, CA: Brooks/Cole Publishing Co.

Luckasson, R., Coulter, D. L., Polloway, E. A., Reiss, S., Schalock, R. L., Snell, M. E., Spitalnick, D. M., & Stark, J. A. (1992). *Mental retardation: Diagnosis, classification, and systems of support* (9th ed.). Washington, DC: American Association on Mental Retardation.

Mithaug, D. E., & Hanawalt, D. A. (1978). The validation of procedures to assess prevocational task preferences in retarded adults. *Journal of Applied Behavior Analysis, 11,* 153–162.

Nosek, M. A. (1992). Independent living. In R. M. Parker & E. M. Szymanski (Eds.), *Rehabilitation counseling* (2nd ed., pp. 103–134). Austin, TX: Pro-Ed.

O'Brien, J. (1987). A guide to life-style planning. In B. Wilcox and G. T. Bellamy (Eds.), *A comprehensive guide to the Activities Catalog* (pp. 175–189). Baltimore: Paul H. Brookes.

O'Brien, J. (1991). *Down stairs that are never your own: Supporting people with developmental disabilities in their own homes.* Paper prepared for The Center on Human Policy, Syracuse University, Syracuse, New York.

Schalock, R. L., & Kiernan, W. E. (1990). *Habilitation planning for adults with disabilities.* New York: Springer-Verlag.

Smith, D. D. (2000). *Introduction to special education* (4th ed.). Boston: Allyn and Bacon.

GLOSSARY OF ASSISTIVE TECHNOLOGY TERMS

The following is a glossary of terms to be used as a resource for people interested in AT devices and services.

AAC   Acronym for Augmentative and Alternative Communication, which is an area of clinical practice that helps people compensate for serious speech limitations by supplementing or establishing a verbal communication system.

Adaptations   Specific accommodations, modifications, and supports to help individuals compensate for functional limitations and challenges.

Alternative keyboard   A hardware device that replaces or enhances a traditional keyboard and is set up to meet the specific user's needs.

ASCII   Acronym for American Standard Code for Information Interchange. A standardization system that converts letters, numbers, punctuation marks, and other characters to unique electronic code that allows information to be transferred from one computer to another or to a peripheral.

ASL   Acronym for American Sign Language, the manual communication system considered to be the "official" language of members of the deaf community.

ATA   Acronym for the Alliance for Technology Access. The ATA is a valuable resource to the disability community.

Aided communication   Communication systems that use equipment and/or devices to provide people with the ability to communicate. Communication modes that use equipment (e.g., augmentative communication aids, paper and pencil) to enhance the communicator's vocalizations or gestures.

Authoring system/language   Software that provides a method or style of delivery, but provides no content. The content must be provided by the user.

Basic life skills   Skills that are associated with a person's ability to interact in society on a daily basis.

Blissymbol   A graphic symbol system used to represent words or concepts that was developed by Charles Bliss.

Braille   A system of raised dots that translates English to a tactile code and vice versa.

Braille input   A hardware device that allows input to the computer via Braille keyboards or standard keyboards with special Braille keys.

Reprinted with permission from the Alliance for Technology Access.

Braille output   A hardware device that produces Braille, either via a paper copy or a refreshable output on or near the keyboard.

CAI   Acronym for Computer Assisted Instruction, which uses the computer to supplement the teaching process.

Captioning   The addition of text to visual displays to supplement or enhance audio features.

CCTV   Acronym for Closed-Circuit Television, which is a magnification system to enlarge images on a monitor.

CD-ROM   Acronym for Compact Disc Read Only Memory, a large-capacity medium for storing graphics, text, and sound.

Communication aid   A device to enhance a person's ability to communicate wants, needs, and so forth.

Communication board   A device made of paper or other material that is used to display choices either by gazing or touching.

Compatibility   The ability for devices (e.g., computers and peripherals) to communicate with one another.

CPU   Acronym for Central Processing Unit, which is the computer's main control center, also called a microprocessor.

Cursor   The symbol on a computer screen that indicates the point of insertion for the user's input.

Direct selection   A system that requires some form of directional movement as a means of pointing.

DOS   Acronym for Disk Operating System, which is a generic term used to describe system software programs that facilitate communication between a computer and peripherals.

Early childhood intervention   Intervention designed to enhance a young child's cognitive, motor, communication, and social skills.

E-mail   Electronic mail that is used to send and receive messages via telecommunications.

Finger spelling   A gestural code for spelling out words. The most common finger spelling system is called the American Manual Alphabet. (Communicating without speech using hand and finger signs.)

Firmware   Software stored in a computer's permanent read only memory (ROM).

Floppy disk   A secondary system to store data. Older computers used 5.25-inch disks, which were replaced by 3.5-inch disks. Zip disks and CD-ROMS are often used today in place of floppy disks.

Font   Typeface.

FM   Amplification system. Sound enhancement wherein sounds are transmitted via FM radio signals.

GUI   Acronym for Graphical User Interface, which is found on computer operating systems with pull-down menus, icons, and windows that represent commands and files.

Hard disk   A secondary storage device used to store large amounts of data within a computer.

Head stick   Adaptive pointer used by people who cannot use their hands to perform computer functions. The head stick usually is usually attached to a helmet or a head strap and the user bends the neck to apply the head stick to a key on the computer's keyboard.

I/O   Acronym for input/output, which refers to how information is transferred between a computer and peripherals.

IEP   Acronym for the Individualized Education Program, which identifies educational and related referrals for students and preschoolers with disabilities.

IFSP   Acronym for Individualized Family Services Plan, a written document that identifies and organizes resources and related services for children under the age of 3 years.

Input device   Any device that enters information into the computer from an external device such as a standard or alternate keyboard, a mouse, and so forth.

Internet   A global communication network that connects computers to the "information highway."

ITP   Acronym for Individualized Transition Plan, a document that coordinates service delivery for students as they move to adulthood.

Joystick   A peripheral device with a movable rod or lever that a user pushes in the direction of an intended movement—the joystick used for a wheelchair, for example.

Keyboard emulator   A hardware device that interfaces with a computer and allows input from a source other than the regular keyboard. Emulators allow the user to run standard software without additional adaptations.

Large print display   A hardware device that enlarges an image that is displayed on a computer monitor.

Large print software   Software that provides enlarged print on either the computer monitor or on paper.

LCD   Acronym for Liquid Crystal Display, an image technology used with many laptop computers, calculators, and digital watches.

LD   Acronym for Learning Disabilities, a condition caused by personal neurological dysfunction that either inhibits learning or causes a loss of information already learned.

Macro command   A user-defined command that causes the compute to execute special instruction.

Menu   A list of options or choices displayed on the computer screen for user selection.

MHz   Abbreviation for Megahertz, a measure of one million cycles per second of CPU clock speed.

MB   Acronym for megabyte, approximately one million bytes, which is a unit of measure for computer memory or storage.

Modem   A hardware peripheral that allows a computer to send and receive information to and from other computers over telephone lines.

Mouse   A computer input device that is used to input information to the computer; moving the mouse to position a pointer on the computer screen.

Multimedia   The combination of various medias for integration into a computer document or presentation.

Morphology   Examination of the smallest units of speech that have memory.

Network   Several computers linked by communications cables.

OCR   Acronym for Optical Character Recognition, a system, that may be a piece of hardware plugged into a PC or software, which translates print into a format that can be "read and spoken" by the computer or translated into Braille.

Output device   A device such as a monitor, used by the computer to communicate information to the operator in a usable form.

Overlay   Paper or other material placed over a membrane keyboard; can often be tailored to an individual's needs.

Peripheral device   Computer hardware (e.g., video monitor, printer) that is remote from a computer yet under the computer's control.

Phonology   Sound system of language.

Printer   A peripheral that produces printed text or graphics.

Pragmatics   Use of language to achieve a specific purpose.

Public domain program   Software that is not copyrighted and therefore can be used by anyone.

Pull-down menu   A list of user's computer choices in the form of a temporary menu that remains hidden until "pulled down" by the computer operator.

QWERTY keyboard   The most common layout of a keyboard in the United States where Q, W, E, R, T, and Y appear in the top row of letter keys.

RAM   Acronym for Random Access Memory, the primary memory where information and software is stored temporarily while a program is running.

ROM   Acronym for Read Only Memory, primary memory where content can be read but not changed in any way.

Scanning   An indirect method of computer access using software that automatically moves along available responses that the operator selects by activating a switch.

Scooter   A three-wheeled mobility unit for personal movement.

Sinem reader software   Software that allows a speech synthesizer to read text in a monitor.

Semantics   Meaningful aspects of language.

Shareware   Software that can be used prior to being purchased.

Speech synthesis   The process of producing sounds similar to human speech via a computer or other device.

Software   Programs that run on computers.

Speech recognition   The process by which a computer can understand spoken commands via translation software.

Speech synthesizer   A device that allows the computer to produce speech.

Spell checker   A program that checks each word in a document to see if it is properly spelled.

Switch   An input device that allows a user with little fine motor dexterity to operate a computer or other electrical device.

Switch toys   Electronic toys that have been adapted and work with a switch.

Tactile graphics   Graphics that have been converted into tactile form.

TDD   Acronym for Telecommunications Device for the Deaf. A device that allows people who are deaf to transmit typed-in messages via telephones lines.

Telecommunications   The process by which information is exchanged with other computers over long distances via telephone lines or some other medium.

Text-to-speech synthesis   Speech output equipment that pronounces text using a speech synthesizer.

Touch screen   Computer input device that is activated for touch; usually the touch screen mounts in front of monitor.

Trackball   A computer input device in which the user rotates a ball to move a pointer on the computer screen; similar to a mouse.

Unaided communication   Method of communication whereby the communicator uses vocalizations, gestures, facial expressions, and sign language, as a few examples to be understood.

Voice sxit   An input method whereby a device sends signals or information to the computer via speech.

Word prediction program   Program that speed up entry by predicting words based on the first few keystrokes.

SECTION 508

§ 1194.22 Web-based Intranet and Internet information and applications.

(a) A text equivalent for every nontext element shall be provided (e.g., via "alt," "longdesc," or in element content).

(b) Equivalent alternatives for any multimedia presentation shall be synchronized with the presentation.

(c) Web pages shall be designed so that all information conveyed with color is also available without color, for example from context or markup.

(d) Documents shall be organized so they are readable without requiring an associated style sheet.

(e) Redundant text links shall be provided for each active region of a server-side image map.

(f) Client-side image maps shall be provided instead of server-side image maps except where the regions cannot be defined with an available geometric shape.

(g) Row and column headers shall be identified for data tables.

(h) Markup shall be used to associate data cells and header cells for data tables that have two or more logical levels of row or column headers.

(i) Frames shall be titled with text that facilitates frame identification and navigation.

(j) Pages shall be designed to avoid causing the screen to flicker with a frequency greater than 2 Hz and lower than 55 Hz.

(k) A text-only page, with equivalent information or functionality, shall be provided to make a web site comply with the provisions of this part, when compliance cannot be accomplished in any other way. The content of the text-only page shall be updated whenever the primary page changes.

(l) When pages utilize scripting languages to display content, or to create interface elements, the information provided by the script shall be identified with functional text that can be read by assistive technology.

(m) When a web page requires that an applet, plug-in or other application be present on the client system to interpret page content, the page must provide a link to a plug-in or applet that complies with §1194.21(a) through (l).

(n) When electronic forms are designed to be completed online, the form shall allow people using assistive technology to access the information, field elements, and functionality required for completion and submission of the form, including all directions and cues.

(o) A method shall be provided that permits users to skip repetitive navigation links.

(p) When a timed response is required, the user shall be alerted and given sufficient time to indicate more time is required.

LISTING OF ASSISTIVE TECHNOLOGY VENDORS

Each year, the Alliance for Technology Access publishes its list of ATA vendors. This listing is reproduced here to serve as a resource for interested readers. Inclusion on this list does not necessarily constitute an endorsement by the authors or the publisher.

AbleNet, Inc.
1081 Tenth Ave. S.E., Minneapolis, MN 55414
800-322-0956
E-mail: customerservice@ablenetinc.com
Web site: http://www.ablenetinc.com
AbleNet develops and markets products and services to meet the needs of children and adults with severe disabilities. Products include simple technology systems and related materials that allow users to actively participate in daily activities. Support services include workshops aimed at parents, teachers, therapists, and care-providers nationwide. AbleNet also provides information and referral services. Call the resource specialist at 800-322-0956 with questions or suggestions about product needs or applications.

Academic Software, Inc.
331 W. 2nd Street, Lexington, KY 40507
Phone: 606-233-2332 or 800-VIA-ADLS
E-mail: asistaff@acsw.com
Web site: http://www.acsw.com
ASI publishes and/or markets several products. The Adaptive Device Locator System (ADLS) is a database of adaptive devices and vendor information for Apple II, Macintosh, or MS/DOS computer systems. The Unicorn Overlay Express produces computer-generated overlays for Unicorn keyboards using picture libraries (e.g., Picture Communication Symbols, KeyPics, Core Picture Vocabulary). The Picture Icon X-CHANGE program allows users to translate pictures from our libraries into programs like LessonMaker, Tutor-Tech, and ToolKit.

From Alliance for Technology Access, 1999b, n.p.

Adaptivation, Inc.
2225 West 50th Street, Suite 100, Sioux Falls, SD 57105
Phone: 800-723-2783/605-335-4445
Fax: 605-335-4446
E-mail: info@adaptivation.com
Web site: http://www.adaptivation.com
Adaptivation designs products for individuals with disabilities to provide them a
means of communication and control. The unique line of switches include Traction
Pads, Pal Pads, and the Vibration Switch. Affordable AAC products include the
VoicePal family, Sequencer, Chipper, and the DEC-AID. There is also a line of wire-
less environmental controls. Adaptivation has many new assistive products com-
ing soon. Call for the latest Adaptivation product catalog.

American Thermoform Corporation
2311 Travers Avenue, City of Commerce, CA 90040
Phone: 213-723-9021
American Thermoform currently offers the Ohtsuki BT-5000 Print/
Printer&emdash, the only printer available that produces Braille and print on the
same page; the Comet personal printer (Braille only), and KTS Braille displays in
80- and 40-cell options.

Antarq
Fernando No. 90, Col. Alamos
C.P. 03400, Mexico, D.F.
Phone: 525-530-2077
Web site: http://www.antarq.com.mx
Offers personal computer technology for special education and rehabilitation for
bilinqual populations in Mexico, Central and South America, Puerto Rico, and
United States. Special equipment is available for visually impaired, deaf-mute, and
individuals with cognitive and physical disabilities and the professionals who work
with them. Applied to all age groups in education, professional rehabilitation,
vocation, and independent living. All products have been selected, adapted, or produced to be applied and used by Spanish-speaking or bilinqual (Spanish/English,
Portuguese/English spoken) populations.

Apple Computer, Inc.
1 Infinite Loop, MS301-3ED
Cupertino, CA 94014
Tech Support: 800-800-2775
Web site: http://www.apple.com
"Apple is committed to helping persons with disabilities attain an unparalleled
level of independence through a personal computer. Every Macintosh ships with
rich, built-in features that support a positive user experience for disabled people."
Through their participation in the Alliance, Apple is demonstrating their intent to
be responsive to the requirements of consumers with disabilities and to work with

them and the ATA developers of assistive technologies to ensure access by all to emerging Apple technology. Apple's Disability Resources web site is located at: http://www.apple.com/education/k12/disability/ The first formal joint activity is participation by the Alliance in Apple's iMac Computer Learning Month sweepstakes along with partners Don Johnston, Inc., and IntelliTools. Assistive Technology will be the focus of the day on October 28 and the Alliance and these two partners and their products will be featured on Apple's website and sweepstakes at http://www.apple.com/education.

APT Technology, Inc./Du-It Control Systems Group, Inc.
236A N. Main Street, Shreve, OH 44676
330-567-3073
E-mail: apt2duit@valkyrie.net
DU-IT designs and manufactures mobility, environmental control, and computer access equipment for severely disabled people. DU-IT prides itself on well-engineered, effective solutions to the difficult control problems of high level (C-5 to C-1) quadriplegics and people with severe cerebral palsy or advanced neuro-muscular disease. DU-IT provides wheelchair control systems and controllers, power wheelchair recline control, and independently operable full-access high-quad SCI computer work station, as well as adaptors and switches.

Arkenstone, Inc.
NASA Ames Moffett Complex, Bldg. 23
P.O. Box 215, Moffett Field, CA 94035
Phone: 800-444-4443
E-mail: info@arkenstone.org
Web site: http://www.arkenstone.org
Arkenstone is a nonprofit organization that has become the leading provider of reading machines for people with visual and reading disabilities. The goal is to make better and more affordable reading systems, so that more people can access print independently. Stand-alone reading machines are available for about $3,500 and PC-based reading systems for about $2,500. The software can convert an existing PC to a reading machine for under $1,000.

Articulate Systems, Inc.
600 West Cummings Park, Suite 4500, Woburn, MA 01801
Phone: 800-443-7077
E-mail: info@dragonsys.com
Web site: http://www.dragonsys.com
Articulate Systems has been the pioneer in Voice User Interface and Voice Communication Technology for the Macintosh since 1986. Articulate Systems' product line includes the award winning Voice Navigator II, which allows users to control their favorite Macintosh application by spoken commands. Articulate Systems' complete line of sound solution products encompasses Voice Recognition, Voice Recording, Voice Annotation, and Voice Messaging.

AssisTech
P.O. Box 137, Stow, NY, 14785
888-ASISTEK
E-mail: info@assisttech.com
Web site: http://www.assisttech.com
AssisTech is a small, energetic company committed to low-cost, mainstream technology solutions. Focused on challenges faced by people with disabilities and their families, their solutions offer alternatives for anyone to have more fun, be more productive and creative, and "just do stuff" more easily. Their growing product line features "way inexpensive," customer-friendly technology creations. Their newest, hottest items make puppetry, mobility, and a new kind of computer play a reality for kids of all ages with and without disabilities.

Assistive Technology, Inc.
850 Boylston Street, Chestnut Hill MA 02167
Phone: 800-793-9227
E-mail: customercare@assistivetech.com
Web site: http://www.assistivetech.com

Atlantis Corporation
804 Westham Parkway, Richmond, VA 23229
E-mail: jcavera@atlantiscorp.com
Web site: http://www.atlantiscorp.com
Atlantis Corporation, a science and engineering consulting firm specializing in data acquisition, analysis, simulations, and control system design, is dedicated to creating systems that are easy to use and accessible to the broadest possible audience, including users with visual impairments.

Aurora Systems, Inc.
Box 43005, 4739 Willingdon Ave., Burnaby, B.C., Canada V5G 3H0
Phone: 604-291-6310, 888-290-1133
E-mail: aurorasw@direct.ca
Web site: http://www.djtech.com/aurora
Aurora Systems provides software to help individuals with learning disabililties and people who require augmentative communication. They have been providing products for Windows and DOS throughout North America and the world for about seven years. Aurora for Windows 2.0 gives AAC, single-finger, and learning-disabled users easy access to Windows applications. Aurora for DOS 2.0 is AAC software that provides easy access to the widest variety of applications software.

Blazie Engineering, Inc.
105 E. Jarrettsville Road, Forest Hill, MD 21050
Phone: 410/893-9333
E-mail: info@blazie.com
Web site: http://www.blazie.com/

Blazie Engineering develops and manufactures products for people with visual impairments, including Braille 'n Speak, Braille Blazer, Personal Touch, Thiel Braille Embosser, and Audiocalc.

Broderbund Software, Inc.
500 Redwood Blvd., Box 6121, Novato, CA 94948-6125
Phone: 800-521-6263
E-mail: lucinda_ray@broder.com
Web site: http://www.broderbund.com/education
Broderbund software is known in the educational marketplace as easy-to-use, innovative and exciting. Best-known titles include Print Shop, Kid Pix, the Carmen Sandiego series, and a brand-new CD-ROM series entitled Broderbund's Living Books. Goals include providing high-quality educational software that appeals to educators and students, as well as continually improving the content of the accompanying materials. Broderbund also looks for new ways of meeting teachers needs and making software more accessible to the special education market.

Brown and Co., Inc.
14 Midoaks Street, Monroe, NY 10950
Phone: 508-352-8822
Brown and Co. is a small company founded to manufacture industrial damper control systems for the asphalt industry. With the advent of the personal computer, Cal Brown, the founder, and Dr. George Markowsky, University of Maine, devised the PC-Pedal to avoid the necessity of reaching for the Shift, Control, Alternate, and Backspace/Delete keys. Using a PC-Pedal, a person with the ability to strike a key and simultaneously close an external switch is able to have full access to the personal computer keyboard.

CAST, Inc. (Center for Applied Special Technology)
39 Cross Street, Peabody, MA 01960
Phone: 508-531-8555
E-mail: cast@cast.org
Web site: http://www.cast.org
Founded in 1984, CAST is a not-for-profit organization whose mission is to expand the opportunities for all people through the use of innovative technology. This mission is achieved through a combination of training, evaluations, and research and development. The ResearchWare products developed out of the needs determined through our research and evaluations of people with disabilities. ResearchWare includes ClickReader, ClickWriter, Talking Calculator, and much more.

Claris Corporation
5201 Patrick Henry Dr., C-56, Box 58168, Santa Clara, CA 95052-8168
Phone: 408-987-7000
E-mail: jeff_orloff@claris.com
Web site: http://www.claris.com

Claris Corporation (a wholly owned subsidiary of Apple Computer, Inc.) develops, markets, and supports application software for Macintosh, Windows, and Apple II computers. It began shipping Claris-labeled products in 1988 to business, government, education, and technical markets. Claris's product line includes integrated productivity applications, word processing, graphics, data management, planning, and CAD (computer aided design).

Closing the Gap, Inc.
P.O. Box 68, Henderson, MN 56044
Phone: 612/248-3294
E-mail: info@closing the gap.com
Web site: http://www.closingthegap.com
Closing the Gap is an information source working exclusively in the field of micro-computers and persons with disabilities. Their goal is to discover ways that micro-computer-related products are being used in special education and rehabilitation and to disseminate that knowledge as widely as possible. Their products include *Closing the Gap*, a bimonthly newspaper, and an annual international conference for special education and rehabilitation professionals.

Compu-Teach 16541 Redman Way, Suite 137C, Redman, WA 98052
Phone: 800/448-3224
E-mail: cmpteach@wolfenet.com
Web site: http://www.wolfenet.com/~cmpteach
All Compu-Teach software is designed by Dr. Roger Schank, Dean of Artificial Intelligence and Cognitive Psychology, and his team at Yale University. Compu-Teach software has multiple levels and is enhanced with colorful graphics, animation, and music to ensure use for many years. Their programs address the subject areas of language arts, reading, math, science, geography, and study skills for skill levels pre-K through college. Compu-Teach also provides teachers tools for testing and grading.

Consultants for Communication Technology
508 Bellevue Terrace, Pittsburgh, PA 15202
Phone: 412-761-6062
E-mail: 70272.1034@compuserve.com
CCT manufactures a line of augmentative communication and telephone access hardware/software products for the speech- and hearing-impaired. Their products include the Handy Speech Communication Aide, Wish Writer, Phone Manager, ToneTalker, Meta4, and other state-of-the-art products at reasonable prices. Their newest program for Windows, Keywi, combines the features of Handy Speech and the Phone Manager in a new, more powerful interface.

Creative Communicating
P.O. Box 3358, Park City, UT 84060
Phone: 435-645-7737

E-mail: mail@creative-comm.com
Web site: http://www.creative-comm.com
Creative Communicating is a small company dedicated to creating practical and affordable materials for children and educational resources for parents and/or service providers. The company develops, publishes, and markets over 50 products, including books, software, videos, and intervention materials. It has brought to the marketplace innovative products in the early childhood and emergent literacy arenas. It developed the Storytime resource books and software. Creative Communicating maintains a World Wide Web site that provides consumer information and support including a free electronic newsletter containing up-to-date topics in assistive technology and literacy.

Dolphin Systems Limited
100 South Ellsworth Avenue, San Mateo CA 94401
Phone: 650-348-7401
E-mail: sales@dolphinusa.com
Web site: http://www.dolphinusa.com
Dolphin Computer Access specializes in the design, manufacture, and distribution of access technology for visually impaired computer users. Dolphin Computer Access specializes in the design, manufacture, and distribution of access technology for visually impaired computer users. Part of Dolphin's development strategy is that visually impaired computer users should be able to enjoy a common standard of access across all their applications without having to resort to special configurations (such as macro files) to achieve this. Dolphin is working to provide intelligent and automatic speech, Braille, and magnification access wherever the Microsoft standards for the Windows operating systems have been applied.

Don Johnston, Incorporated
26799 West Commerce Drive, Volo, IL 60073
Phone: 847-740-0749 (U.S.); 847-740-7326 (global) Fax: 800-859-5242
Tech Support: 800-999-4660
E-mail: info@donjohnston.com
Web site: http://www.donjohnston.com
Don Johnston, Inc., has become a leader in the field of adaptive equipment and computer access. DJI develops, manufactures, and markets materials for persons who are nonverbal and who have physical disabilities. Many products are specifically used for training in the areas of augmentative communication, physical access, and control of the environment. The DJI catalog reaches schools, hospitals, training centers, and families around the world. DJI exhibits at major augmentative communication and computer conferences.

Dorling Kindersley Family Learning
14614 N.E. 82nd Street, Vancouver, WA
Phone: 888-225-3535

Dorling Kindersley is the world-renowned British publisher of award winning CD-ROMs, videos, and lushly photographed books including the popular "Eyewitness" series. Their mission is one of impacting literacy in homes, schools, centers, and agencies.

Dunamis, Inc.
3423 Fowler Blvd., Lawrenceville, GA 30244
Phone: 800-828-2443
E-mail: dumanisben@aol.com
Dunamis develops software and hardware products to allow people with disabilities to use computers to enhance their lives and work more independently. Dunamis is sometimes called upon to help fit students to the right software, computer, and adaptive devices for use at school and at home. Dunamis carries a comprehensive line of software and adaptive devices, including the Powerpad touch tablet.

Echo Speech Corporation
6460 Via Real, Carpinteria, CA 93013
Phone: 800-377-3246
E-mail: mark@echospeech.com
Echo Technology Corporation (formerly Street Electronics) has sold the Echo speech products to the schools and special needs market since 1980. There are hundreds of Echo-compatible programs available from over 100 software manufacturers. The goal of the company is to produce high-quality, state-of-the-art speech output products at reasonable prices that can be used by a variety of users. The special-needs community has always been a primary focus in both design and marketing of the Echo product line.

Edmark Corporation
6727 185th Ave. NE, P.O. Box 97021, Redmond, WA 98073-9721
Phone: 800-362-2890
E-mail: maryannt@edmark.com
Web site: http://www.edmark.com
Edmark is a leading developer and publisher of high-quality, award-winning educational software. Serving both the home and education markets, Edmark combines rich multimedia technology with solid educational methodology to create products that inspire creativity, develop thinking skills, and engage children in the learning process. In its early years, the company focused on the special education market, publishing both print materials and software for the Apple, and manufacturing the TouchWindow, a touch-sensitive input device for the computer. These products are available for the education market.

Education TURNKEY Systems, Inc.
256 North Washington Street, Falls Church, VA 22046
Phone: 703-536-2310

E-mail: turnkey@ix.netcom.com
Education TURNKEY Systems has provided services to the special education community for more than a decade. TURNKEY also provides services to vendors of communication aids and devices and special education software publishers through market research, consultation, and the use of electronic software distribution. TURNKEY also conducts national video teleconferences on communication aids and devices.

Educational Press/Learning Well
1720 H Bellmont Ave., Baltimore, MD 21224
Phone: 410-561-5912
E-mail: 73444.2412@compuserve.com
Educational Press is a publishing company that develops material exclusively for the special education market and older learners with very low reading abilities. The target audience is special education students in middle school and high school who are reading at a third-grade level. Materials are either in workbook format or computer format. Computer software is accompanied by workbook material to help in the transition from the computer to printed materials. Most materials focus on the transitional student and teach employability skills, including the social skills necessary for success on the job.

Exceller Software Corp.
2 Graham Road West, Ithaca, NY 14850
Phone: 607-257-1665
E-mail: exceller@aol.com
Web site: http://www.exceller.com
Exceller Software publishes linguistic and reference software for education, home, and business markets. Software products include multimedia English grammar learning for ESL students; bilingual dictionaries in Spanish, German, Italian, and Portuguese; and Webster's Spanish/English Dictionary for Macintosh and Windows. Software is enabled for people with disabilities. Most titles have text-to-speech pronunciation for both source words and the respective definitions, including example sentences. For the Windows platform, the software also has variable size (larger) fonts and resizable user interface.

Fellowes (formerly APT, Inc.)
1789 Norwood Ave., Itasco, IL, 60143
Phone: 800-945-4545
Appoint was formed in 1989 to offer affordable, state-of-the-art input device technology. A strength lies in their ability to predict market needs and react with innovative, well-engineered solutions. MousePen Pro is the first mouse shaped like a pen. Because of its design, it is more comfortable and natural to use than a traditional mouse. Thumbelina is the world's smallest trackball. Designed for versatility, this thumb-driven device is ideal for portability and hand-held presentations, and because of its ergonomic shape and design will not cause carpal tunnel syndrome.

FutureForms
903 Chicago Drive, Grand Rapids, MI 49509
Phone: 616-475-1227
E-mail: info@futureforms.com
Web site: http://www.futureforms.com
FutureForms can convert existing or create a new paper-based form in an electronic format. Forms and documents are maintained in their electronic form library for clients' safety and convenience. FutureForms has proven products and services that will allow an organization to increase productivity and reduce costs. They offer an additional tool to aid people with disabilities in gaining employment.

Gus Communications, Inc.
1006 Lonetree Court, Bellingham, WA 98226
Phone: 360-715-8580
E-mail: gus@gusinc.com
Web site: http://www.gusinc.com
The Gus! Multimedia Speech System for Windows is the world's most popular AAC software product. It converts any Windows-compatible computer into a dynamic display communication device. Digitized and synthetic speech (synthesizer included), 2-72 buttons/page, unlimited layers, scanning. Includes the Gus! Talking Keyboard, Gus! Abbreviations, and Gus! Mouse. Also the Gus! Touch Screen for Portable Computers. Works with any Windows-compatible portable computer for finger/touch access.

The Great Talking Box Company
2245 Fortune Drive, Suite A, San Jose, CA 95135
Phone: 877-275-4482; 408-456-0151
Fax: 408-456-0184
E-mail: inquire@gtb-sym.com
Web site: http://www.gtb-sym.com
Featuring the EasyTalk, the Great Talking Box Company offers affordable augmentative communication devices. Individuals of all ages and disabilities can benefit from the EasyTalk's flexibility and ease of use. Due to digitized recording there are no language barriers. The EasyTalk has 8 recording levels and up to 54 minutes of extended recording time. Messages can be of variable length, with no time limits per key. Used as a speech device or learning tool, the EasyTalk is utilized worldwide by adults and children alike.

Hartley Courseware, Inc.
9920 Pacific Heights Blvd., Suite 500, San Diego, CA 92121
Phone: 800-521-8538
E-mail: mbradley@jlc.com
Hartley Courseware specializes in software programs for students with learning difficulties. Hartley publishes over 200 programs in reading and mathematics for grades Pre-K–12. Many secondary programs are also appropriate for adults.

Best-known programs are First Connections: The Golden Book Encyclopedia; Write This Way, a writing processor for learning disabled and hearing-impaired students; and Dr. Peet's Talk/Writer, a simple writing processor for younger children and visually imparied students. Hartley offers software for Macintosh, Windows, DOS, and Apple II compatible computers, and has over 40 CD-ROM titles.

Humanities Software
P.O. Box 950, 408 Columbia St., Hood River, OR 97031
Phone: 800-245-6737
E-mail: hinfo@humanitiessoftware.com
Web site: http://www.humanitiessoftware.com
Humanities Software is the world's largest publisher of whole language, literature-based software, offering over 150 titles for grades K–12, including programs for students with special needs, ESL, Remedial, and Emergent Literacy. This innovative software integrates process writing, literature, and word processing, and addresses all major areas of written language development. Chosen from the WRITE ON! titles, the Special Needs Collection contains titles of clear, carefully structured lessons, providing practice with basic language skills and offering opportunities for self-expression through open-ended writing.

IBM Special Needs Solutions
Bldg. 904, Internal Zip 9448, 11400 Burnet Rd., Austin, TX 78758
Phone: 800-426-4832
E-mail: snsinfo@us.ibm.com
Web site: http://www.austin.ibm.com/sns/
IBM's Special Needs Sytems develops and markets products that enhance computer access and learning for people with disabilities. Also see info about IBM's VoiceType at http://www.ibm.com/products. Once there, find VoiceType.

In Touch Systems
11 Westview Road, Spring Valley, NY 10977
Phone: 800-332-6244
E-mail: 74425.1633@compuserve.com
In Touch Systems produces the Magic Wand Keyboard (IBM or Apple), a miniature computer keyboard and mouse designed for anyone with restricted or no hand/arm movement. Both keyboard and mouse work with the slightest touch of a wand, using either a hand-held wand or mouth stick. No pressure is needed, only contact. The Magic Wand Keyboard was by created Jerry Crouch, president of In Touch Systems, for his wife, Susan, who is quadriplegic. Susan now uses a computer to manage sales and marketing for the company.

Information Services, Inc.
28 Green Street, Newbury, MA 01951
Phone: 800-462-9198

E-mail: sales@is-inc.com
Web site: http://www.is-inc.com
ISI is a Canadian-based company with offices in Canada and in Newbury, MA. Working with the Institute on Applied Technology at Children's Hospital, Boston, ISI jointly developed WriteAway, a DOS-based software writing tool-kit designed specifically for children and adults with learning and physical disabilities. Write-Away, available for the DOS and Windows 95 Operating Systems, integrates word-processing features with word prediction, text readback, built-in scanning, and alternate keyboard-access modes. The product has been used successfully by children and adults with a wide range of disabilities.

Innocomp
26210 Emery Road, Suite 302, Warrensville Heights, OH 44128
800-382-8622
E-mail: innocomp@aol.com
Web site: http://www.sayitall.com
Innocomp manufactures and distributes products relating to augmentative communication. Products include the Say-It-All II Plus and the Say-It-Simply Plus now with Clarity Speech. Clarity Speech is a revolutionary new speech output designed by Innocomp to have human-quality speech in a text-to-speech system. It is available in male, female, and child's voice. The goal is to provide quality speech output in an easy-to-use and lightweight device and to provide this in a product that is economically feasible.

Innovative Products
830 South 48th Street, Grand Forks ND 58201
Phone: 701-772-5185
Fax: 701-772-5284
E-mail: jsteinke@iphope.com
Web site: http://www.iphope.com
Innovative Products (IP) manufactures the GO-BOT and GBI, which allows standing or seating with full support for the head, knees, back and torso areas of the body. The GO-BOT and GBI can also be outfitted with an optional tray system for daily use and support. The enhanced electronics package with speed control for the GO-BOT offers many of the features needed by children with disabilities to function to their potential in everyday life, with controls such as proportional joystick, switches, and a wireless radio remote control with emergency on/off for safety.

IntelliTools
55 Leveroni Ct., Suite 9, Novato, CA 94949
Phone: 800-899-6687
Fax: 415-382-5950
E-mail: info@intellitools.com
Web site: http://www.intellitools.com

IntelliTools produces and distributes IntelliKeys, the high-quality alternative keyboard, and a host of software products for people with physical, visual, or cognitive disabilities. Software includes the award-winning series of creativity tools: IntelliTalk, a versatile talking word processor; Overlay Maker, a drawing program for designing custom overlays for IntelliKeys; IntelliPics, an easy-to-use multimedia authoring program; and ClickIt!, a powerful utility providing mouseless access to point-and-click software. IntelliTools also publishes a growing number of ready-to-use curriculum resources, including instant access to Edmark and Living Books software; Hands-On Concepts, an integrated early reading and math series; Math-Pad; and Exploring Patterns. IntelliKeys works with Macintosh and PC-compatible computers. All software is available for the Macintosh with a growing line of Windows products including Overlay Maker and IntelliTalk.

Judy Lynn Software
278 Dunhams Corner Road, East Brunswick, NJ 08816
Phone: 908-390-8845
E-mail: judylynn@castle.net
Web site: http://www.castle.net/~judylynn/
Judy Lynn Software was founded in 1991 by Elliot Pludwinski, a programmer, who could not find lower-level single-switch software for the IBM PC for his daughter Judy, who was born with microcephaly. With encouragement and guidance from Judy's teacher, the programs were written for children with a cognitive age level as early as nine months. The six software titles in the product line are Cause & Effect, Cause & Effect Carnival, Visual Tracking, Fundamental Concepts, Switch Art, and Visual Motor Skills (1994 Parent's Choice Honor).

Keyboard Alternatives & Vision Solutions
537 College Avenue, Santa Rosa CA 95404-4102
Phone: 707-544-8000
E-mail: keyalt@keyalt.com
Web site: http://www.keyalt.com
Keyboard Alternatives & Vision Solutions was founded in 1989 by Jon Simkovitz, selling magnification devices, screen magnification software, and reading machines for the visually impaired and blind. Jon quickly recognized a growing need for ergonomic products for the workplace, such as keyboards, mice, keyboard trays, adjustable furniture, and the like. The company now provides hundreds of products of this type as well as voice dictation software, telephone headsets, fluorescent lighting filters, magnification systems, and Braille products. The company prides itself on finding appropriate solutions for people in need rather than attempting to "sell products." They offer customer assistance in product selection, training, and technical support to maximize product usefulness and customer satisfaction.

Laureate Learning Systems, Inc.
110 East Spring Street, Winooski, VT 05404
Phone: 800-562-6801

E-mail: laureate@laureatelearning.com
Web site: http://www.laureatelearning.com
Laureate is dedicated to the innovative use of computer technology for special education and rehabilitation. Laureate offers programs for language development, concept development and processing, augmentative communication, and instructional games. Laureate programs are easy-to-use, flexible, and above all, effective. Natural-sounding speech and colorful pictures motivate and guide the learner, making most of the programs appropriate for nonreaders.

Lawrence Productions
1800 S. 35th St., Galesburg, MI 49053
Phone: 800-421-4157
Lawrence Productions has been a producer of interactive educational software since 1980. Lawrence programs span a wide range of reading and interest levels and are designed for pre-K, elementary, secondary, college, and adult education classes. Lawrence now offers a complementary line of educational videos.

LD Resources
202 Lake Road, New Preston, CT 06777
Phone: 860-868-3214
E-mail: richard@ldresources.com
Web site: http://www.ldresources.com
LD Resources creates HyperCard stacks that are simple, easy-to-use, and inexpensive. They have reference, entertainment, clip art, language learning, story-telling, and many other kinds of stacks ranging in price from $5 to $20 and aimed at a variety of ages and abilities. Free and shareware stacks can be found on most online services and in many Macintosh user group libraries. Their commercial stacks can be ordered directly from them. Their goal is to help make the people who use their products happier and more independent.

Little Planet Publishing
4004 Hillsboro Road, Suite 237B, Nashville, TN 37215
Phone: 800-974-2248
E-mail: psloan@littleplanet.com
Web site: http://www.littleplanet.com
Little Planet Publishing develops and publishes curriculum-based software for early education. The Little Planet Literacy Series is a language arts series with current titles for kindergarten to third-grade levels. The series is the result of four years of joint research and development between Little Planet Publishing and the Learning Technology Center (LTC) at Peabody College, Vanderbilt University. The LTC is internationally known for its research into how technology may be fully integrated into the classroom curriculum.

Lorien Systems
Enkalon Business Centre, 25 Randalstown Road, Antrim, N Ireland BT41 4LJ
Phone: 011-44-1849-428105

E-mail: info@loriens.com
Web site: http://www.texthelp.com
Lorien Systems set about developing software products that would allow people with various disabilities, ranging from literacy difficulties to motion and dexterity problems, gain a much greater degree of access to the computer. Products have evolved, through listening to the requirements of the professionals and the end users, into some of the most innovative and easy-to-use products for the computer user with disabilities, either as a means of communication or as a means to fulfilling employment.

LS&S Group
PO Box 673, Northbrook, IL 60065
Phone: 800-468-4789
E-mail: lssgrp@aol.com
Web site: http://www.lssgroup.com
The LS&S Group specializes in products for the visually impaired, with a large selection of CCTV and computer products.

Madenta Communications
3022 Calgary Trail South, Edmonton AB, Canada T6J 6V4
Phone: 800-661-8406
Email-: madenta@madenta.com
Web site: http://www.madenta.com
Madenta develops products in pursuit of its goal of providing quality assistive technology for people with disabilities. Doors! is a collection of products that provides complete control of the Macintosh. Possible access methods include point and click, single or multiple switch, adapted keyboard, and voice. Innovations such as built-in word prediction, resizable on-screen keyboards, cursor scanning sequences, and transparent background operation make these products revolutionary.

Marblesoft
12301 Central Ave. NE, Suite 205, Blaine, MN 55434
Phone: 612-755-1402
E-mail: marble2@winternet.com
Web site: http://www.winternet.com/~marble
Marblesoft is a special education software company. All programs focus on early childhood development (Early Learning) with various hardware accesses utilized. 128K versions offer input through Touchwindow, Powerpad, Light Pen, Keyboard, and Switches. All use the Echo, DoubleTalk, or Cricket speech synthesizer, run on Apple family computers, are laser-compatible, and have a student records management program that allows for a screen or written printout.

Mayer-Johnson Co.
P.O. Box 1579, Solana Beach, CA 92075
Phone: 619-550-0084

E-mail: mayerj@aol.com
Web site: http://www.mayer-johnson.com
The Mayer-Johnson Co. is the originator of the Picture Communication Symbols. Their symbols are used in augmentative communication. Their products include educational materials and software. The software is used to make communication boards, educational materials, and overlays for different computer access devices and for speech output. Presently software is designed for Macintosh and Windows.

Microsoft: Accessibility and Disabilities Group
One Microsoft Way, Redman, WA 98052-6399
Phone: 800-426-9400
E-mail: greglo@microsoft.com
Web site: http://www.microsoft.com/enable
Microsoft has established the Accessibility and Disabilities Group to make computers easier to use for people with special accessibility needs. This group works to make Microsoft products and services more accessible as well as promote accessibility throughout the computer industry. It also supports the development of a rich variety of third-party accessibility aids.

Microsystems Software, Inc.
600 Worcester Rd., Framingham, MA 01701
Phone: 800-828-2600
E-mail: billk@microsys.com
Web site: http://www.handiware.com
Microsystems publishes award-winning PC-access software providing powerful, efficient, and affordable long-term solutions for adapted access, augmentative communication, and low-vision needs. The flexibility of the software enables customization to physical needs and provides for maximum hardware and software compatibility. The HandiWARE family includes HandiKEY, HandiCHAT, HandiCODE, HandiWORD, HandiSHIFT, HandiVIEW, and SeeBEEP. Microsystems provides quality solutions for individuals with disabilities and prides itself on customer satisfaction.

MicroTalk
917 Clear Creek, Texarkana, TX 75503
Phone: 903-832-3471
E-mail: larry@screenaccess.com
Web site: http://www.screenaccess.com/
MicroTalk produces a program called ASAP, a screen reading program, and two speech cards, DoubleTalk and LiteTalk. ASAP reads whatever you type on the computer.

Millennium Software
3155 Fujita St., Torrance, CA 90505
Phone: 310-530-0356
E-mail: peuapeu@aol.com

The immediate goal of Millennium Software is to publish products such as Labeling-Tutor that carefully use discrete trial methods to address the needs of learning disabled children. These products will allow the parent or therapist to tailor the software to the specific cognitive, motor, sensory, and perseverative handicaps of the child, allowing for modication of and additions to the material being taught. The company also seeks to provide exceptional user support, yet keeps prices low enough for home users.

Mindscape Educational Software
1345 Diversey Parkway, Chicago, IL 60603
Phone: 800-829-1900
E-mail: mcoyne@mindscape.com
Web site: http://www.mindscape.com
Mindscape is a division of Software Toolworks, publisher of educational, curriculum, test preparation, and applications software for the home and school market. All educational software is distributed exclusively through the Society for Visual Education. Of Mindscape's 170 software selections, 45 are targeted for intensive use and thorough testing by special needs populations.

OMS Development
610 B Forest Ave., Wilmette, IL 60091
Phone: 847-251-5793
E-mail: ebohlman@netcom.com
OMS Development is primarily a custom programming and product development firm. OMS markets standard products, including powerful and affordable adaptive software. Tiny Talk is an affordable and small memory screen reading program for the IBM. Keycache, a word prediction program, is also available for IBM-compatible computers and works with nearly any program that uses keyboard input.

PageMinder
3623 South Avenue, Springfield, MO 65807
Phone: 888.882.7787
E-mail: pageminder@pageminderinc.com
Web site: http://www.pageminderinc.com
PageMinder provides a welcome solution for individuals struggling with memory deficits, or trying to keep up with a complicated schedule. With the use of paging technology, customers receive text reminders for medication times, daily living skills, appointments, or other routine tasks. The system is portable, easy to use, and requires no initiation on the part of the user. It can be adapted for many languages.

Prentke Romich Company
1022 Heyl Road, Wooster, OH 44691
Phone: 800-262-1933
E-mail: info@prentrom.com
Web site: http://www.prentrom.com/index.html

PRC's company mission is to help people with disabilities achieve their potential in educational, vocational, and personal pursuits. To this end PRC provides quality language and assistive technology products and services to people with disabilities, their families, and professions. Products include augmentative communication systems, computer access technology, and environmental controls. PRC services include toll-free sales and service numbers, a trial rental program to ensure applicability prior to purchase, and a service loaner program so that a user is not without a device while it is being serviced.

RJ Cooper and Associates
24843 Del Prado #283, Dana Pt., CA 92629
Phone: 800-RJCOOPER
E-mail: rj@rjcooper.com
Web site: http://www.rjcooper.com
RJ Cooper makes special-needs instructional software, access software, switch interfaces, and adapted trackballs and joysticks. RJ produces everything he makes for Mac and Windows, as well as his "old" library of Apple II software. Free demos are available. RJ has what may be the only online interactive, real-time, single-switch arcade game. Download his Movie Viewer to be able to play the games at his web site.

Raised Dot Computing, Inc.
408 South Baldwin Street, Madison , WI 53703
Phone: 608-257-9595
E-mail: dnavy@well.com
Web site: http://www.rdcbraille.com
RDC is dedicated to helping people with vision impairments make the maximum use of microcomputers. Their continuing goal is enabling people to work independently to discover the pleasures and challenges of computers. Their software is used to move information rapidly and accurately between print and grade II Braille, increasing the available Braille. A new product gives access to AppleWorks. They recognize that many people with vision impairments are not Braille readers. Their software supports large-print output on screen and paper and voice output.

Rhamdec, Inc.
P.O. Box 4296, Santa Clara, CA 95056
Phone: 800-469-3372
Web site: http://www.mydesc.com
Rhamdec is a manufacturer of attractive, high-quality productivity products for children and adults. The company's first product line is the patented MYDESC Custom Desktop, which is an adjustable tilting work surface available for wheelchairs, scooters, sofas, beds, tables, or floors. The MYDESC line was developed with input from end users, educators, and health-care professionals. The company believes that comfort and mobility can be achieved through good products designs that are both functional and attractive.

Roger Wagner Publishing, Inc.
1050 Pioneer Way, #P, El Cajon, CA 92020
Phone: 800-421-6526
E-mail: rwagnerinc@aol.com
Web site: http://www.hyperstudio.com
RWP designs Apple-specific software for use in the office, home, or school. Their current leading program, HyperStudio, is the top hypermedia product available. The recent Apple Achievement Awards recognized HyperStudio as the Best Software of the Year, Best Multimedia Product, and Best Apple IIgs Software. RWP is strongly dedicated to education and special needs. Many of the new features in HyperStudio v. 3.0 are specifically for the educational and special needs user. With these added features, HyperStudio can now reach many more new and first-time users.

Semerc
ProMedia, 790 Bloomfield Avenue, Clifton, NJ 07012
Phone: 800-462-0930
E-mail: info@promedia-semerc.com
Web site: http://www.promedia-semerc.com
SEMERC is a British company that specializes in hardware and software for special needs. Their software is used by educational institutions around the world and is now being introduced in the United States. They also manufacture a unique line of access products that include an infrared touch screen, computer track balls, and joysticks. More products are under development. SEMERC products feature a broad range of skill development beginning with cause and effect and advancing to full-featured word processing. Programs in their product line offer educational, creative, and recreational experiences for students with disabilities.

Sentient Systems Technology, Inc.
2100 Wharton Street, Suite 630, Pittsburgh, PA 15203
Phone: 800-344-1778
Web site: http://www.sentient-sys.com
Since 1983, Sentient Systems Technology Inc. has provided advanced augmentative communication solutions to thousands of people with speech, language, learning, and physical disabilities from around the world.

Simtech Publications
134 East Street, Litchfield, CT 06759
Phone: 860-567-1173
E-mail: switchedon@hsj.com
Web site: http://www.hsj.com
Simtech Publications was established in 1991 with a goal of developing and marketing low-cost switch accessible software for children with disabilities. All of Simtech's programs are extremely simple and user-friendly and focus on developing concepts and motor skills related to switch control. Bill Lynn, Simtech's owner

and software developer, is a speech-language pathologist with 20 years experience in the area of assistive technology and augmentative communication. A demo disk is available at their web site.

Skills Bank Corporation
Parkview Center 1, 7104 Ambassador Road, Baltimore, MD 21244
Phone: 800-847-5455
E-mail: cstaffor@skillsbank.com
Web site: http://www.skillsbank.com
Skills Bank products are designed to support teachers of basic skills, by providing student activities and evaluation tools that would require one-on-one teaching in a traditional educational setting. All Skills Bank products provide individual tutorials that evaluate the student, suggest lesson plans automatically or according to the instructor's choices, give hints and prompts, and reinforce learning in other pedagogically sound ways.

SoftTouch/kidTECH
4182 Pinewood Lake Drive, Bakersfield, CA 93309
Phone: 805-873-8744
E-mail: jomeyer@aol.com
The goal of kidTECH developers is to create software that the young child with disabilities will enjoy and at the same time learn from. kidTECH's software is based in song. The programs include songs common to the regular and special early childhood curriculums around the country. Each program includes a scanning mode for single-switch operation with an option for an auditory or quiet scan. Access options include mouse, TouchWindow, IntelliKeys, and Ke:nx. Printed overlays for the IntelliKeys are available both in print and on disk.

Special Needs Project Worldwide
3463 State St., Ste. 282, Santa Barbara, CA 93105
Phone: 800-333-6867
E-mail: books@specialneeds.com
Special Needs Project sells books about disabilities through its catalog and at conferences and consults with public and private agencies. Special Needs Project is directed by Hod Gray, an active parent with a special interest in assistive technology and an established California bookseller. SNP is an unmatched resource for books about disabilities and offers one-stop shopping for all current titles.

SSK Technology, Inc.
5619 Scotts Valley Dr., Suite 280, Scotts Valley, CA 95066
Phone: 408-461-8900
E-mail: wriTalk@aol.com
SSK Technology, Inc. stated goal is to provide "access" that is natural and easy through technology. The WriTalk is a technological breakthrough allowing real-time

written or typed communication over the telephone lines. Anyone with speech or hearing losses can communicate with family, friends, and co-workers using the WriTalk. Future SSK products will be compatible with the WritTalk. The WriTalk Palm (a cellular unit, software for communication between the WriTalk and a PC), and other software to enhance the applications of the WritTalk are available.

Stone and Associates
7910 Ivanhoe Ave., Suite 319, La Jolla, CA 92037
Phone: 619-693-6333
Stone and Associates, founded in 1983, is a nationally recognized publisher of educational software. The company was one of the first to anticipate and fulfill the needs of the IBM PC home educational marketplace. Now, with over 10 educational titles for home and school computers, Stone and Associates software also operates with the Apple II and Atari ST families of products. The hallmark of Stone and Associates published products is the style in which brightly colored graphics are used to teach reading and math skills.

Sun Microsystems Accessibility Group
901 San Antonio Road MS UCUPO2-103, Palo Alto, CA 94303
Phone: 415-863-3151
E-mail: access@sun.com
Web site: http://www.sun.com/tech/access
Sun Microsystems has developed Java Accessibility API, which will enable Java developers to write applications that many more of America's 40 million people with disabilities can immediately access and use. The Java Accessibility API is designed to allow assistance technologies such as screen readers, screen magnifiers, speech recognition systems, and Braille terminals to access Java applications. It is available for public review at http://java.sun.com/products/jfc/" http://java.sun.com/products/jfc/. It was created through an open design process based on input from licensees and developers, as well as experts in the assistive technology field.

Sunburst Communications
101 Castleton St., Pleasantville, NY 10570
Phone: 800-321-7511
E-mail: service@nysunburst.com
Web site: http://www.sunburst.com
Sunburst produces quality educational software in nearly all curriculum areas, for all grade levels, for Macintosh, PC-compatible, and Apple II platforms.

The Spinoza Company
1876 Minnehaha Ave West, St. Paul, MN 55104-1029
Phone: 800-282-2327; 651-644-7251
Fax: 651-644-7252
E-mail: spinoza@spinozabear.com
Web site: http://www.spinozabear.com

Spinoza, the bear who speaks from the heart, was developed by a communications specialist and a special education teacher. The 17-inch teddy bear has a cassette player inside and comes with a collection of nine tapes designed to build a positive self-concept. Spinoza is used effectively by parents, teachers, and health-care professionals to promote literacy, emotional health, and social skills. Also available with a Talking Book player (to play four-track tapes as used by people with visual impairments).

Synergy
412 High Plain Street, Suite 19, Walpole, MA 02081-4264
Phone: 508-668-7424
E-mail: synergy@ma.ultranet.com
Web site: http://www.speakwithus.com
The Synergy mAAC and Millennium PC are durable, weather-resistant, portable AAC/computer systems. They accept multiple access methods: built-in touch screen, switch input, HeadMouse, and more. The Synergy AAC system allow users to do anything they can do on a desktop computer. The company offers a free trial program, funding counseling, communication packages, and three-year warranty.

TASH International, Inc.
Unit 1-91 Station Street, Ajax, ONT L1S 3H2 Canada
Phone: 800-463-5685
E-mail: tashcan@aol.com
Web site: http://www.tashint.com
TASH offers a wide range of quality switches, as well as access hardware for both PC and Macintosh computers. TASH provides special keyboard and mouse control for anyone who cannot use the standard keyboard and mouse. TASH also has a variety environmental control systems for accessing the telephone, TV, computers, and appliances, as well as a line of digitized communication aids.

TeleSensory
420 Almanor, Sunnyvale, CA 94086-3533
Phone: 800-227-8418
E-mail: smiller@telesensory.com
Web site: http://www.telesensory.com
TeleSensory manufactures and distributes a wide variety of products for blind and visually impaired children and adults. These products include low-vision reading aids and access peripherals for IBM, Apple II, and Macintosh that include speech access devices, computer screen enlargers, Optacon print reading aids, Braille printers, OCR devices, and refreshable Braille display.

UCLA Microcomputer Project
UCLA Intervention Program, 23-10 Rehab., 1000 Veteran Ave., Los Angeles, CA
   90095
Phone: 310-825-4821
E-mail: twebb@pediatrics.medsch.ucla.edu

The UCLA Microcomputer Project develops software that is physically accessible and developmentally appropriate for preschool handicapped children (eighteen months to five years of age). The team strives to create software that will promote language skills, motor skills, and socialization, and enhance play. The software is accessed either by a single switch or by the Power Pad accompanied with picture overlays. Also available are a hardware/software resource pamphlet and a booklet providing general guidelines for beginning computer use with preschool handicapped children.

Universal Learning Technology
39 Cross Street, Peabody, MA 01960
Phone: 508-538-0036
E-mail: ult@cast.org

Voice Communications
P.O. Box 29, Wilton, CT 06897
Phone: 203-775-3204
E-mail: keghtesadi@aol.com
Voice Communication Interface is in the business of developing custom wireless voice activated systems for command and control of industrial, commercial, and business office applications. The Voice Link product line provides bi-directional wireless communication for speech recognition applications where mobility, flexibility, and ease of use are crucial in a structurally complicated environment.

VoiSys International
34 Linnell Circle, Nutting Lake, MA 01865
Phone: 508-667-8145
E-mail: voisys@tiac.net
Web site: http://www.voisys.com

WesTest Engineering Corporation
810 West Shepherd Lane, Farmington, UT 84025
Phone: 801-298-7100
E-mail: mary@darci.org
Web site: http://www.darci.org
The DARCI TOO, is a universal alternate input device for both Apple and IBM computers. Because this device has a number of operating modes and can be used with a variety of interface devices (joysticks, switches, matrix keyboards, and so on), it is especially useful as a tool to assess a person's control capabilities. The Morse Code Darci Card uses the PCMCIA bus to provide a transparent method controlling a computer with Morse code. All keyboard and mouse functions are available as well as the use of switches, joysticks and pointing devices to enter single-, double- and triple-input Morse code.

William K. Bradford Publishing Company
16 Craig Road, Acton, MA 01720
Phone: 800-421-2009
E-mail: wkb@wkbradford.com
Web site: http://www.wkbradford.com
William K. Bradford Publishing Company produces K–12 educational software. They carry the school versions of product lines like Explore-A-Story and Explore-A-Science. Additionally, William K. Bradford Publishing Company produces home versions of certain D.C. Heath titles, as well as many other titles from a variety of developers. Home versions are configured with brief user instructions, appropriate disks, and any other support materials needed for operation.

World Communications
245 Tonopah Drive, Fremont, CA 94539
Phone: 800-352-1979
World Communications strives to offer simple, practical, and useful solutions for computer access and augmentative communications to people with disabilities. They currently offer HelpWare products such as Help U Type, Help U Key, Help U Speak, Freedom Writer, and the new Windows 3.x products such as Mouse Keys and Help U Type for Windows. The products cover a wide range of disabilities and are upgraded as better technology becomes available. The HelpWare products have become very useful and practical since over the years they have evolved by incorporating suggestions and advice of many researchers, users, and educators.

REFERENCES

Alliance for Technology Access. (1999a). *ATA resource centers* (n.p.). Available: http://www.ataccess.org/MemberDirectory/atacenters.html

Alliance for Technology Access. (1999b). *ATA vendors* (n.p.) Available: http://www.ataccess.org/MemberDirectory/atavendors.html

Closing the Gap. (1999a). *Glossary* (n.p.) Available: http://www.closingthegap.com/rd/rdGlossary.html

Closing the Gap. (1999b). *Organizations* (n.p.). Available: http://www.closingthegap.com/rd/otherorg.html

National Association of Protection and Advocacy Systems (1999). *Direct links to P&As/CAPs websites* (n.p.). Available: http://www.protectionandadvocacy.com/demofile.htm

Public Law 105-394. S. 2432. (1998). *An act to support programs of grants to states to address the assistive technology needs of individuals with disabilities, and for other purposes. Approved Nov. 13, 1998.* Washington, DC: National Archives and Records Administration, Office of the Federal Register.

RESNA (1999). State contact list (n.p.). Available: http://www.resna.org/taproject/sta_acomp.html